ALWAYS APPRENTICES

THE BELIEVER MAGAZINE PRESENTS TWENTY-TWO CONVERSATIONS BETWEEN WRITERS

ALWAYS APPRENTICES

THE *BELIEVER* MAGAZINE PRESENTS
TWENTY-TWO CONVERSATIONS
BETWEEN WRITERS

Edited by VENDELA VIDA,
ROSS SIMONINI,
& SHEILA HETI

BELIEVER BOOKS

a tiny division of

MCSWEENEY'S
which is also tiny

BELIEVER BOOKS
a division of
McSWEENEY'S

849 Valencia Street
San Francisco, CA 94110

www.believermag.com

Cover design by Dan McKinley

Illustrations by Charles Burns

Printed in the United States by Edwards Brothers Malloy

ISBN: 978-1-938073-25-0

TABLE OF CONTENTS

Notes and Apologies:

★ Most of these conversations occurred between 2007 and 2012. Earlier conversations have been collected in *The Believer Book of Writers Talking to Writers*.

★ If you are looking for a *Believer* conversation from 2007 to 2012 that does not appear in this book, please visit the archive on our website: *believermag.com*.

★ These conversations were conducted in person, over email, over the telephone, and sometimes via postal mail. They took place in pubs, on stages, in writers' kitchens or living rooms, and outside.

★ The contributors and interviewees in this book are writers of fiction and nonfiction. Conversations with poets and playwrights will be included in the *Best of the Believer Interviews* book, which will most likely be published in 2014.

DON DeLILLO

TALKS WITH

BRET EASTON ELLIS

"GOOD TIMES OR BAD TIMES FOR WRITERS, WHAT DOES THAT REALLY MEAN?"

Some misconceptions cleared up herein:

That DeLillo and Ellis met at a party in the company of Barbara Feldon
That The Great Gatsby *is not a nightmarish tragedy*
That Ellis is the dark prince of decadence or whatever

hen asking Bret Easton Ellis and Don DeLillo to sit and have a conversation, I was not only unsure that they'd agree to do it, I simply didn't expect them to enjoy it. Both writers—living literary legends—had not met before, and, on the surface, they seem to have nothing in common. In the media, Ellis is known as a decadent, public figure of the '80s, DeLillo as a Salingeresque recluse, silent to the media. (Both deny that these characterizations are accurate.) I would never have imagined they'd get along so well.

Don DeLillo was born in 1936 in New York City. He was raised in an Italian American family and earned a degree in communication arts.

The literary world was an unknown territory for him when he quit his job and began writing his first novel. According to Ellis, DeLillo's work represents "a new phase in fiction." His refined style and philosophical themes—paranoia, language, truth, modern urban living—have indisputably influenced a spate of contemporary American writers.

Some of these themes also nourish Bret Easton Ellis's work, work which has become a touchstone for younger authors writing about youth culture. Ellis was born in 1964 in Los Angeles. A graduate of Bennington College, he published his first book, Less Than Zero, *in 1985. It was a stunning and violent portrait of a ruthless civilization. Although he had not written the book expecting publication, it immediately established him as one of the decade's leading artistic figures.*

Their conversation took place in a large Louis XIII room, with old armchairs and an impressive fireplace, in mid-October 2010, in the Hôtel d'Aubusson in Paris. Both monstres sacrés were in Europe promoting their new books (DeLillo's Point Omega *and Ellis's* Imperial Bedrooms*). DeLillo arrived first. Then came Ellis. And then an hour or so of almost-private and friendly conversation.* —Didier Jacob (September 2011)

I. "I WAS TOTALLY WRONG ABOUT THAT."

DIDIER JACOB: You and Bret have never met, I think?

BRET EASTON ELLIS: I remember a long, long time ago, meeting you at a party at someone's place—I can't quite remember whose place it was—and why do I want to think you were with the actress Barbara Feldon?

DON DeLILLO: No… The name Barbara Feldon is familiar, but I can't place it.

BEE: For some reason, I was standing in a corner and thinking, That's Don DeLillo. This was in the '80s, and I believed you were standing with Barbara Feldon. She played Agent 99 in *Get Smart,* the original TV show. I was wrong, I was totally wrong about that. I had never met Don; I know many people who know him, but, yes, we had never met.

DJ: This is funny because in France, writers often know each other because they've met on television talk shows, or while they were doing promotion for their books.

DD: I'm not usually meetable. [*Laughs*]

BEE: And I'm not a professional writer in the sense that I give a lot of interviews or make myself available without promoting a book. So I have these silences of about five or six years, and then I come out and I do all these things. I'm not that available, either.

DJ: You two have never met, and we don't want to go into excessive back patting, but could you perhaps discuss your respective bodies of work?

DD: Bret started earlier in life. Your first book was published when you were twenty-one, whereas it took me forever to get going. It's a very strange thing to think about now, but it seemed normal at the time. I had a job, which I quit. People assumed that I quit so I could write, and that was a fair assumption. But what I really did was go to the movies. What I wanted to do was go to the weekend movies in empty theaters and watch the nouvelle vague and all the interesting movies that were coming out in the '60s. Eventually I got to start working on my first novel, *Americana.* It took forever because I didn't have the discipline. I'm not sure I can explain why, but it took me a long time. It was not until about two years into the book that I decided that yes, I was a writer, that *even if this book doesn't get published, I will keep writing.* I just began to believe that because I sensed a kind of development in my writing.

I was writing about things I didn't know I knew, which is the best kind of discovery you can make about yourself. Anyway, that's how it began. It took four years for me to do it.

BEE: It's so strange to hear that, because when I read *Americana,* without going into the whole lovefest aspect of it all, it seemed such an assured book. It's interesting because I began writing at a very, very early age. I began writing picture books or children's books when I was six, seven, eight. I was also into comic books, and I made my own comic books. I was into horror and sci-fi, then I graduated into writing my first novel when I was fourteen. I'd thought I'd had a very interesting summer and I wrote a novel about that summer. After re-reading it, I came to the conclusion it wasn't an interesting summer at all. So that was my first attempt at a novel, and I suppose what happened next became the *Less Than Zero* project. In a way, it was a collage of my journals, my attempt at writing the kind of nonfiction that Joan Didion was doing in her *Slouching Towards Bethlehem* essays—a kind of personal nonfiction. I was trying to ape that style, because we were reading her in high school in Southern California. I don't know how many other high schools were teaching *Slouching Towards Bethlehem* to eleventh graders and I don't know how many of my classmates responded to it, but I was the alienated writer and I really dug Didion. So that's what I was doing.

Less Than Zero kind of began and evolved over time. There were many attempts at it until there was this version that my teacher at Bennington College at the time, as well as an editor and an agent, thought was ready for publication. I had no intention of publishing *Less Than Zero.* I thought it was practice for something I would do further on, another novel. My narrative in terms of how I got it published was, at the time, quite odd. It was a strange combination to be that young and also to be published. For a while there, after the success of the book, many young writers seemed to be getting published, many at a much younger age than I had been. Then, of course, when that wasn't working out anymore, it stopped.

DD: I remember living in the middle of Manhattan, and I had no connection whatsoever with the publishing business. I didn't know how to get an agent. Today, young writers know all these things whether or not they succeed, but I didn't know quite how to start. Luckily, I had published a short story in some small quarterly, and I got a letter from an editor at Houghton Mifflin asking if there were anything else I might show him. So there it was, a manuscript of about six hundred pages, and I just sent it to him. I did not even know how to mail the damn thing. Finally, he replied that they were interested, and I had a meeting with him and a younger editor, and they were very helpful. The book needed work, and it's interesting how clearly I was able to see it. Only about two months after having finished it, I made plenty of changes myself and it became, as they say, publishable. Then I changed it again many years later when Penguin wanted to do a new paperback reprint. I went through the book—the only time I re-read one of my novels—and I cut about fifteen pages. I didn't add anything, I just cut, and that's what's now available, at least in paperback.

BEE: When was that?

DD: It was after I published *Libra,* so it was the late '80s. But there was a paperback in the original form.

BEE: OK, then maybe I read the original version of *Americana,* because I read the book earlier than that. I remember very clearly the first time I read one of your novels. I was maybe seventeen or eighteen and I picked up *The Names* in the Vintage paperback. It was a greenish cover with a shirtless boy on it. At the time, I would haunt bookshops and I would look for books and buy them. That's what I would spend my disposable income on. I remember picking up that book—that was my introduction to Don's work, picking up *The Names.* At eighteen, it seemed very haunting and full of dread. I found it very mysterious. Then I went back and read his earlier books, and in 1985 *White Noise* was a big event on the campus where I was going to school. I've read *The Names,* like, three times since then, at ten-year intervals, and it means something different to me every time. I read it when I was eighteen, then twenty-eight, then thirty-eight, and each time it took on a different meaning. Well, I say that, but I don't really know what that means. The same thing happened to me with *The Great Gatsby.* You read it when you're a kid and you find it mercifully quick, then at twenty-eight it means something else, and at thirty-eight, as you get older, it becomes much more of a nightmarish tragedy.

DD: It's about time for me to read *The Great Gatsby* again, I think. [*Laughs*] But *The Names* was important for me because it was sort of a rededication to the novel. I was living in Greece and surrounded by new things, new voices, new sounds. And these things were very invigorating and found their way into my book almost on a daily basis. I found myself paying more attention to the language of my book, perhaps in part because I was surrounded by foreign languages, not only in Greece but in other places I was traveling. It began to occur to me that the alphabet actually is an art, a visual art, as I was looking at old Greek ruins inscribed with ancient words, and studying them in terms of shape and size as much as anything else. I began to look at my own sentences in a curious way, almost as if they were foreign objects to be scrutinized. It was a very important book for me, and I think I became a more serious writer at that time.

BEE: As a reader of all of your books, that definitely marked a new phase in the fiction, I think.

DD: *Less Than Zero* was published in 1985, and it created a great amount of attention.

BEE: It was published the same year as *White Noise.* Eighty-five was a very good year for both of us, actually.

DD: Except that I was middle aged and you were a kid.

II. A VERY PROBLEMATIC RELATIONSHIP WITH THE NOVEL

DJ: Would you agree that although your books share common topics, your writing approaches are very different?

DD: Bret's work was highly skilled and seemingly professional for a man who was so young at the time. It seemed you had the skill and the knowingness of an author who should have been much older.

BEE: I was depressed. I was a depressed teenager.

DD: I think you probably depressed a number of young writers who couldn't reach a level like that at nearly the same age.

BEE: It was bad news for many of my peers. I had a core group of male friends at college and we all wanted to be writers. We were in workshops together and we were looking at those novels. I thought there were writers who were better than I was, and they thought they were better than I was, too. There's no denying that part of the attraction of *Less Than Zero* for publishers was that it felt like a book that had been written by an insider in—let's put it this way—a commercially exploitable way. It had elements that seemed to be easily sellable, I think, for a first novelist. And there was a kind of narrative to that book that people could cling to or grab on to easily. When this book was published, my other friends, my colleagues, my peers, freaked out a little bit at the success of it. I lost friends out of envy and jealousy. I remember very clearly that there was a writer in our group who was the best writer of all of us and who had written a manuscript that he could not get published for the life of him. I even tried later on to get it published. He was a little unwieldy and he was very stubborn about things, but he seemed to be the one who was going to be the most serious and most dedicated writer of us all. So, yes, there was an immense amount of jealousy surrounding the publication of *Less Than Zero*.

I tried to be as down-to-earth as possible about it, but you have to understand, this wasn't a book I intended to publish. At twenty, when your teacher and these New York professionals and their agents want to represent you, and they're moving forward, pushing things along, of course you go along with it. Even in retrospect, of course, I would have gone along with it. But I didn't have any idea that it would become the book that it did become. It was a surprise. The publishing house paid no money for it, they paid the lowest advance they could get away with. There were a lot of fights between the editorial board, with the older editors not understanding why anyone would publish this book and the younger editors defending it. Finally, they said, "Look, no money for advertising, nothing. If you want to publish this one book, go ahead and do it." It was very much a word-of-mouth book. It was not a successful book until six or seven months after it was published. My relationship to that novel is very different than the relationship the novel has to a reader. I did not think more than two hundred people outside of my peer group would read it. Now, twenty-five years later, it's in a twenty-fifth anniversary edition at Vintage and in the U.K. And it's like I'm standing in the shadows, smiling ironically at all this. I have a very problematic relationship with the novel in terms of the fact that it was not supposed to be what it ended up becoming.

DJ: It did change your life, though.

BEE: It certainly did. On certain personal levels it was good, because I was able to support myself independently and no longer had to depend on parents or jobs. In that way it was—maybe not the best thing for me, I don't know—it was a very interesting and very confusing moment in my life.

DD: And you have a history in the movies. Several of your novels have been adapted.

BEE: This is true, yes. Out of the seven books, four have been turned into films. But I was a big moviegoer, too. One of my biggest pleasures—still is, for that matter—was going to the films during the day. There are certain theaters I like to go to because I know I will be one of the only people in there. Matinees on a weekday are my favorite times to go to films, or in the late afternoon. I did that a lot when I was writing as a teenager. After school was when I would go see a lot of European films. I also discovered the nouvelle vague when I was in high school—at revival houses. They don't have these anymore. Well, there aren't any in L.A. anymore. I don't know about New York.

DD: Well, occasional revivals at the Film Forum. But it's not strictly the revival house as it was in the '60s or '70s.

DJ: Your own books have often been optioned, but never turned into films.

DD: People keep taking options but they never make the films. There's a plan for next year by David Cronenberg of *Cosmopolis.* We'll see if it happens.

BEE: Who was trying to adapt *White Noise* for the longest time? Wasn't that Stephen Schiff?

DD: I don't know. The option hasn't been renewed for some reason. I don't know how that business works.

BEE: It's so strange. I'm always surprised when my books are optioned or even turned into movies, because they weren't conceived as movies. They were conceived as books. They're language based, and I do write screenplays as well, and those I think would make much better films than adaptations of my novels.

DD: Have you had any luck with screenplays?

BEE: I've had luck in the sense that I've been able to sell scripts and that I've been hired to write scripts. But the one time that I did have one of my scripts turned into a film was an adaptation of one of my books, a collection of short stories called *The Informers*. I wrote and produced that film, and it was a disaster. It really did not turn out well. It had nothing to do with the screenplay not working, it had to do with elements that I was not aware of. I had sold scripts before, I had seen adaptations of my books made, but I had never participated in the making of a film. And it was incredibly instructive. It was a big learning experience. There were a lot of mistakes made, a lot of things unforeseen, a lot of bad luck—just bad luck.

DD: Where was the filming done?

BEE: The filming was done in Los Angeles, Argentina, and Uruguay, which doubled as Hawaii, because one of the sections of the film takes place there and it was too expensive to shoot in Hawaii. Unfortunately, in *The Informers* it looks like Uruguay. It doesn't look like Hawaii at all, so that was another part of the problem. When you see these beach scenes, you go, What? How did they shoot this? It was very disappointing because it was the one time I felt I had control over an adaptation of mine by being the producer and the writer on it. And I'd had some mixed feelings over adaptations of my novels. Also, just thinking that they'll never make the movie, you just take the money. Ninety-eight percent of all books that are optioned or bought never see the light of day. So you can have the best of both worlds—you get the money and the book stays there. Or if you're very—if you're super lucky—it's turned into a terrific film that not only helps sell your last book but your entire backlist.

That's never happened to me before, but if it does, that's wonderful. Usually it doesn't happen, though. And usually literary books make bad movies, that's just how it is. Very rarely does a literary novel produce a good film. I was just reading Jonathan Franzen's *The Corrections,* and as much as I love it, or *Freedom,* I think they would be terrible films. The rights to *Freedom* are being bought right now and the deal is being closed. That's a staggering novel, but do I really want to see this on a screen? Do I really want to see these characters and these scenarios filmed and acted out by people, rather than the pleasure that I had creating these scenes in my head? I don't know.

DJ: Do you think the status of writers in Hollywood has improved since the days of Faulkner and Fitzgerald?

BEE: It's still terrible, but it's always been terrible for actors, as it's always been terrible for writers. I think it's worse now, in a way, because there used to be a time when, as a writer, you were employed and had a contract with a studio. It was a steady job, it was an income, people went out there and did it. Now everyone is scrambling for work, and certainly this writers' strike that happened two or three years ago did not help matters at all. I think it hurts the industry for writers. So, no, I don't think it's a good time for writers at all. But you know, it's an old-school way of thinking—good times or bad times for writers, what does that really mean? It's not a great time creatively for *anyone* in Hollywood. We're in a transitional phase, and I don't know what's going to happen. People always want to see movies, and people will always want to make movies. There's always rich people coming to town waving their checkbook because they want to get into what they consider to be a very sexy business. And yes, they will write you a check to write a script you want to write about two artists who can't deal anymore and want to kill themselves. They'll go, "Sure, can we meet Angelina Jolie if we give you the money to write your script?" and you'll say, "Yeah, sure, I can get you to a party." The business will always attract that sort of people, and, interestingly, they are the ones who ultimately do fun and interesting films. But they are in the business for reasons that have nothing to do with making a good movie.

III. TIME, MOTION, AND THE OCCASIONAL FACE

DJ: Don, what prompted you to write *Point Omega?*

DD: I went to the showing of a video work at the Museum of Modern Art in New York—this was three or four years ago. It was called *24 Hour Psycho,* by the video artist Douglas Gordon. I didn't know about it, although it had been shown in other cities quite a few times. I found myself interested almost immediately by the movement of the characters, by familiar characters in familiar situations. Of course, it's a famous movie.

It began to occur to me that this was a kind of study in time and motion, and in what we're able to see: how we see, what we see, what we miss seeing under normal circumstances. These circumstances were not normal, obviously. I just stood there in this dark, cold room with no chairs or benches, a freestanding screen that you could walk around. It was very interesting because on the other side of the screen we see everything in reverse. There were very few people, and many people would come in for a moment or two, be utterly bewildered, and then leave. And other people—a few—would stay for ten or fifteen minutes or so, and I found myself going back three or four times and staying for an hour and a half or two hours by the last time. That's when I decided to write something, and it eventually took the form of fiction.

Now, why did Douglas Gordon choose *Psycho* over a thousand other movies? I'm not sure. It works quite well in that film most of the time. The most interesting thing about *24 Hour Psycho* is the scenes in which nothing is happening, even in normal motion. In other words, the emptier the scene, the better it is to watch it in slow motion. It becomes very abstract. There are scenes that take perhaps three seconds in the original version that take three minutes in this version, and they are just scenes with rugs or cracks in the floorboard, and those are the best scenes in the entire movie. There is no sound at all in *24 Hour Psycho,* and all the suspense of the original film is drained away in slow motion. It's nothing but time, motion, and the occasional face. And it's surprisingly compelling, at least to me. And I haven't even seen the entire film. I've seen about six hours' worth.

DJ: Were you influenced by Hitchcock?

DD: No, not at all. I mean, I admire him. *Vertigo* is a very good film, and *The Birds* is also very good. But he is an audience-pleaser; he will manipulate ruthlessly to get an audience reaction, which is OK for that kind of movie.

DJ: It's also a film about violence and homicidal madness.

DD: There was a murder somewhere in the Midwest and someone wrote a newspaper article about it. Then a novelist spotted the story, which inspired him to write a novel. Then a screenwriter did a screenplay for Hitchcock based on that novel, which became *Psycho,* which then bred two remakes, *Psycho II* and *Psycho III.* Then Gus Van Sant did a remake of the original *Psycho,* and that was called *Psycho,* too. Then Douglas Gordon did *24 Hour Psycho.* Who knows what's next? Well, my novel, obviously, so now we need a film version of it. [*Laughs*]

DJ: Was Hitchcock an influence on you in terms of suspense and violence?

BEE: No. The older I get, there's a romance to Hitchcock that

I find myself relating to more and more. *Vertigo* meant nothing to me at eighteen. I didn't get it; I thought it was boring. Now I find it to be one of the most crushing, wrenching films ever made about love, the futility of romance, and how we keep repeating cycles. Certainly, that period of Hitchcock when he made *Vertigo* and *Psycho* and *The Birds,* which I think are his three masterpieces, is him at his best. But as a writer, no, I really can't point to any filmmaker and say, "Yes, they influenced my work." I think cinema influenced my work and made it cinematic in a way. But for me it was novelists and writers who influenced me the most. And you really don't need a lot, you only need maybe two or three. I mean, if I look back really early on, it was maybe Hemingway and Didion. When I was intensely into minimalism, it was maybe Raymond Carver. Then later Don was a big influence, and when I look at the people who really shaped my way of writing, there are not a lot of them. I don't think I would necessarily point to filmmakers.

DJ: Speaking of Carver, what did you think of the new, not-so-minimalistic edition of his works?

BEE: I don't think it's going to make me very popular to talk about this—Don can go first.

DD: Gordon Lish was Carver's editor when he was at Random, and I didn't know him very well when he was editing Carver. I just knew him at a distance and I didn't realize how much work he'd done on Carver's manuscripts. Over the years, it became a serious matter in publishing. I do think he improved the stories considerably and I enjoyed reading most of those stories. I did find the Hemingway influence a bit strenuous at times, but they're nevertheless very good stories and very much in the American tradition of short-story writing. As far as the subsequent controversies are concerned, as original Carver work became available and as a biography was published, I don't really have much of an opinion, to tell you the truth.

DJ: But did you read both versions?

DD: I read some of Carver's work that he wrote after he and Gordon separated as writer and editor, and I didn't think it was as good as the early work. That's about as far as I would go.

BEE: And I completely agree. So I don't need to add to that. That's exactly my opinion as well. That's perfectly stated.

DJ: Don, you live a fairly reclusive life—

DD: Oh, no, it's not reclusive. I mean, I have friends, I go places— here I am in Paris. There are things I don't do, definitely, that other writers like to do, but that's always been the case. When I began, the tradition of writers doing publicity was not nearly as developed as it is today. For about six books, I was not even asked to do an interview. That's the way it was and that was fine with me. And then, I don't know, I guess when *Libra* came out—that was at the end of the 1980s—I think I did a few interviews, although I didn't do any traveling for the book. Actually, I went to London, but that was all I did. I did a little more for *Underworld* and that's about it, with the occasional trip to Europe, to France or Germany, and not much else. In the States, my editor understands how I feel about this and she asked me to do only one interview and a reading for my last book.

DJ: Because you don't feel like it, or feel it's not part of the job?

DD: That's an outdated feeling, but it's not part of the job. That's how I feel, anyway. But younger writers today are very different. They're eager to do this.

DJ: As for you, Bret, you only do tours when your books are published, but you stay out of the public eye between novels.

BEE: I feel guilty. If I didn't have to, I would definitely not do a tour. I think it's bad for you in a lot of ways: bad for your ego, bad for you physically, as tours are very long. I don't really know how much it affects sales, so I do it kind of out of a guilt-trip in a way. I feel I owe these tours to my publisher, although I sometimes refuse to do this or go there. But I also suppose I am more comfortable with it than Don. On a certain level, I don't know what it was never to have to do any publicity. I remember being twenty-one and having to go on the *Today* show, having to talk to the *New York Times,* and doing those photo shoots for *Rolling Stone.* My having been raised in that kind of atmosphere makes it more accessible for me, and I'm OK with it.

But I'm not like a professional type of writer who does the panels and writes reviews for the *New York Review of Books* or does any kind of readings outside of that area of time when the book is published. I don't feel comfortable enough or smart enough to do these things. I'm perfectly content in my private life not to do this. It's strange that I have this reputation as a kind of publicity-hungry, brat-pack-loving novelist, when I never felt that to be the case about me. It's a painting of me that the press liked to build up, and I never felt that that was me. But it was a very interesting and very sexy narrative about me—they were trying to make this connection between my personal life and what I was writing about. I'm always amused when I'm painted that way: the dark prince of decadence or whatever.

DD: And once an image is established, you're a dead man.

BEE: You're screwed, yes. The irony is that when I try to show them my real, authentic self, they're completely disappointed. You just can't win this one.

IV. THE END OF THE EMPIRE

DJ: Do you think the lives of writers have changed a lot?

DD: It's changed in my lifetime as a writer in an extraordinary way. I don't know about yours, Bret. It's pretty much the same for you, isn't it?

BEE: You know what, I think it's different. I think the empire is kind of over, in terms of the idea of novelists being able to support themselves through literary fiction and balancing the writing of a novel with maybe teaching half the year or writing journalism and paying the bills that way. There was a moment like that, which I refer to as "the empire," from 1945 to about 2001, or maybe a bit after 9/11. But now you can't make a living as a novelist. There's of course always that exception when someone gets an advance, but usually these advances go to authors who are creating vampire franchises. They're not going to serious literary novels, whose audience appears to be dwindling, regardless of when there's a *Freedom* or Don's *Underworld*. It seems to be happening less and less, and the idea of the book taking part of the center stage of literary culture seems to me to be almost an empire thing. It doesn't seem to be happening anymore, regardless of what's going on in America right now with, again, the Franzen novels. It's very touching to me how *Freedom* is good enough to withstand all the praise that it's getting, but it seems to me to be the last gasp of something that was once more prevalent in the culture: a book would come out and people would talk about it. I think that has changed since I came out, and I think it's very different now.

DD: I think everybody with a computer will be able to become his or her own novelist, and will be able to sign his or her own novel as everything becomes more individualized on the web. You'll be able to consult a program that will make you the main character. That's what's going to happen, to my mind.

BEE: I think there will always be the need for large-scale stories being told and not just short little bites, regardless of whether it's being done on television, or some kind of novel for the iPad with images and sound and music as you're reading a text. I don't know—I'm really flailing here.

DD: We don't really know how technology will affect narrative. That's the question. See, people used to say that the novel is going to die, but they would never say that movies will die with it, when in fact all forms depend on the narrative. I think if one of them fails, the others are going to fail as well. Maybe this will happen to both forms, and maybe movies will take a totally different direction with fiction.

BEE: Narrative is evolving in terms of the kind of narratives people are responding to. A lot of my younger friends will tell you that reality television is a kind of narrative. Following the arc of a celebrity on an hourly basis, or noticing announcements on Twitter or Facebook from this person they're following, has a narrative that they respond to. And the narrative of video games is a big thing among young people, where they follow part one, part two, part three, and part four. The interactive element also helps them create the narrative of the video game by deciding to shoot this person or climb that mountaintop or whatever. The ways people respond to narratives in different forms is very interesting. I'm just an old writer, so it's hard for me to get my head around that kind of idea, and I'm more comfortable with the pages of a book.

DD: I still write on an old manual typewriter. I don't think I could write otherwise.

BEE: Really? That's amazing. Even *Underworld*? I wrote four drafts of *American Psycho* on an old typewriter in the late '80s, and it didn't seem that tough to me with the little white-out thing.

DD: It's like the eighteenth century. Changing a typewriter ribbon... What I really enjoy is the sensual feel of the hammer hitting the page and having a slightly larger type on my typewriter.

Watching those letter-shapes form means something. I also write by hand, but not at great lengths. I know other writers who use the typewriter. Paul Auster does.

BEE: I write by hand at first sometimes, and then I transfer everything into the computer. But I agree with you. In this digitized age, I do miss the sensuous feeling of typing, the clocking of the keys, seeing the ink hit the page. It's the same way with holding vinyl, with films and with books. Everything is digitized now I don't know if people of twenty-two or twenty-three years of age would be having this conversation, because that's what their whole lives have been like. But for someone who's been in that transitional phase of moving from one era to the next, there is definitely a sense of loss.

DJ: One last question: could you each describe to me the place where you write?

DD: Sure. It's a room in an old house where I live. I don't go somewhere else to write. After I finish breakfast, I walk into the room. There are paintings made by an old friend of mine who's now deceased, and a photograph of Charlie Parker taken at some old club in New York in the 1950s. There are books and a couple of windows, and a typewriter on a table—it's not a desk, it's just a table with a lot of junk on it. That's where I work. The door is shut and most of the time it's quiet, except when there's an automobile accident on the nearby parkway and a helicopter hovers for about twenty minutes, making a deadly sound. But that's it.

BEE: Do you mean anytime, or just now at this point of my life? Right now, it's an office that's in the place where I live. I just walk down the hallway and my office has a view of the city I live in, which is Los Angeles. I like to keep it very clean. There are no paintings and no posters, just a small bookshelf off to the side. There's a TV screen that's sometimes on CNN, but mostly it's off.

I have a glass-topped desk with a couple of computers on it and a stack of notes. Even though there's a view on the city, the view from my desk is at such an angle that I only have a view on the sky, and not the city. And the window is usually open. ✻

PAULA FOX

NICK POPPY

"YOU DON'T HAVE TO STRUGGLE AGAINST
THE THING IN YOURSELF THAT KNOWS HOW
TO SAY SOMETHING—BUT YOU HAVE TO FIND
A WAY OF SAYING THESE THINGS,
FOR GROWN-UPS AS WELL AS CHILDREN."

Appropriate elements for children's fiction:

Sentiment
Racial things
Sexual things
Death

Paula Fox is most famous for her novel Desperate
Characters, *which finely fillets the mores and anxi-*
eties of urban intelligentsia. We could stop right there,
except that she is also the author of five more fine nov-
els for adults (including Poor George, The Widow's
Children, *and* The Western Coast*), twenty-odd novels for young people*
(including the Newbery winner The Slave Dancer*), and two very engaging*
*memoirs of her early years (*Borrowed Finery *and* The Coldest Winter*).*
Any of these would confirm her status as a writer of the very first order.

In her books, Fox has a nearly endless capacity for sympathy and under-
standing, but also for something harsher that looks at times like cruelty. It

isn't. The worlds she describes are not neat moral universes, and her characters, never purely this or that, are often put through painful paces. Children are kidnapped, orphaned, and cast out into the world with no assurance of safety; grown-ups are as likely to hurt as to help. Running through almost all her books is the harsh birthing of adult consciousness, and this is equally true of her work for adults as of her children's books. Fox is terribly honest, and sometimes that means being honest about terrible things.

I visited Fox at her Brooklyn home a few days after the Virginia Tech shootings and a few days before her eighty-fourth birthday. On the way there, I stopped at a flower shop, and on the florist's suggestion, I picked up some daylilies as a hostess present. This turned out to be a lucky good choice, as Fox had a vase full of nearly wilting daylilies in her kitchen. She put the fresh flowers in water, and we sat down to talk.

—Nick Poppy (September 2007)

I. SENTIMENT AND SENTIMENTALITY

NICK POPPY: This is a thrill. I've read many of your books, and now I get to meet you. One thing I'd like to ask—I only came by your work at the turn of the millennium, when a lot of your novels were reissued. I wonder if you could talk about that?

PAULA FOX: I can tell you literally what happened. Jonathan Franzen wrote a piece for *Harper's*. We already knew each other for a couple of years, but he had been teaching at Swarthmore, and he wrote me a note saying that he had found *Desperate Characters* and he would like ten copies if I had them. So I called my daughter who lives in Portland, and she went to Powell's, the famous bookstore, to see if she could find *Desperate Characters*. She sent them directly to Jonathan. And then he came up to New York, and he was gradually beginning to gather materials for the article. I was sort of like a motif going through it, in a large symphony where there were other instruments. But he was persistent. Tom Bissell, who was an editor at Holt, wrote to me after he read the article. And that same day I sent him my last copy of *Desperate Characters,* by return mail. He read it and thought it was OK, so he presented it to the board and then they decided to publish all of my novels that were out of print. Gradually, people wrote prefaces to them, and Jonathan Lethem wrote the preface to my first novel, which was called *Poor George.* He's a very nice man, a great writer.

So that's how it started. I was suddenly "taken up," as they say. And then, fortunately for me, I was dropped within a year. Because when you get taken up, something happens to you. You become self-conscious, and that's very bad for writers. And for anybody. Virginia Woolf used to say she knew she was in trouble when she started looking for her name in the newspaper. You become outside yourself. You're not the person, the writer, the painter, so forth, who works without thinking—you think about too much outside of the work. You think about yourself, but it's not the self that works well.

NP: But while this was going on, and even before, you had a parallel career, writing children's books.

PF: I had been writing children's books—I've written twenty-two books for children, and many of them won prizes—in fact, I won the Hans Christian Andersen medal, and that was pretty steady. It was a source of income, and a certain kind of audience response. Children would write me, "Dear Ms. Fox, I just read *One-Eyed Cat.* I like Judy Blume much better than you."

NP: Ouch.

PF: I just sold *The Slave Dancer* to China two days ago, isn't that exciting? I'm really surprised that it sold there. Anyhow, I had a reputation in Europe, but I didn't know I was going to get in on China.

NP: Well, it's a big market.

PF: When I call AOL, it's always somebody from India that answers, you know? I like to ask them, "Where are you?" "Bombay." Anyhow, that's how it all began. But I had something of a kind of minor reputation in this country. And I was published in France. The French published *Desperate Characters* and *The Widow's Children*. They got very good reviews, but they were considered caviar for the general, they appealed to very few people. Which is true. And now I'm at work on a novella. The book concerns a Cathar heretic and is set in the south of what was not yet France, Languedoc, in a village in the Pyrenees. It takes place in 1371 AD.

NP: A very good year.

PF: A very good year… for wine!

NP: Thinking about literary reputation, I'm interested in what happens to a book after you're done with it, after you've sent it off into the world. What's your attitude toward this thing you've made?

PF: Well, you know, I've had a very rough time of it, in my writing life. Three of my books, *The Western Coast, A Servant's Tale,* and *The Widow's Children*—between the three of them I think I racked up two years of rejection from publishers. *A Servant's Tale* and *The Widow's Children* got most of them. *A Servant's Tale* was rejected by seventeen publishers. *The Widow's Children* was my third novel from Harcourt Brace. I sent it to my editor there, and he said, "This is the best novel you've written, but you have a really bad track record." Meaning, I didn't sell vast numbers of books. Not even little vast numbers. So then I looked around for a publisher for a year and a half, and finally I found one, a lovely man named Henry Robbins, from E. P. Dutton, who died in the Fourteenth Street subway station, I'm sorry to say. But he published *The Widow's Children,* and it got a review in the *New York Times* by someone I had known for two years. And you're not supposed to know the person you're reviewing. She said the book lacked a certain kind of human warmth, and that it was very sentimental.

NP: I don't think of your books as being at all sentimental. It seems like the inverse would be true—that there's a human warmth and sympathy for the characters, but also that you're not afraid to have things go very badly for them.

PF: Yes. Well, I think that's called sentiment, as opposed to sentimentality. You know, it's like when you go to a very bad movie and somebody dies, and you cry, and you come out and you say, "What a wonderful movie!" [*Laughs*] That's a good definition of sentimentality.

NP: So that's caviar for the masses. Or fish sticks.

PF: Exactly.

NP: But it's interesting to me—in both your children's books and your novels for grown-ups, what you do to your characters. Sentimental is not at all what you're after, and in fact, I was struck in reading *The Slave Dancer* and *Monkey Island* and some of your other children's books, how your characters go through very hard times.

PF: Did you read *One-Eyed Cat*?

NP: Yes.

PF: I think the cat in the story has the strength of life. And I think probably that means a lot to me. Life can be very fragile, frail, but there's some kind of persistence about it, so far. And that's about the cat having the strength of life, which is the heart of that book. And I think what I feel mostly is obliged to tell not "the truth," because we don't know what that is, but the truths we know. You know, I realized one day, I was looking at a manuscript, I was lying on my bed, looking at it on the floor, turning the pages, and I suddenly thought, I have to mean every word I write. *A* and *the* included. And then I remembered Mary McCarthy accused Lillian Hellman of lying in her work, even about the words *the* and *a*! [*Laughs*] I was very gratified.

NP: It's striking that in some of your children's books, what you're describing are things you wouldn't want to expose a child to.

PF: I think children, even the kind of children who lead neat, contained lives, go through all kinds of strange things, things that come in the night, or the morning. Coleridge wrote a famous essay about writing for children. He said, a little boy comes home, says, "Mama, mama, I gave a penny to a beggar," and she says, "Oh, you're such a good boy!" He says this is the worst kind of trash you can write for children. I mean, it makes them so conscious of goodness. But there is goodness in people, there is goodness, but it must not be flattered, or thinned out by someone telling you. And you can't have one without the badness, either. You know, there's that psychopath who went on the shooting rampage, that blank person, who answered his name with a question mark. Something was missing. His person was missing. The answer was missing. And so I feel that children are exposed to a lot more violence in this country, but then we have these child safety tops on medicine that take fifteen minutes for an adult to undo. On the one hand they're terribly overprotective, and the middle-class children I've known, their rooms look like toy stores, which is why I wrote my first book, *Maurice's Room*.

NP: How did that come about?

PF: We were living in Greece, around 1963, on an island, and we went out with a fisherman, and he said to my husband and myself, "In America, there are many things." And it came to me to write a book about a child who rejects toys and loves rusty bedsprings and very strange things. So I instantly started that. Because I never had time before to write. I'd been working all my life, and I had six months then to write. And there was nothing for me to do but cook and shop. But I had all this time, and I had a typewriter, a little portable Italian one, and so I wrote *Poor George* and *Maurice's Room*. And I sold them both. That's how I started down this terrible path. [*Laughs*]

NP: The upbringing you describe in *Borrowed Finery* and some of your other autobiographical writings does not immediately suggest that you'd become a writer. It seems like there were many paths that you could've taken.

PF: I think I always wanted to write. You know, when I lived with my grandmother, I remember that I would gather a group of children, and I was about ten or eleven, I guess, in the back steps of our apartment house in Kew Gardens. One time I started reading *Kidnapped,* and when I looked up, they were all gone. And it is very boring for children. But not for me it wasn't. I loved to read to people, to children. I always wanted to write, I think for a number of reasons. My father was a writer, not a very good one. He was a screenwriter. And I'm sure you'll recall from *Borrowed Finery,* my mother said that Graham Greene had seen a movie my father had written, called *The Last Train from Madrid,* and he said it was the worst movie he ever saw!

NP: At least it was something superlative.

PF: Yes, it was the *-st* of something. But not best, worst. Anyhow, I think I always had that kind of drive. I was diverted for a while by music, but my father didn't pay the bills for music school, so that ended. And then I went to the Art Students League for a few months, but he didn't pay those bills either. And then I had to model there, so I became a model. For William Zorach, among other people.

I went down various little bits of roads, but it was all summed up for me in writing, and so then I began to write seriously when I was nineteen or twenty, and every story was rejected. And then two were taken by the *Negro Digest,* which was then edited by a man named Hoyt Fuller. By then I had gotten a teaching job in my thirties, at Ethical Culture, and they had a publicity service, and they picked up all the wire mentions, and one of the mentions was of the two stories I sold to the *Negro Digest.* And so the two women in the public relations office of the Ethical Culture school on Sixty-third Street came in looking for a black woman. And it was me. [*Laughs*] So then I was very encouraged. Hoyt Fuller had written to me, and he was trying to find out if I was black. And I wouldn't tell him! When we went to Greece, I had been teaching at Fieldston, which was the high school for Ethical Culture, and I had in mind the story for *Poor George.* Because someone had said to me that he knew someone who had taken in a boy like one in the book. I thought it was a terrific story, it seemed to me, a person like this, a teacher, who goes up against the boulder that is this boy. Fordham schist that can't be effectively moved. He's just set. And I thought about that battle in people, to shape themselves and to shape others, and so that's how it came to me. But I wrote it because it was the story of a man taking a boy in who then proceeds to steal his wife, and everything. And who is himself killed.

NP: That failure of good intentions is something pretty easily ascribed to Americans.

PF: But there's something awful about giving up, too. You have to examine it. What you intend to do is not the same as what you're doing. I think the tendency to want to do good for people is very strong. *Poor George* isn't the story about the defeat of good intentions, it's the story about someone who is blinded and self-indulgent with good intentions.

II. TOOTH AND CLAW

NP: Walking to your house, I noticed a lot of the retail has to do with very nice stores for children, baby boutiques, that kind of thing. I wonder what those suggest about how we treat our children.

PF: My thought is, and it's just the beginning of a sense of things, that we're affected by everything. By baby shops and Imus and that awful shooting in Virginia. But I think one is too quick to jump and say self-indulgence. It's true, there is self-indulgence, but I don't know if one can draw a conclusion from the proliferation of children's shops around here. Children in the nineteenth century weren't children so much as little human beings, and mostly they were treated like automata. Except for the people who loved them. Now they have the upper hand, seemingly. But—there's more child abuse in this country than I think in most industrialized countries. And yet we put those caps on medicine bottles. The contrast is so great, between the care—the irritating care on the one hand, and the terrible violence on the other. It's a conundrum, it's puzzling. I'm writing about heresy in the fourteenth century, and, you know, I don't think life has changed so much. Because there is still such terrible, beastly behavior by one group against another. And it's true, it's beastly, in the literal sense—we have chimp cousins. [*Laughs*] It's interesting how we share a certain bloodthirstiness. Because they kill, chimps.

NP: I wonder if some of that bloodthirstiness, for better or for worse, has allowed us to build cities and so on?

PF: It's possible, I don't really know. But alas, nature is tooth and claw. So I think, in answer to your original question, from which we've strayed—I think you can't read *Anna Karenina* to a five-year-old, but you can, I think, tell the truth about all kinds of things. Racial things. Sexual things. AIDS, which I did in *The Eagle Kite*. I think all that can be somehow shown in a certain way. There's a way in which you can do it decently, because it is a decent thing. When a man falls in love with another man, and his son sees them embrace on the beach, and then the father has AIDS and leaves his wife, to die. The boy visits, and he knows there's something wrong but doesn't know how to understand it. And then he remembers the kite on the beach, and he remembers seeing two men embrace. And then the father dies. They have a terrible fight before he does, but it never comes out why he dies. I think children can read that. They're exposed to so much in the news that's just out there. I think all these things have a way of being told. I think after terrific struggle—you don't have to struggle against the thing in yourself that knows how to say something—but you have to find a way of saying these things, for grown-ups as well as children. There's a way of writing truthfully that doesn't have to do with simply saying things that are taboo. That's easy. But to get at the truth of something, you really have to think about it. You have to think and feel about it. And somehow whatever that process is, thinking and feeling, you have to lend yourself to it. So you can see it from every angle.

NP: The care you have to take in writing for a young audience—it seems like there's a delicate balancing act between protecting them in some way and teaching them. Or is that not so?

PF: No, I think it is. I was starting to say I wouldn't read *Anna Karenina* to a five-year-old, because judgment is a function of time, and they haven't had time. They don't understand about time yet, and what it does to people. And how time is a huge element in everybody's lives, and determines not only its length but how we grow, how we grow up, and how we do various things. And it isn't that I would keep sexual matters away from a five-year-old—I would, in fact, but I think for a child of five to get *Anna Karenina,* it shouldn't be read to him or her at that age. It's too good. It's too wonderful a novel. I think by the time you're seventeen or sixteen, you're ready. And then you have to read it again when you're thirty. I read D. H. Lawrence's *Sons and Lovers,* partly because of the title, when I was in boarding school in Canada, when I was sixteen. The title grabbed me, and then I discovered the book, I discovered Lawrence. And it was like a huge awakening. Everything in life was in Lawrence. Because you know Lawrence was a passionate writer. Every word, every feeling, every color. *The Rainbow, Women in Love,* I remember the descriptions of the stockings the two sisters wore, the brilliant colors, and the moonlit pool that in *Women in Love* one of the couples passes by, and the description of the birds sitting in the tree in the moonlight. I didn't like his blood passages and sex and all of that stuff. But all writers have that ailment. They're not perfect. But he was pretty close to perfect for me at that age. It seems to me when you're young, you read Lawrence. And when you get past fifty, you don't quite read him anymore. Except for certain pieces and essays he wrote. He's a younger person's writer. And he's wonderful. Wonderful. I loved him, and it awakened something in me, awakened a desire to know more, to come to some sort of grips with life, to not be as dreamy in the way I tended to be at fifteen. But I think, to go back to my original statement, of not reading *Anna Karenina* to a five-year-old, I think a five-year-old would miss too much. Not because they're not capable of understanding it—because they're only capable of understanding certain things at that age. Because they haven't experienced time. They haven't gone through the years. Otherwise, you could read it to them.

NP: Maybe as a soporific.

PF: Right, exactly. [*Laughs*]

NP: When I read *Slave Dancer,* there were certain passages that a reader of any age or level of experience would find difficult to process. You didn't candy-coat it.

PF: But I was very selective about what I chose to write about. I didn't write about castration, for example, which was done to a lot of slaves. Because I knew the audience for that book, and that would be too hard for them. You have to be very selective about what you're going to write about, at the same time that you write truthfully about what you do write about. But you select. I had to do a bit of research for that book, and then I had it checked by a historian, and it was mostly OK. But I found out, for example, that on slave ships, and on most ships of that period in fact, to use the bathroom, you had to go on the side of the ship, to a lower chair with a hole in it. And that was how I described it. And the ship's hold, where Jesse was carried by the slaves, when he was flung down as punishment. They carried him up, and I felt that they were closer to goodwill than the slave owners. They were closer to the original instinct to protect a child than Captain Cawthorne.

III. SUGGESTED DEPTHS

NP: One thing I want to ask you about, which has nothing to do with what we've been talking about so far, is *Desperate Characters*. I understand the book was turned into a film.

PF: Yes. I didn't like it much. And Jonathan Franzen thought it was pretty bad. And Tom Bissell thought it was pretty bad. I was happy with the money I made. We bought this house—we got $35,000 and put it right down. It was a very low-budget film, it was made for $350,000. Shirley MacLaine was in it. Lew Grade, who was a British businessman known as "Low Grade," provided her with the money in exchange for her being on a sitcom for a while. And I was involved in a lot of it, as a gofer. You know, people began to treat me like an errand girl! But I remember one night when a scene was shot on Court Street, and there were five hundred people out to watch Shirley MacLaine, and it's the only way you can silence a crowd, by shooting a movie. There was a crowd, with drunks, and dogs barking. And a man from the movie company, with a finger to his mouth, went running down the street, "Shhhhhhhhh." And then they were able to shoot the scene, which took two minutes. It took hours to set up, it involved a bar up here on the corner, which Shirley and another character went into, and there was nothing but silence. I mean, even the dogs were silenced. So there it was. Frank Gilroy, who wrote the screenplay, was somebody I liked a lot. He wrote a very good play called *The Subject Was Roses,* which won the Pulitzer Prize years ago. But there was something about the movie, it didn't work. Kenny Mars played Otto. He was in *The Producers*—he played the one who sang "Springtime for Hitler." If you just looked at him, you'd start laughing, because he was so funny. I remember going to rehearsal, and he was telling people about his wife's kidney operation, and it made everybody break up with laughter. And I think he spoiled the whole movie, because he was too funny for Otto. The whole thing lacked a certain kind of inner gravity. And the part that was best in it was the Flynders part. But it wasn't very good, it wasn't successful. I like *The Stranger* a lot, Albert Camus, that was a French movie that was done with a lot of panache and style, pretty good. But I don't think books make good films— except books like *Gone with the Wind.*

NP: Probably not much of a book.

PF: Exactly.

NP: So, as far as adaptations, I wonder if there's a decent one of *Anna Karenina.*

PF: Garbo. She was wonderful, and Basil Rathbone was Karenin, and Fredric March was Vronsky. I still remember how Garbo looked when she threw herself onto the train tracks at the end of the movie. Or the beginning. It was a failure as a movie. It just had this great actress, great-looking woman in it.

NP: With *Desperate Characters,* what was it like to have this thing you made put in other people's hands, who maybe didn't do it justice?

PF: I took the money and I spent it. We got this house out of it. I didn't feel particularly possessive. I didn't feel any emotion. I'd done my work, that's how I felt about it. They could have turned it into a musical comedy, as far as I was concerned. I didn't get hung up about it. Somebody has an option on *The Slave Dancer.*

NP: I think that would make a great movie.

PF: Yes, I think it would too. It gets very stark in certain places, scenes. I can see it as a movie. *Desperate Characters* is too interior for celluloid.

NP: There are some absolutely gripping passages in that book. But the power of that writing, of your descriptions and so forth, couldn't be easily translated into film.

PF: Right. You could copy the stage directions, but… I'm thinking about movies that I like, like *Chinatown* or *On the Waterfront.* They all have a lot of obvious stuff in them. It suggests depths, but not depths suggestive of obvious stuff. There are certain things that movies do that people can't do in books, and certain things that people can do in books they can't in movies. I like movies. But I think the greatest arts are poetry and music.

NP: Have you written any poetry?

PF: Oh, no!

NP: You never tried your hand at that?

PF: When I was in high school, the brief time I was in high school,

I wrote one poem, which I saved a copy of, called "Little Boy." I was thirteen. And it's got that "note" that's in all my books. You want to see it?

NP: I'd love to.

PF: OK, I'll show it to you. It's upstairs in my study. ✻

BARRY HANNAH

TALKS WITH

WELLS TOWER

"FICTION WRITERS ARE GOOD PEOPLE, USUALLY.
THERE'S A LOT OF PRETENDERS,
BUT I HAVEN'T MET A LOT OF SONS OF BITCHES."

Good places to write:

Motels

The kitchen table

Bad places to write:

*Robert Altman's wooden tower in California with Plexiglas windows
and gulls all around you*

Barry Hannah is America's greatest living writer" is something I started saying when I first read Hannah's work in the late 1990s. I'm sad I had to stop saying it on March 1 of this year, when Barry passed away.

In July 2008, Barry invited me down to Oxford, Mississippi, where he lived. I spent three days in Oxford, riding around, chatting with the tape recorder, rolling and smoking cigarettes, a habit I picked up for the weekend. It wasn't a convenient time for Barry to entertain a guest. His wife, Susan, was going through chemotherapy, and Barry's health wasn't too good, either. He ran out of breath a lot. His oxygen tank kept clanging around in the back of his Jeep. Still, he was a gracious and *ambitious tour guide. He showed me Faulkner's home, and took me to Square Books, Oxford's venerable bookshop, and one afternoon he took me out to the catfish pond of the late writer Larry Brown. Larry's gravestone sits near the shore of that pond. While we were there, Barry started talking to the stone, telling Larry how much he missed and admired him, an affirmation of love between friends that puts a rock in my throat when I think about it still.*

Barry's work drove people to fanaticism. I know a writer who memorized the first five pages of Hannah's novel Ray, and someone else who claims he's bought two hundred copies of Airships just to hand out to people who haven't read it. Yet it bothered Barry that he didn't have a broader audience, that he had only one "airport book" with his last novel, Yonder Stands Your Orphan. Why he didn't have more airport books is a mystery to me. Even though Hannah populated his novels and stories with serial killers and devils and a guy who kills his lover with a razor strapped to his loins, I'd argue that any one of Hannah's sentences picked at random holds more hope and joy than the entire self-help section at the O'Hare Barnes and Noble. Hannah loved Flaubert as a fellow member of the mot-juste tribe, though Hannah wasn't satisfied with just the right word, it had to be the fiery, ecstatic word, too, a Molotov cocktail against syntactic dreariness.

—Wells Tower (October 2010)

I. PRETENDERS V. SONS OF BITCHES

[*It's a weekend afternoon in Oxford, Mississippi, July 2008. Barry Hannah asked me if I'd ever been to Rowan Oak, Faulkner's estate. I never had. Barry seemed to think it was important that we go have a look around. We're driving over in Barry's Jeep.*]

WELLS TOWER: Do you still read much Faulkner?

BARRY HANNAH: Yeah, there are only about five books I re-read. I re-read *As I Lay Dying*. With the insanity and tragedy, it's the best dysfunctional family ever written. There's not a speck of love lost there. I taught at Middlebury, and since I was Southern, I had to teach Faulkner. I'm glad I discovered Faulkner late, it would have messed with my style. I'd have felt inadequate. I like Hemingway much better. It gave me life. I wanted to go to Paris so bad after reading *The Sun Also Rises,* just to have a Pernod or a coffee or something. [*We drive past a banner advertising the upcoming McCain-Obama debate.*]

Hey, did you know we're having the presidential debate here? We're gonna be on the map some. We're having McCain and Obama, there's gonna be three thousand journalists here in two months.

WT: Why Oxford, I wonder.

BH: The country's just running out of places that are decent, and Oxford's very decent. A handsome town, very literary.

WT: How do you feel about the election?

BH: Waiting, still waiting. I like Obama. There's the Grisham house. My publisher Sam Lawrence loved Oxford so much that he lived there, and when he died, Grisham bought it. Grisham's generosity has totally changed my teaching; the MFA program's almost totally John. It's highly ranked and everything. I don't care. I really want to be below the radar, but hell, all this money from John—I didn't wanna let him down. Two Grisham fellowships. We're not ever going to be Iowa, but we'll be good in a small way. Georgia State was a drag. On the third floor there were these gypsies selling fake silver shit. It was crazy. [*At Rowan Oak. We walk over to the house to peer in the window of Faulkner's office.*]

Faulkner bought this place for twenty-five thousand dollars after he had a hit with *Sanctuary* in 1929. The curtains are parted. No, they're not, goddammit, how rude. I've got a handkerchief for the dew... It all has to be air-conditioned to the right temperature to preserve it.

It was not in this good of shape when he was here. Then he went up to Charlottesville. He said he liked Charlottesville because everybody was a snob, like him—they left you alone—and he rode horses. His death was brought on by a combination of alcohol and horses—he fell off one. He'd ruptured a disk. He was drinking for pain (as well as for his alcoholism) at the end. The dry-out clinic is up the road, below Memphis, about an hour from here—Byhalia. His back was killing him. He died in Byhalia. It was just his time.

There's a deer. Look at the deer. Sweet little yearling. I don't know how people shoot 'em.

WT: I feel like shooting them. They eat everything I plant.

BH: They're just incredibly beautiful. I think they're wonderful. He's not trained to survive. I could walk right up to him. Do you see any spikes?

WT: No, I think it's a doe.

BH: The males know you wanna kill 'em. Every now and then one comes by with a rack. They're just so glorious. They beat each other to death to get to mate.

Here's the marker for his Nobel Prize. Around here, no one even knew what the hell that was. Some Swedes give him a prize. Shit, why's that important? I'm not kidding.

When I first came here, I just heard Faulkner Faulkner Faulkner. His kinfolk and all of it—I was just bored by it. But then I grew to like to have these ghosts around. I find it amenable. He was a little man who did a hell of a lot. Underdog story.

I spent about six or seven years outside of the South. Two years in Vermont at Middlebury, a few in Montana, California. I didn't think I'd come back here at all. I grew up during the civil rights era and I'd had it with these horrible goddamn cowards killing blacks and all the rest. It was a shame. But there are certain worthy things about Mississippi. It's one of the most integrated states in the Union. Oxford, at least on the surface, is very gorgeous. It wasn't Faulkner or any of that that brought me back. It was the people.

WT: So you don't feel an urge to flee the company of other writers, or their ghosts?

BH: The good ones are so few. But fiction writers are good people, usually. There's a lot of pretenders, but I haven't met a lot of sons of bitches.

WT: Well, if you stick with it, it beats you into a certain humility.

BH: Right, humility.

II. A CANNED DREAM OF THE SOUTH

[*I spent the afternoon with Barry riding around on the small roads outside Oxford. We paid a long, warm visit to Larry Brown's grave, which lies on the shore of a catfish pond Larry owned. Afterward, we went to Barry's house, a modest 1950s ranch in a suburban neighborhood not far from the university.*]

BH: Kawasaki 1500. It's the best bike I've ever owned. It's just a joy. You want a beer?

WT: Sure. That'd be great.

BH: I got Miller in glass, and I got straight Bud in a glass.

WT: I'll take the Bud.

BH: Sit here. It's a good chair.

WT: Are you mostly working on the typewriter these days?

BH: Always. That's all I use. Pencil, pen, and typewriter. I put a tin roof out here just for the rain.

WT: It's a great sound. I wish you could get it on a white-noise machine.

BH: We got a pool out back, so it's a better house than an Eisenhower house. We put the decks around it, added a pool. I've got very musical students so we play some over here. I play bass and flugelhorn but I always envied the guitar, the way you handle it. When I got very ill and almost died Susan built this library, all the shelves. I came back and Susan wants to give me an environment to write in. It's not necessary, I told her. I write in motels. I write at the kitchen table, but she's from Southern California money and you're supposed to look like a writer. I don't get off on being imperial. I was just flat bad when I tried to write for Robert Altman [*Power and Light*]. At his house, I was in a wooden tower with Plexiglas windows and gulls were all round you and the Pacific Ocean came under the house and I said, "Shit, this is heaven, I don't have a subject, it's just too good."

WT: He optioned *Ray*?

BH: No, he didn't. He liked *Ray,* but I went out there. I thought there was gonna be a future in it but there wasn't.

There's too much crap in here. I always thought I'd live among books, you realize when you move, you're moving stuff you'll never read again. I'm just giving away a lot of stuff now. It's my time in life to give it away to someone who's gonna read it. Most of these books are history, all of Cormac McCarthy, Bukowski, Larry Brown, Flannery O'Connor, Hemingway, Faulkner.

I'm just like an elder modernist. *Postmodern* is a very flat, meaningless term to me. I'm nothing like John Barth or Robert Coover. I don't like games about writing.

WT: I recently came across an interview with someone who couldn't stop calling you a "difficult writer." It seemed to piss you off.

BH: I'm disheartened by others who've said that. I never thought I was that difficult. I thought I was writing for a fairly hip, intelligent crowd; I just thought there were more of them out there. But they're not. They're not out there waiting. They're not gonna use their intelligence on your book. They'll use it on television or something—so I was kind of brokenhearted that I was called difficult. I always intended to be light and open. I misjudged the American audience. On the other hand, I've had students at Iowa who've sold a lot of books, there just aren't huge numbers of writers who are doing well. It's not impossible. I guess it's the plot element that I don't care enough about. I don't really care about plot; I want to have a page-turner in a different kind of way.

WT: *Yonder* was pretty complexly plotted, but it wasn't a book whose satisfactions were necessarily in the plot.

BH: My stories do have plot. They're not just scattered language; they're controlled, toward an end. I do love storytelling. I start out in a very plain, old-fashioned way. I'm obviously not connecting with the thousands of people I thought were out there. Maybe because I grew up with smart peers, people up on music, science, the world. I grew up with some smart damn people, and that might have hindered me as a writer. You had to be quick.

WT: Do you read magazines?

BH: If someone would rave about a story in the *New Yorker*, I'll read it. But you get a lot of that Woody Allen–New Yorker–Hamptons fiction. My [students] have to send off to the little magazines. I get the sense that only grad students read those.

WT: Writer's writers?

BH: I don't like that term, because I wouldn't buy somebody's album on a dare if they called him a musician's musician. I don't write to be a writer's writer. I don't want to be like the little-magazine writer. I don't want to be that.

Categories are bad news. Being Southern will just kill you sometimes. It's not always a graceful adjective. Sometimes it means, don't bother because it's gonna be [*Sings a lick from dueling banjos*]. It's gonna be: porch, banjo, Negroes. There's a canned dream of the South that a lot of people get into, and I've resisted that stuff my entire so-called career. Ready-made Southernism just disgusts me, just makes me nauseated. I mean, you can't see a movie without hearing that goddamned slide guitar. Shit, I'm just so tired of it.

WT: Well, at the same time, you've exchanged in readership what you've gained in esteem. Fifty or a hundred years from now, it seems pretty likely that people will still be reading *Airships* or *Geronimo Rex,* but they probably won't be reading *The Firm.*

BH: John is honest about what he does. Knowing his audience is what made him rich. His novels plug into anywhere—black, Indonesian, whatever's hot in Hollywood, let's ram it in there. Got something about a drunk in a busted trailer? Call Cate Blanchett. Put her in.

But Grisham, he's a lawyer. He's not literary, and that helped him. He found an audience that none of us knew existed. People who have never owned a book. Lawyers don't read and Walmart people don't read, but they will read a Grisham.

["A Creature in the Bay of St. Louis"] is the kind of story that's gonna have an audience, that's the kind of thing, if I wrote more of those I'd be a lot more famous. I think my wife even finds me too literary, she's a good critic: "Where's the plot, where's the story, let's keep it moving."

WT: How do you revise?

BH: I tell these students there's no use in revising something that's bad. I believe that, for short stories. It's brief, very brief, from four to twelve pages, getting something done. I don't believe in rewriting this one goddamned story. If the first draft is no goddamned good, it's no good. It's stupid to revise it, to me. The first draft has got to be loaded with most of it. Does it not? It can't just be a shell of what's going to be. I think it's got to be exciting.

I had my first airport book with *Yonder Stands Your Orphan* when I was sixty. It's going to be a middle seller, but I love the short story. I don't know why more people don't jump on them. They are the breath of life.

III. THE PISTOL THING

[*We are having lunch at Proud Larry's restaurant, off Oxford's downtown square.*]

BH: I didn't ever mean to be a teacher. I thought I'd sell a hundred thousand and be off. My model was Kerouac, and *On the Road*. You write a book, get a New York publisher, and sell a hundred thousand and you're set up to smoke opium out in the casbah and write book after book. I'm not kidding. I was so blissfully ignorant. But I've taught consistently except when I was with Altman, which was a good life experience but it meant nothing to me artistically. Nothing. But I'm glad I did it. I'm glad I got to know California pretty well for three years. I was there because I didn't want to teach anymore. I'd been fired in Alabama for drunkardly behavior.

WT: Was that the pistol thing?

BH: Yeah. I never pulled a loaded pistol on anybody, but it got around that I did. It got turned into lore. It's a myth. There's so much bad gun stuff. I've pulled away from guns. They're not funny anymore. There was no one, when I was in school, who talked about going in and blowing up students. The teachers were very stern and hateable, but nobody ever mentioned murder. But I do enjoy the teaching, and it's also a pleasurable distraction when the writing's not going well. It keeps you going. I'm re-energized, though, I think, having found the answer to this novel. I did this with a Jeb Stuart novel I thought I wanted to write, and I spent months and months on it, and I ended up with three short stories, which was all I was interested in, and the Jeb Stuart stories are in *Airships*. I've made this mistake before, it was just that reception to *Yonder* was so good that I wanted to do another novel. That was the market talking, it wasn't me. It's fun to see your book in an airport. It's fun. I hope we'll still see yours in there. Will you send me a copy? I imagine I'll like it.

WT: I don't know. My book's really an apprenticeship at the form. I mean, there are some OK stories and a few dismal failures.

BH: Are you the only one calling them dismal failures? They were all published in magazines. Why would they print them?

WT: I think they're fairly clean stories. I cared a good deal about the language. They show some effort, I think.

BH: You never know, man. It might get in the airport and sell a bunch. I sure hope it does.

WT: Yeah, we'll see. I've got no illusions about making a lot of dough with the fiction. It's tough enough trying to write something that I believe to be worth a shit without worrying about whether lots of people will want to buy it or not. I did a fair amount of work on it, lots of serious revisions, trying out different ways of telling each story.

BH: I know that feeling of knowing that a story could be better, different, but I got used to the idea that there's no inevitable one way to tell a story, there are always a number of ways, third person, first person, and often it's worth trying. So you went to Columbia for your MFA? Did you like it?

WT: Sure. It's a pretty vast program, but I had a great mentor there with Ben Marcus. He was a brilliant teacher and an incredibly generous advocate for my work.

BH: I think it's a useful degree. It should teach you discipline, and you should find out whether you've got endurance. I don't really believe in a creative-writing major as an undergraduate. It's a bad idea, terrible. I've met creative-writing majors from other places and they don't know a goddamn thing. They're the worst students. They just think they're good because they could pass.

WT: Yeah, they get very good at building these well-armored little stories, elliptical and spare and hard to wedge your critical pry-bar into, mainly because the story's not trying to *do* anything.

BH: They're too young. Why would you major in something you're not ready for? That you wouldn't be ready for until you know the world? There are no seventeen-to-eighteen-year-old novelists and very few in their twenties. The average age for a first novel now is forty-two.

WT: Do you think *Boomerang* will be the end of your straight memoiristic writing?

BH: I almost didn't release that one. I didn't feel it was all that mature, but I just didn't have anything else to say at the time. So I just structured the book with a slight plot that allowed me to pretty much tell the truth, a book about my friends and the places I was living. I was very hesitant to print it, but since then many people say they've enjoyed it.

IV. "ALL MY HEROES WERE ALCOHOLICS."

WT: I remember this reading you did at the New School, and the room was crowded with all of these young writers, and you said, "Before you all embark on this weird career, I'd encourage you to ask yourselves whether you really want to spend your scant years on the planet stalking life in the peculiar way that writers must." How do you feel it shook out for you? Is there much to regret?

BH: No, because the other side of the coin is so rich. You get to live more than others, too. You get to be more people, and certainly, if you're successful, you get to go more places, but it does make your relationships difficult.

WT: How do the "bad Barry" years—the wild years—look to you now?

BH: I wasted a lot of time. I don't care whether alcoholism's a disease or not, you're still guilty of the ugly things you said. Some of the ugly things I said to my second wife, I'd love to take them back. But it's too late. The wild stuff is all so overrated. Drinking, you don't feel good all the time. There's a lot of down, a lot of misery. Had I just had a series of beautiful women and that had been the extent of the wildness, that'd be great, but it wasn't like that. But, you know, all my heroes were alcoholics: Joyce, Hemingway, Faulkner. How many more do you want?

The alcohol had the code and mystery about it as a writer's drug, but I'm glad that's been debunked. But the trouble with the drinking, much as I hate to admit it, is it helped the work. The first two drinks were always wonderfully liberating. You think better. You're braver, and you'll say anything. If you could just hang in there with two or three, it'd be beautiful. The trouble was I couldn't.

And the hangovers were terrible, and to stop them you go back to the hair of the dog, eventually, and then you're drinking more and more. I was reading this book about Led Zeppelin and there's a bit where Jimmy Page is talking about his heroin habit of ten years, and he never realized how close health could be. He was shocked he'd been strung out for so long.

It was terrible. I hate to be fatalistic about it, but alcoholism, man, it's just in your genes. We had some of it in my family, and it just got me.

WT: What was that piece you did for the *O.A.* [*Oxford American*], "Christ in the Room," where you said you'd had an encounter with Jesus?

BH: I was not on any hospital drugs, I know the mind plays tricks, and this was such a close-up, tangible dream that I woke up weeping. It made sense; it was not surrealistic; it was Christ with the mountains behind him, red, brown. And it was just a big thing in my life. I think I became a better guy. I don't know, I'm still thinking about what lobe of the brain gives you that. Why not Buddha? Obviously it's cultural and I'm generally agnostic. I'm a pantheist at best, but I love Christ—who doesn't? But when you start getting the Bible you understand why young men and women go to divinity schools and come out atheists. It's not that these places are cradles of atheism, it's that they finally read the book, and they're just confused!

WT: What do you do with an experience like the one you had?

BH: It transfers to something prayer-like, an appreciation of the word, but you don't have to be religious to get it, but if you're a young Baptist, you might as well be a young communist, they get to you early and indoctrinate you. Children will listen to anything elders say to survive, and if you grew up without an elder telling you there was a god, what did your parents say to you? Still, I wish the religious less ill than I used to.

WT: I grew up without any religion. Though I guess the faith that life matters more because of stuff people made up—books, music—isn't a bad approximation.

BH: Music, absolutely. That's where I've always felt like a failure, you want the pure music and you never get it.

WT: I'll fight you on that one about your work.

BH: Everything's a failure, when you compare it to music.

WT: *Bats Out of Hell,* there's something about the fierceness of the wit, the electricity in the language, and structural rigor of the stories that seems to me both braver and more disciplined than the earlier stuff.

BH: I think that one's my best work, frankly. People love *Airships* a lot more.

WT: Well, the thing I've always admired in your work is that the language itself is a force of joy. The vitality and gunpowder in every word is itself an agent of life. It's like Melville. It's not about the whale; it's about the pleasure with language. There's so much joy and exuberance packed into the wordcraft, every sentence is about to blow six gaskets.

BH: I'm one of those who never finished *Moby-Dick.* I couldn't get through the thick Shakespearean stuff. I would have advocated for editing that. If it had been, it'd be accessible and great. The purists want to read all that fucking cetology, man. You know, though, I love the water and fish. I should adore the whale and fish. Maybe I should try again. ✶

ALEKSANDAR HEMON

COLUM McCANN

"I DON'T CARE WHAT OTHER BOOKS ARE LIKE, BAD OR NOT. I AM GOING TO KEEP DOING THIS. I CANNOT BE STOPPED."

Ways in which writers suffer from reduced moral authority:

Banality of language
Acceptance of the ordinary

leksandar Hemon is the author of four works of *fiction, including the novel* The Lazarus Project *(Riverhead 2008) and a short-story collection,* Love and Obstacles *(Riverhead 2009). He was born in Sarajevo, Bosnia-Herzegovina, where he lived until he ended up in Chicago, where he lives now.*

Colum McCann is the author of seven works of fiction, including the National Book Award–winning novel Let the Great World Spin *(Random House 2009),* Zoli *(Random House 2007), and* Dancer *(Metropolitan Books 2003). He was born in Dublin, Ireland, and now lives in New York where he teaches in the Hunter College MFA Creative Writing program.*

This conversation is an email continuation of a series of conversations between Hemon (a.k.a. Sasha) and McCann. The most memorable one took place in Lyon, France, some years back, which ended in a bar with an unreal collection of whiskeys, with both men singing "Waltzing Matilda" to the accompaniment of a choir of humming Frenchmen. That much is recalled— the rest is supplied by the imagination and the whiskey's after-kick.

(January 2010)

COLUM McCANN: What are we doing here? Why aren't we in a pub?

ALEKSANDAR HEMON: Because you live in the provinces, far away from everything.

CM: So, we're here… to talk (as the bishop to the hooker). The next question is: why are we here? That, of course, is easy to answer. But, seriously, sometimes I wonder if we—I mean, we, us, as writers— have to increasingly justify ourselves, you know, like visual artists, whose primary mode of entry into their art seems to be the pains-taking explanation of it. Forget the painting. There's a whole busi-ness built up around it. The artists have to acquire a specific language. Have you read any of those "statements of purpose" (!) by some of the contemporary artists? It's like stepping through acres of fresh tar. You pick one foot up only to find the other sinking further.

AH: Actually, I have not read any of those statements of purpose, but I can imagine what they look like. I wouldn't be so hard on artists, though. On the one hand, all artists, writers included, have an ethics and an aesthetics, whether they can formulate them or not. I happen to think that it is good to be able to formulate—it is good to know what you are doing and to be able to talk about it. On the other hand, art is so widely (and often thinly) spread, that anything can be it. A lot of it is nothing but a gesture, not an object, not a thing unto itself, and it literally does not exist without interpretation. I am all for interpretation, but for the past century or so, an interpretation can be slapped on everything and anything. Literature, on the other hand, is always something—it is either story or poetry, ideally both. That is, you always know what it is and even if the interpretation is not available, the experience of language is. Language is so inherent to humanity, so necessary for even basic thinking, that stories and poetry are available to anyone who can process language. So it's easy for us.

CM: I happen to think that an ounce of empathy is worth a boatload of judgment. A writer can disease himself or herself with his or her own position, thinking about it too much. But, that said, I'm slightly off-put by our world getting increasingly rarefied, like the world of art, where we must justify ourselves with our meaning. Imagine constantly explaining ourselves. Like a football commentary or something...

AH: What do you mean "our world"? You mean the literary world? What is that? I don't know what that is.

CM: A book that matters.

AH: Many books matter to many people.

CM: I love finding one that matters to me. It doesn't happen every day.

AH: What I do know is this: I spent the day reading books that are out of print. I read them as part of my research for a future project. And then I spent time staring out the window imagining people and situations in places I have not visited (and probably won't), at the time I did not experience. It will be a while before I put the pen on the paper, if indeed I ever do. But I will continue obsessing about these people—they have names already—and I will keep imagining landscapes, their lives and deaths, and I will love them. I will spend years doing that, not really talking to anybody about it. It is crazy, there is no reason to do it. But that's what I've been doing all these years and it is well past any need for justification. And once I write the book, and it gets published, if I'm lucky, then it exists and it will keep existing. And that existence is well past justification.

And I am not sure who it is you think we must justify ourselves to?

CM: Well, to our children, for one. To ourselves, for another. I never knew my great-grandfather, but he walked the streets of Dublin on June 16, 1904. I can understand my great-grandfather now, and the line of fathers that came after him, so much better because I happen to have read *Ulysses,* because I have walked through those pages. Those small corners. The odd riff. The jaunt down from Eccles Street. Davy Byrne and Blazes Boylan. The National Library. Literally my great-grandfather (whom of course I never met) becomes flesh and blood for me in the pages of a novel. The novel (a "fiction"!) invents his human form for me.

As you yourself say, in *The Lazarus Project,* "All the lives we could live, all the people we will never know, never will be, they are everywhere. That is what the world is." That to me is the essence of literature, and why I used your quote as the epigraph (I almost said epigram) of my own new novel. We become alive in bodies and geographies and times not our own. That's the justification. That's enough purpose because I think what it does is it expands our ability not only to justify, but to criticize that self-justification.

I want to delve into your novel a little more. For me it's the best book I've read in years. On the most basic level it just opened me, continually, opened up the synapses and the veins too. Literature is not an Olympics, but my god, I really think you created something lasting and purposeful here. When I think back on my first experience of reading it—and I've read it now twice—I recall thinking that it restored my belief in the possibility of literature and what matters, the music of what matters.

AH: Thank you. That is a beautiful thing to say to a writer.

CM: It's a great contemporary novel. It cross-weaved in the most extraordinary way, in the sense that it is European and American also, it went right to the dusty corners of the twentieth century, then jumped right up to present-day Sarajevo, went into the kitchen, opened the can of sardines (or "sadness" as Brik says), excused itself to the street once more, and a few pages on found itself in Abu Ghraib before circling back to Chicago in the early part of the twentieth century. It had such access, it was like a Whitman poem. In fact, I was reminded of a line from Mandelstam that goes something like, "I desire this thinking body— / this charred bony flesh, / alive to its own span— / to turn into a street, a country."

A question, then. I detected a necessity, if that's the right word. And a necessity that required anger. So, how much anger did it take to write that novel?

AH: I want a book to contain a world—indeed the world. Writing is my main means of engagement with the world and I want the scars of that engagement to be left in the language. I write and read with the assumption that literature contains knowledge of human experience that is not available otherwise.

Rilke said that art can come only out of inner necessity. I write because I must. Or because I cannot not write. Danilo Kiš said that he started writing only after he overcame his disgust with literature. As for anger—unfortunately, it constitutes me. I put a lot of anger into *Lazarus* when I was writing it, then I took out a lot of it when I was editing it. What is left is no longer my anger. But I have plenty more in me for future projects.

CM: The anger is still there. It's so necessary to the book. It propels it. Another question, not too distant from the first: we don't seem to have a lot of anger in us, our own generation of writers, the forty-somethings—we seem rather tame and afraid of upsetting one another. I'm not necessarily advocating a scrap, but we all seem scared, mea culpa. Shall we have a fistfight?

AH: Get your hand back first.

CM: Yeah, being just out of hospital (a hand/wrist problem) I realize we need a lot more than a good fist for a fight. I want to engage on a level that lets me know that my blood's boiling.

AH: Not living in New York, I am sure I miss a lot of literary spats and mouth-offs, but I still think there is a lot of conflict. The problem is not the shortage of writerly conflicts, the problem is their irrelevance. The ones I caught, though I can't remember a single one at this time, seem so personal, petty and inconsequential. They're like upstairs neighbors fighting: noise, drama, someone else's life. I don't know what your model for a productive scrap might be, but I think that a necessary ingredient ought to be something that matters—there ought to be something at stake: an aesthetics, an ethics, a world—so that confronting another writer is related to some kind of vision, or, if you wish, a future. For a fight to be productive, or at least relevant, writers should fight over different demands they put upon writing (as an individual, private act) and literature (a network of relations in which we are all involved). There is no shortage of conflict, but there is a shortage of ethics and aesthetics. I am itching to criticize some well-regarded writers' works, but I am not doing it because I am perfectly aware that my critique could easily be reduced to envy or just plain meanness.

There is also the fact that literature seems so fragile these days (What is happening to reading? What is happening to books? What is happening to publishing?), so there is instinctive solidarity among writers as professionals—you don't want to get someone fired. We are all swimming in the same sea of shit.

CM: Well, something poisonous has certainly been let loose in the past several years, and I suppose the idea of having a spat against an individual means nothing in the larger scheme of things. The English call it *handbags,* as in slinging handbags at each other. A lot of it went on in previous generations of writers (nothing as good as fifth-century Greece, I suppose) but now we're backed up against a different wall, and perhaps the fear is that nobody's watching and so we need to make noise. I think this prospect of irrelevance is what we buck up against, and perhaps that brings us together. But I'm worried. Here we are, post-Bush, but still in the middle of a national regression to the robber-baron mentality, the continued opposition to enlightened social legislation, the ongoing kowtow to the lowest common denominator. There's an idea that Obama's going to save us all. I danced as much as anyone the night he was elected, but we're in such a deep swamp I'm not sure we're going to get out of it that easily.

AH: I agree, but at least I don't feel that I'm living under occupation any more. It's like we've been fucking liberated.

CM: No kidding. I can actually go back to Ireland and not be embarrassed about living in America. When thinking about America the line returned: "You can't go back to the country that doesn't exist anymore"—I'm so glad. It was torturous living here. Imagine having to be tortured here.

But speaking of legislation and enlightenment, I've a question about books, the country of books. I've been reading a lot about Émile Zola, the French writer in the nineteenth century, and his rage, his belief in the novel as a social tool, the possibility of a novel restoring the value of a life which has been devalued by others. He was interested in the notion of "living out loud." He wanted to dilate the nostrils of the young French writers, get them fired up. He brought the novel out into the streets, the mines, the brothels. It's all rather dizzying stuff and whenever I talk about him I just watch people's eyebrows beginning to raise, up up up. But he had *cojones*. He didn't want his audacity to be pardoned.

AH: Yes, but he was writing when there was not only a possibility of revolution, but a few had taken place. Workers would go on strike, the army would shoot them, cities burned. Social conflict and political war were daily occurrences. Europe—and the world—was rife with serious revolutionary movements. Zola did not invent or own that rage, nor was his agency limited to writing. For Zola's work to have social impact, there had to have been a movement or movements, and for him to have any agency he could not stand outside of that. Having grown up in a socialist country—moribund as it was—I still caught the tail end of socialist realism understood as a legitimate aesthetics. You could find a Stalinist novel in the library, in the classics section. In college, I read interpretations of Chekhov and Kafka that claimed to have discovered revolutionary spirit in their works. I've read books in school that were written by ideological rote—they were brainwashers. Therefore, any art, any literature, that has a clearly defined political goal is repellent to me.

If I may offer a critique of your position as I understand it, you are a romantic, attracted to noble individuals, far too noble, far too beholden to their inner necessities to be respected and cherished by the world. Zoli, Rudi, Petit, et al. They are heroes, in the Greek sense: the people with hubris, perhaps even saints, inasmuch as they are infused with some divine spirit. That is great stuff for literature, but the worst stuff for political change. (And Obama is a perfect example—he is seen as a hero, someone above politics, but he is a first-class politician, if we are lucky.) Therefore you are fascinated by Zola's hubris, by his noble stand, but only because he had the balls. The balls do not make a writer, and I believe this is where we might disagree.

CM: But I'd say that I was interested in using that hubris not to talk about hubris, which is uninteresting, but, again, the music of what matters. In writing *Dancer* I didn't care one whit about Rudolf Nureyev nor his very obvious hubris. I cared about the shoemaker, the rentboy, the smaller characters at the edges. In this new novel I want to use the obvious arrogance of something like the [tightrope] walk across the World Trade Center towers not to talk about the walk itself, but all the people who live *below* the walk. The novel starts out big, but ends up being very intentionally local, on a little Bronx backstreet. The forgotten thirty-eight-year-old grandmother is the heart of the novel. It pretends to be a novel about a tightrope walker, but it is absolutely nothing of the sort. What is at stake here is so much more. It's an intentional critique of how we order our stories. If that doesn't come through, then I have failed.

AH: It does come through, gorgeously. But Petit's presence, walking up in the sky, allows for the space in which Corrigan and Tillie and all the other beautiful people you create will exhibit their saintly hubris, much like Rudi's presence, like a flash of lightning, illuminates all the other characters around him. They are pseudo-prophetic presences who allow the others to come to light.

CM: Tillie commits suicide, she loses her family, but yes, still she has a purpose. Like your Rora, she is able to grieve. She discovers the ability to grieve. And yes, I think we do disagree, though not as much as some might think. I have the obvious visceral reaction to being called a romantic. I can feel my skin prickle. Might it be as easy to call me a cynic? I'd prefer to balance the contradictions. The political is in the local. You say that writing is the only thing you can do. You cannot live without it. And I understand that. But, Sasha, I can live without it, I think. I mean, I could survive. But if I can tell my kids a story that shifts their world sideways a little, then I will do it. And, by extension, therefore it is the only thing

I want to do. Which is not only romantic, but hopefully fierce, or hopelessly fierce.

AH: I admire that. On the one hand, it latches on to a worthy tradition, including the actual Romantics. On the other, it takes belief, a willingness to die for the cause, so to speak.

Don't die, though.

CM: Robert Stone said something along the lines that we have to make sure we don't die. At least not yet.

Of course, elementally, one of the functions of writing—even if unread—is that it lasts. But so much writing in the past few years—so much of what seems to garner praise—is housebroken and mannered and so very well behaved. Want to say a couple of bad words? Say *social novel*. Want to say a really bad word? Say *lyrical*. Want to sell a lot of books? Write about the prep school. Or the creative writing program. There seems to be an exhaustion around the narrative form, at least until recently, when it seems more and more young writers are taking the bull by the horns. I've been noticing more of an engagement, an excitement in the air. But in general I think it's true that a lot of writers are taking on less of the world and sitting back in stunned submission to the publishing execs.

I may be overreaching my claim here, and there are notable exceptions, of course, but I think we as writers suffer from a reduced moral authority, and a lot of the blame has to do with us, because we have been so fucking well behaved, no Guantánamo novels, no Katrina novels that I know of yet, no *Grapes of Wrath*. There's a fashionable modesty of idea, a banality of language, an acceptance of the ordinary.

AH: Here is the news, Mr. McCann: novels do not solve problems, though ideally they cause some. And if a Katrina novel would be a noble effort, that does not mean it would be any good—and if it is not good, then the pain and suffering and humiliation would have been misused for a literary tryout. You don't practice your craft on other people's tragedy. Moreover, the tragedy of Katrina was broadcast live. Painfully so. You also seem to demand immediacy. That is, you need a Guantánamo novel, and Guantánamo is not even closed yet. What's the rush? It's not that war crimes stop as soon as a novel about them is published. Literature operates slowly, it is always inching toward bliss, never quite getting there.

CM: But I've never even dreamt that novels can solve problems. If they could we'd have no problems, or more likely no novels. And you're right, the Guantánamo novel will probably take twenty years. But here is the flipside of the news: stories have to be told over and over again, lest we forget them. Here, I think you make a mistake. You're assuming once told is always told. Which I fear is the problem of how history is presented.

AH: Some are told over and over again, I know. I've heard a lot of them. And stories will not be forgotten. There is something called narrative paradigm. It is a term from psychology and, for me, it boils down to this: people understand their own life as stories. They see themselves as characters in the stories of their life. Storytelling is a cognitive framework. But the models for those stories often come from the outside—they used to come from books (Emma Bovary imagined her life as a romantic novel, but lost control of the plot), and these days come from movies and television. As long as there are living human beings, there will be language and stories.

What you demand from storytelling is a moral—even political— import. I tend to shun that didactic aspect.

CM: But I'd hate to think that you or I or anyone else would tell people how to think. The space to undergo experience, or empathize, is a different space from the didactic space. Allowing space for change is allowing space for grace. That's what I get from good writing. That's what I get from your books. And I have to agree,

I have nothing to say that will change anybody's mind. Nothing. Being didactic is uninteresting. But allowing space for people to remake their minds about things, to change—or to get angry—is a viable literary purpose. That I fail at this over and over is my reason to continue. Failure is edifying. We break the lights.

AH: I like the idea of a book being a democratic space which readers enter, carrying their own thoughts, and participate in a conversation, or experience of grace. But what's important here is that there is no *we*. There is no inherent solidarity—of purpose, of ethics or aesthetics—among writers. There may be some shared experience of irrelevance, but that just makes people pissy and lonely. We are not engaged in a common project. There are a few writers I could loosely define a common project with—the project being the kind of literature that respects the individual sovereignty of human beings—and with them I can talk and argue, but that does not mean we may not be in conflict beyond repair in some other field. And there are many who are engaged in entirely different projects, aesthetical or political.

CM: I agree, I agree, I agree. But I hear you favoring the lonely outpost, which is in itself an acutely romantic idea. There's a real danger in flying the lonely flag. It reinforces stereotypes of the writer, and it suggests, to the reader, that it doesn't ultimately matter.

AH: Whatever solidarity I have established with other writers individually, it is usually organized around books. We connected as readers, as it were, not writers. To me, the solidarity of readers is far more important than the solidarity of writers, particularly since readers in fact find ways to connect over a book or books, whatever they may be. And no book will get all the readers, not even books like the Bible, which strives to get all the readers. Books with a fashionable modesty of ideas will find the readers who respond to banal language and accept the ordinary unquestioningly. And some other readers will carry a book of Brodsky's poems in their pockets at all times. And there are readers who engage with books in both of those modes.

It was always clear to me that I would have to earn my readers, some I would have to find, some to create. No reader owes me anything—I am owed nothing for my noble efforts, because my writing was always unconditional, always coming out of inner necessity. Another way to say it: I don't care what other books are like, bad or not. I am going to keep doing this. I cannot be stopped.

CM: Yes… breaking the traffic lights. I love it! It's never too late to let a reader finish a book for you.

AH: Let me ask you something about *Let the Great World Spin*. It is clearly a book about the city of New York, a celebration of it. But it is entirely devoid of fashionable glamour that taints so much of writing and art and whatnot coming from New York. Could your book have been written for and/or in any other city?

CM: Oh yeah, I hope so. Chicago. Dublin. Paris. But New York is where it felt right. And I know New York pretty well now. But I also wanted the under- and overcurrent of the towers, which come down, which fall. And then there's something about New York and just what an international city it is. I love it here. And I have to say that I had so much fun doing this novel. When I found the voice of Tillie I felt that she had a kinship with Molly. Just like when—as a reader—I found the voice of your Lazarus I thought I had entered a breathing space that I'd always wanted. Come forth Lazarus, and he came in first, or fifth, it doesn't matter.

I have to say I enjoy every inch of it, even the slow painstaking parts, the building up and smashing down. The touring. The teaching. I love teaching. As I said earlier, I spent a period in hospital recently and—apart from my own family, Allison and the kids—I missed my students the most. So I'd have to say that I like the life.

And even the parts that other people sneer at, like the New York literary parties. I actually enjoy them—why not? If it's no fun I'll just leave. It's easy. How about you? How much do you enjoy it, the writing life? The work, the territory, the travel?

AH: I hate traveling and being away from my family. But I like meeting my readers, as what I write is actualized in them. Those encounters are exhilarating to me. I was in Sarajevo recently and had a reading attended by my parents and my sister and family friends and my friends of thirty years and kids young enough to be my children and professors from whose books I studied language, etc. It was like a perfect funeral, except it was a fulfillment of something—a community reconstituted. And after I was done, it broke apart.

CM: Pub now, come on. Let's go! ✳

MARY GAITSKILL

TALKS WITH

SHEILA HETI

"VIRGINIA WOOLF—I'M SURE SHE WOULD
HAVE BEEN A GREAT WRITER, REGARDLESS,
BUT SHE HAD A LOT OF HELP, TOO.
LEONARD WAS A WIFE. THAT'S INVALUABLE.
WOMEN DO NOT HAVE THAT VERY OFTEN."

Pop-culture examples of people loved for their hideousness:

Buffy the Vampire Slayer
Tony Soprano
Dexter, America's Favorite Serial Killer

Iwent to visit *Mary Gaitskill on a pleasant October day in the comfortable, chalet-like home she shares with her husband, also a writer, on the campus of Bard College (though neither of them teaches there).*

She had recently submitted to her publisher her latest story collection, Don't Cry, *her fifth book in twenty years. Her first,* Bad Behavior, *was also a collection, published when she was thirty-three. This was followed three years later by the novel* Two Girls, Fat and Thin, *then the story collection* Because They Wanted To, *and, eight years later, in 2005, the novel* Veronica, *about a former fashion model, which was a finalist for the National Book Award and the National Book Critics Circle Award.*

Perhaps due less to her writing than to the film Secretary, *which was based on her short story, her name is often associated with images of degradation, sexy sadomasochism, and female weakness. But her themes are richer and more vast. What is most amazing about Gaitskill is her ability to portray the heart of human longing and suffering, and to see in each gesture of our lives the disturbing and conflicting pool of drives that marks our every gesture.*

In Don't Cry, *she speaks more directly about America than in previous works. One story traces what transpires in an airport between a widowed old woman and a young, fatherless boy, set against the backdrop of the Iraq War. Another follows a single woman who travels with a friend to Ethiopia to adopt a baby. In these stories, we find the same loneliness, attempts to connect, and flashes of beauty.*

Soon after I arrived at her home around midday, she served me large cookies and apples and made tea. We sat for over two hours at a wood table in her dining room, across from each other. Her demeanor was fragile, powerful, and tough, her voice gentle and steady, and she always made very direct eye contact. She laughed often, intent and friendly.   —*Sheila Heti (February 2009)*

I. THE UNKNOWABLE

SHEILA HETI: Henry Miller says that when he was younger, he was mainly imitating other writers and was interested in plot and these other things, and that then he discovered "the vital thing," and after that he was able to write in a different way—in a way that was closer to his real preoccupations and that truly expressed himself. He never says what that "vital thing" is, and I wonder if for you there's a vital thing in writing—something that has to be there.

MARY GAITSKILL: Yeah, but it's very hard to say what it is, and I should preface my answer by saying that when I was first interviewed, when I published *Bad Behavior*, I really didn't know how to answer interview questions, because I never thought analytically about what I was doing, so I would answer very clumsily. I heard myself on a live radio show and the interviewer was

Michael Silverblatt, and I was dumbstruck—there was just this silence. Since you can't have dead airtime on the radio, he would answer for me, and I would be like, *Yeah, yeah, that's what I meant.* When I listened to that, I was horrified—I thought I sounded stupid. It's not good to let other people define your work for you. They're going to do it anyway, but you should at least step up to the plate when you're asked. So I cultivated a method. I began to think analytically, which I had to do to teach, anyway, and I began to cultivate an approach where I would answer questions in a very thorough way. But after listening to myself talk and talk and talk, I now think the more intelligent response was the silence, because I don't think people know. It's only after writing it do you look at it and go, *Oh yeah, that's what I was doing*—but most of the time when you're actually writing, you don't have that clear an idea. I think you do in some unconscious way, but it isn't that thought-out, analytical thing you call upon when you're answering questions.

Having said that, I think the closest thing I can come to defining what that vital thing is for me—is that there's a sort of soul quality in writing, if it's any good. It has a spirit or an energy to it that is very integral to who the writer is on a deep level. It's almost a cellular thing. It takes place in the cells of the writing, and it is what makes it alive or not. That's why most writers have a cynical attitude toward writing programs. You can teach people a lot about craft and various techniques, and you can certainly teach them to appreciate, but you *cannot* give them spirit or soul if it's not there.

SH: And do you think that's a gift? Do you put that ability into the realm of the unknowable?

MG: Yes. And it's something that critics don't much write about because most of them don't understand it, and I think even when they're sensitive to it, it's very difficult to. It's something that takes place almost under the skin or under the flesh of the plot of the story or the characters.

Sometimes when I teach a class I read a paragraph from *Bleak House*—a description of Lady Dedlock. On the one hand she's a very flat character, and we never cease to be aware of exactly what she's like. She's cold, she's rigid, she's self-tortured, she's proud. It's reasserted over and over again, both by the narrator and by her actions and words, but in the paragraph in which she's introduced there's this description around her of where she lives and it's just this vast, moving, wet, dripping, surging world that is mysterious and strange and infuses her with this power—this female power. So on the one hand she's like this static playing card, but on the other she's representative of this incredible force of nature—this primeval force and thwarted fecundity—a death and fecundity at once. And that's not something that's simple. That's not something that most writers have any understanding of how to do.

SH: Do you think it's also something most writers simply don't pay attention to in life?

MG: I think a lot of people don't *feel* it. And then many people feel it but they don't necessarily have the power to put it down on the page.

II. LONGHAND

SH: Nabokov is one of your favorite writers, and he talks about his characters as "galley slaves," and I wonder to what degree your characters have a mind of their own, or to what degree you have a sense beforehand of what's going to happen in your stories.

MG: Sometimes I don't have a sense. Other times I'll have a vague idea of what the story will be, but I can't find a way into it. Then I'll get an image that sometimes doesn't seem to have anything to do with the story but for some reason it's my way into it, but then I have to feel my way around and kind of—I make little notes in the margin of what I want to happen next, or what I want to talk about next.

SH: Do you write longhand, then?

MG: I used to write longhand exclusively. I've switched over now, partially. I usually start in longhand, then at some point I'll go to the computer. Actually, the last few stories I wrote totally on the computer. I'm not sure I like the change.

SH: How is it different?

MG: It's for some reason easier to write on the computer. I started to turn to it when I felt really blocked and frustrated writing longhand. Somehow sitting down at the computer was a little more freeing. It seemed more casual. I don't quite know why that is.

SH: But you like the casualness or you don't like the casualness?

MG: At times I do. If I'm having trouble getting anything on the page, I'm willing to go for that. I feel that when you're writing longhand, you really get heavily immersed in your own being, because your writing is so much you. Typing is ideal for revision because there's a distance to it. It's more impersonal. But there's another thing which is more practical. I've noticed that when I'm writing longhand, sometimes I'll write something and I'll go, *Oh, that's awful,* and I'll cross it out and I'll write something over it. And frequently when I go back, I decide that what I crossed out was actually better. When you're writing on the computer, you don't cross it out, you just delete it. But now, if I'm not sure, I don't delete it. Instead of making the revision, I just put it in a bracket and write my second idea, and I can look back and see which I think was better, because sometimes the first thing is actually better.

III. FREEDOM
AND SENTIMENTALITY

SH: Before a writer is published there is such a privacy, and I wonder if it's possible to get back to that same privacy. Was it very hard to write after your first book, *Bad Behavior,* was published?

MG: When I was writing the stories in *Bad Behavior,* I kept saying to myself, *It's OK, it's OK, it doesn't have to be good, no one will look at it.* And that was very liberating. I wasn't even thinking of it as a book. I was looking at it as whatever story I was working on at the moment. But after publishing *Bad Behavior* I was very self-conscious. I knew people would be looking at *Two Girls, Fat and Thin* and that I was going to be looked at more harshly, but also that the people who liked *Bad Behavior* would not turn their back on me if they did not like *Two Girls.* The third book was scarier because I didn't feel that I was going to be cut slack. I felt if that book was a flop, I was dead. That's kind of a ridiculous way to think, but I did have that fear.

SH: And with *Veronica*?

MG: I actually did feel very free. It had been so long since I put out a book that I felt that in some way I was no longer on the scene. I felt that people who read were aware of me, but that I wasn't really a focal point, there wasn't a spotlight on me, and it made me feel like I could do what I wanted, and I wasn't concerned with pleasing people. I actually thought that people wouldn't like it.

SH: Why?

MG: I felt it was very different from what I'd written before. I thought people might find the shifts in time confusing and would just be impatient with it, though I made an effort to have it follow subliminally, so the images would subliminally connect, and

I guess I succeeded, because it did not seem like many people found it confusing. But I was worried about that. I was worried that people would find it sentimental or gushy and mystical somehow.

SH: Sentimental? Why?

MG: It's not to me, because sentimental is false-feeling—but a lot of people now seem to confuse sentimentality with expression of strong emotion, and there *is* emotion strongly expressed in the book.

SH: Did people say it was sentimental at all?

MG: I didn't read most of the reviews, but my impression is that that wasn't a complaint.

SH: Why didn't you read them?

MG: I thought most of them would be bad, but also I don't want other people's voices in my head right now.

SH: Because you're working on other things and it could throw you off?

MG: Yeah.

SH: Do you worry about timeliness at all? If you're writing a story and it's taking years—

MG: I do worry. Perhaps I shouldn't. Perhaps it's small of me, but it's such a concern now. I think our sense of history has sped up and things change so much faster now. *Veronica* was originally written back in the '90s. I did worry and make an effort to bring the point of view up to a more current time, but I think it was fine still to talk about the '80s and '70s.

SH: Is that part of the reason you don't use brand names? I notice there are rarely pop-cultural figures in *Veronica*—

MG: Well, I refer to them every now and then. Doris Day, Jo Stafford—I have no problem referring to those people. What I don't usually like is when people just drop names in. I think it's lazy. It's assuming your reader is going to have a particular emotional or mental response to that thing or that singer or that person, and I don't think everybody *does* have the same response. So if I *do* use somebody like Judy Garland, I'm going to describe what Judy Garland looks and sounds like to the character. I may not describe it in enormous length, but if it's worth noticing—if the character's noticing it and she's having a response to it, then I want to say what that response is. To take the reader into a deeper experience of it.

IV. IN THE WORLD

SH: Re-reading all your books, then going out into the world, I started to see things in a much more granular way, like little shifts in people's perceptions of each other, and how feelings are so molecular, and how they change instant to instant. It made me go through the world with a heightened sensitivity to how every little gesture changes somebody else's little gesture. Do you feel like that's an accurate reflection of the way you go through the world?

MG: Sometimes, not always. One of the unnerving things that happened when *Bad Behavior* came out was that I was actually a very shy person and very socially awkward, and suddenly I found myself in these very sophisticated social circles, which I was not used to, and people seemed to expect me to have this X-ray vision and to be coming up with these witty, snappy comments, and that's not what I was like at all! I don't pay attention a lot of the time. When I'm sitting down to write something and I'm imagining a situation or remembering a person or whatever it is, that's when I really think, *What is going on here?* I think probably everybody in some unconscious way absorbs a great deal, but you're not consciously thinking about it all the time. If I'm puzzled by something or I'm not understanding a person, then I'll home in on them. Sometimes somebody does grab my attention in a very strong way, and I'll pay attention, but I don't pay attention like that all the time with my mind.

SH: Would you be able to explain what your basic attitude is toward people that you meet? Like if you go into a room or go to a party, is there a basic disposition you have toward humans going through the world?

MG: [*Slightly defensive*] Could *you* answer that question?

SH: Yeah. I think for me I would say that I basically admire the distinctness of people, and I feel that I start off with a kind of admiration that gets chiseled down, but my fundamental attitude is curiosity and imagining mostly that they have qualities that I would admire.

MG: That's very thoughtful. It really varies with me. A lot of it depends on the context, my mood. I mean, my attitude toward coming into a classroom of students is going to be different from my attitude going to a cocktail party, or to an interview, or answering the phone and I'm in a bad mood and I stub my toe and I pick it up and it's somebody trying to sell me something. I think in the past my baseline was probably very guarded. I think that because once someone who knew me very well said, "When you meet people, the door is locked, and if somebody says something that interests you, or you talk to them awhile and decide you're interested, then you unlock the door, but from their point of view they're just looking at a closed door." [*Laughs*] And I thought that was a great metaphor and interesting and possibly true for me at that time.

V. DISSOLVING

SH: I'm curious about your titles. Do you come up with a lot of different titles and choose the best one? *Because They Wanted To* is a title I love.

MG: Yeah, that one just came to me. *Bad Behavior* wasn't my title, although it certainly has a lot of resonance for many people, so I'm not unhappy about it, but it wasn't my idea.

SH: It was the publisher's?

MG: Yeah. Or her boyfriend's title. He was the one who came up with it.

SH: What was your title?

MG: It wasn't a very good one, but I still like it better than *Bad Behavior* and I would have preferred to have called it that.

SH: Called it what?

MG: I wanted to title it *Daisy's Valentine.*

SH: [*Laughs*] Right. Would you say that the characters you portray are the common run of humanity, or extreme cases—if there is such a thing as an extreme case?

MG: I don't think they are extreme cases. I think there *are* such things as extreme cases. I haven't written about that many of them. Most of my characters aren't very extreme. You read about the extreme ones in the paper. [*Laughing*]

SH: A reviewer, writing on *Veronica,* calls a model "the single most explicit expression of physical, superficial beauty in a contemporary setting." I wonder if that's what a model is for you.

MG: Yes and no. Death is a big theme in the book, illness. What is that? It's a fact that human beings—no matter who they are, no matter how healthy or strong or beautiful they are—are going to age and become weak and ugly by a certain standard, and die. And I think that's a terrifying idea for people to get their minds around. It's a very strange thing the way we exist: that we appear in the world out of another person's body in this discrete, small form, and that we have all of this life force pouring through us—as does everything alive, animals, insects—yet it must take this very specific form of a personality, a body that looks a certain way and that functions a certain way. Our eyes and our mouths and our noses are so particularly formed. Human beings look so different from each other, voices are so different, everything about us is so individual, and that's so exciting and juicy and appealing, and we're attached to these things and they're so fascinating and beautiful—I don't just mean model-beautiful, but all the individual forms that people can take.

And yet in another way, we're going to fall apart, kind of dissolve back into this vast soup from whence we came, whatever that is. It's almost like these beings pop out of this massive sludge and then they get sucked back into it, and that's a really hard thing to comprehend. I think people try to make the most of their time on earth and also to *fix* their time on earth. They try to fix external verities, things that are true for all time, ideas that are true for all time: Rome will last forever! America will last forever! Beauty, as defined by the fashion industry, is one of those things—*this* is beautiful. *This* will always be beautiful—and hold it in a way that has some sense of permanence about it, and absoluteness. And yet it's not.

Then take a young teenage girl who happens to be born in this definition of this thing. On the one hand, it must be very powerful and extraordinarily exciting for a girl of that age to be infused with this importance, and yet how confusing. I mean, she's just a very young, unformed person who's being asked and demanded by her job to take this very intense form that has all this meaning for people. That's a heavy thing. Also in the '90s, when I began writing the book, it became just monstrously, grotesquely important. This idea of the model. I mean, it had always been there. When I was hanging around in New York in the '80s I met models, and models were fixtures in nightclubs, but at least people I knew didn't make such a fuss over them. I mean, some men did, but certainly the women I knew didn't consider models to be the ultimate in what they might want to be. Then suddenly in the '90s it seemed like this was the ultimate of what a young woman should want to be, which seemed insane to me. I think it's changed a bit now—I hope. I'm not that attuned with popular culture but it seems like that's a little bit different now?

VI. WIVES

SH: Do you ever feel like you would rather have been born a man, or are you happy to have been born a woman?

MG: I think, for my type of personality, I might have been better as a male. When I was a kid, I did want to be a boy. I didn't like to play with dolls, and most of my friends were kind of sensitive, sissy boys. But as I got older, the mystique of being a girl began to interest me. It was confusing what sexuality was, and the responses of other people, but it didn't make me feel terrified or vulnerable. Then once I got into being a girl I did like it, although I was very conscious of and angry about certain inequalities or ways that women were treated. I became aware of that early and I didn't like it.

One thing I'm very envious of men for is when they get married—this is less true than it was, but I still think it's true—their wife is going to help them. Look at Nabokov. He was a brilliant writer. He would have been a brilliant writer no matter what. But do you know how much his wife *did* for him? She did the shopping. They would drive to the store together—she would drive. She did all the dealings with the landlord, she shoveled the walk. She typed his manuscripts, she edited them. I don't think most women would go that far, but women are far more willing to do the support work, which is really, really helpful. Virginia Woolf—I'm sure she would have been a great writer, regardless, but she had a lot of help, too. Leonard was a wife. That's invaluable. Women do not have that very often.

Also, the fact that women are expected to have children and most of them *want* to have children. That is *a lot* of work. Men can have children and enjoy that and have the pride and love but they're not expected to do most of the child care and they don't. Even if they want to, most children, when they're young, the connection is with the mother more than the father.

My husband and I have a pretty mutually supportive relationship, but sometimes we joke about, *Somebody needs to be the wife around here! Where's the wife? Will somebody please be the wife!* I mean, we sort of take turns being the wife to some extent, but both of us would really secretly like a wife.

SH: But would you have respect for a man who would be your wife?

MG: No! That's the problem. I mean, I would *appreciate* him, but I think that most women—not all, but most women—would have some degree of difficulty with that, whereas men don't.

SH: I would find it hard to be very sexually attracted to somebody who was doing everything for me.

MG: Well, Virginia Woolf and Leonard didn't really—I mean, maybe they did, sometimes—but I don't think that was their primary relationship.

SH: Is not having children part of wanting to write?

MG: Well, I never wanted children, up until my forties. Then at forty-one I got married and started to think of it. I think I still could have conceived. My sister had children when she was forty-three and I probably could have, too. If things had been different, we might have, but both of us were in very bad shape financially, and I had to teach, and I was trying to write *Veronica,* and it would have meant giving up being a writer, and I wasn't in a position to do that for ten years. So it did involve a decision based on writing. It was something that I did feel a degree of sadness about, because children are wonderful. They are. And it is part of the gift that women have, that they can do that. Not being able to have a child is another way in which it's hard for me to imagine being a man.

SH: Do you think it's more of a role to be a man in the world than a woman?

MG: I don't know. It's certainly been the conventional wisdom. I think there's a sense where you have to prove being a man, where you don't have to prove being a woman. But I think there's a great deal involved in the woman's role as well, and having children is proving that you're a woman. I think that if you don't have children, people are very critical of your femininity. There's a strong tendency to feel that a woman who doesn't have children is somehow failing in her role as a woman.

SH: I like that Susan Sontag quote, where she says, "The easiest thing in the world for me is to pay attention." What would you say is the easiest thing in the world for you?

MG: To sit and stare into space. I experience that as very nurturing. I like that.

VII. REPETITION

SH: You said in an interview for *Because They Wanted To* that you used to think it was wrong to tell the reader what to think, but sometimes now you don't think it's so bad. In *Veronica* you say even more what people are feeling, and I wonder where that decision came from.

MG: I don't know. It may have come from reading people like Dickens again and noticing the power of him—it's like the feeling comes in waves, it's like these waves crashing over you—you get it on a mental level, then you get it on an emotional level, then you get it on a deeper emotional level, then it comes and knocks you out of the picture. I just find that that's very true to life—that as you get older, you have an experience, you think you know it, then it comes again and you understand it more deeply, then it comes again and you understand it, and then you understand it to the point that it almost tears you to pieces.

I think for it to work in fiction, some of it depends on timing—when the reader is ready to have that other wave hit them, and when they're wanting it—when they're wanting what they're feeling about the book to come pouring out at them, almost like an answering to their own feelings.

SH: Do you experience a lot of repetition in life?

MG: Yep.

SH: Do you think that's created by one's own character?

MG: Yeah. And also just the nature of things.

SH: That there are only so many possible experiences?

MG: On a daily basis you tend to experience the same things, to the point that you often don't recognize when something new has happened, or you're very disoriented when something new happens.

People tend to set themselves up in patterns; something happens, it hurts them, then something similar happens, and—*it's happened again!* It seems much bigger then, and they get worried and go through life looking for that thing, and because they're so concerned and looking for it, when anything that happens resembles that thing, they're sure it's happening again. So sometimes people think things are repeating even when they're not.

VIII. DIGNITY

SH: Do you think dignity has much to do with being able to consciously choose what one does?

MG: Yeah, I think that's certainly part of dignity. There's a character in the story "Secretary" who behaves in a somewhat degraded manner. She's told to bend over the desk and she's spanked, and she had a mixed reaction to it. On the one hand she's very excited, on the other hand she's really humiliated and shocked.

What gives the character a certain dignity is that she's called by a reporter after she's quit that job, and he wants to write an exposé on her boss because he's running for public office, and she just hangs up. She's young, in my mind, no older than eighteen, and she doesn't know why she doesn't want to cooperate. Some people would feel, *He made me do this and my self-esteem was so low and I couldn't say no.* But in my mind, she chooses not to testify against him, because she feels on some level that she was part of it. This understanding is intuitive. It's not in her head, but I think on some gut level she understands that what happened was as much her choice as his. To me that's dignity.

SH: And what is shame?

MG: It's interesting what shame is. The best definition I've heard is that guilt is about what you've *done,* shame is about who you *are.* If something's out of my control, I don't feel shame about it, because what could I have done? If you're guilty, you can at least try to atone for it or make it better or not do it again. If it's who you are, you can't do much about it except change yourself, and that's pretty hard.

SH: Your characters often like the ugly things in other characters—that's what they're drawn to—and in popular culture, people are never presented as liking those things in other people. It's always that they love their beauty, or they love their kindness or generosity or this sort of thing.

MG: I actually don't think that's true. I think popular culture is full of people being loved for hideousness. Like Buffy the Vampire Slayer. Who does she love? Angel—another vampire. Girls falling for bad guys is huge in popular culture. Tony Soprano is a murderer, a horrible person. Lots of people love him—viewers and characters. His mother is a monster and he loves her. I saw a poster on the side of a bus in New York that was showing this smiling young man with blood all over, and it said: DEXTER—AMERICA'S FAVORITE SERIAL KILLER. He's got an audience. He's a murderer. I think popular culture is very enamored with horrible people and is in love with liking the ugly parts of people. Which is fine. I think it's realistic, but I don't think people think of it that way. I don't think people think, *I love him because he's aggressive and cruel and stupid* or whatever. I think the good parts are often wound up in the bad parts, like somebody may have a lot of meanness to them, but the way they express it, it feels fun; it's like something else is getting mixed in with it that has a feeling of excitement or of something happening or playfulness, and I think that's what people are responding to.

IX. THAT'S GOOD.

SH: I love the story "Mirror Ball" in your recent collection. I can't stop thinking about the boy's soul and the girl's soul. It's almost like a great new myth of what goes on between women and men who have sex with each other. It's almost a perfect crystallization of one of the things you communicate in your writing—that there is so much going on in our humanity that we aren't aware of, and our lack of care and sensitivity is a kind of tragedy, a tragedy of coarseness which diminishes us, though we are not exactly to blame.

MG: Actually, "Mirror Ball" was one that I couldn't place anywhere, yet on these first readings I've been getting, you're the third person to especially like it.

SH: Do you remember the first story you ever wrote?

MG: I think it was in first grade. To the extent that I remember it, Billy Blue Jay builds a nest, and he sits in it and he realizes he's lonely, and he goes out and tries to find a girlfriend, and he goes out and finds Betty Blue Jay, and he asks her to come live in his nest with him, and she does. [*Laughs*] The end.

SH: Did you have an audience for it?

MG: I had to read it to two boys in detention after school. They were probably second-graders who whispered in class. But they seemed like juvenile delinquents to me at the time. I was so scared. I didn't even look at them. I just looked down and saw their toes and read in a mumbling voice.

SH: Did they like it?

MG: Yes! They were really nice. They said to me, *That's good.* ✱

CHIMAMANDA NGOZI ADICHIE

TALKS WITH

JOSHUA JELLY-SCHAPIRO

"I LISTEN TO WHAT MY FATHER WENT THROUGH
AND THINK: MY GOD, IF ALL THAT HAPPENED TO ME,
I WOULD BE A BITTER, BITTER PERSON.
I'D JUST BE ANGRY WITH THE WORLD,
AND I WOULDN'T BE ABLE TO WRITE ANYTHING."

Three categories of contemporary Nigerians' reactions to their civil war:

*People whose families were Biafran, who are still burning
with neo-nationalist zeal*

Skeptics who feel strongly that we should talk about it

People who say, "Let's let the past be the past"

66 **T**hings *began to fall apart at home," go the first lines
of Chimamanda Ngozi Adichie's acclaimed first novel,*
Purple Hibiscus, *"when my brother, Jaja, did not go
to communion and Papa flung his heavy missal across
the room and broke the figurines on the étagère." The
reference to* Things Fall Apart, *Chinua Achebe's masterpiece about colonialism destroying tradition, marks Adichie's debt to her Igbo forebear but
also signals her differing concerns. The sentence could perhaps be read to
distill the larger ambitions of Adichie's work thus far: to engage the themes*

93

that long defined African literature—the legacies of colonialism, the cause of nation building—but to do so in a way expressive of a new generation's ironic view of these questions, and in a way attuned to the intimate lives of her characters.

Purple Hibiscus, which won the Commonwealth Writers' Prize in 2005 for best first book, depicts a teenage narrator and her brother coming to terms with their authoritarian Catholic father as Nigeria begins to fall apart under a military coup. Adichie's second novel, Half of a Yellow Sun, is set during the Biafran war, the horrific 1967–70 conflict begun when south Nigeria's Igbo citizens declared independence from their new country's government in its Muslim north. The novel depicts the war through a story about how it is lived by a small coterie of characters—a pair of middle-class sisters (one pretty, one plain) and their respective mates (a revolutionary mathematician, an English expat); a houseboy and a University master. In 2007 it was awarded the prestigious Orange Prize for fiction.

Adichie was born in 1977 in Enugu, a small village in Anambra state, in southeast Nigeria. She grew up, though, in the university town of Nsukka, where her parents still work, and where she spent her childhood in a house that was once home to Achebe himself. (Of discovering his work at the age of ten, she has recalled: "I didn't think it was possible for people like me to be in books.") She briefly studied medicine ("It's what educated Nigerians are supposed to do"), but having hoped from a young age to be a writer, she soon quit her course and moved to the United States to finish college. Joining her sister, a doctor living in Connecticut, she completed a B.A. in political science at Eastern Connecticut State University. Since that time Adichie has studied creative writing at Johns Hopkins, spent a year teaching the same at Princeton, and returned to Connecticut two years ago to complete a masters in African studies at Yale. In addition to the two novels, she has written numerous short stories and essays for publications including the New Yorker, Granta, and the New York Times. In September 2008, she was named a MacArthur Fellow.

Adichie speaks in a sonorous voice inflected with the Nigerian-British cadences of home, her precise diction joined to a ready laugh. Our conversation took place on a warm May day in New Haven across the street from the Yale University Art Gallery. —Joshua Jelly-Schapiro (January 2009)

I. "I HAVE NIGERIAN FRIENDS WHO CAN LIST EVERY MONARCH IN ENGLAND FROM THE NINTH CENTURY, AND KNOW NOTHING ABOUT NIGERIA IN 1954."

JOSHUA JELLY-SCHAPIRO: You're just finishing school, eh? Congratulations! What brought you back? How has it been?

CHIMAMANDA NGOZI ADICHIE: Oh, must we? [*Laughs*] I'm glad to be done. It was an ill-advised decision to come. It's not that the program is a bad program so much as it is that I'm just not a good fit for it. I don't like academia, in a way; I find it constricting. I started the program because I wanted to learn about Africa. It's one thing to be from a country in Africa, but there's just so much that you don't know; our education system just doesn't prepare us for knowing who we are. I have Nigerian friends who can list every monarch in England from the ninth century, and know nothing about Nigeria in 1954. So I wanted to make up for that. I probably would have done better simply continuing my own self-directed reading. Academia is often about academia and not about the real, messy world.

JJS: Your fiction is overtly engaged with these themes of history, and politics—the history of Nigeria; the legacies of colonialism; Biafra. What does approaching these questions as a novelist afford that might differ from how a historian does?

CNA: I think it's probably that I'm interested in the exceptions. One of the things about historical work—some of it, not all—is that it's very much interested in generalities: that this is what people in general did. Sometimes historians refer to countries as though they were people—they'll say: Britain did this. As a novelist, I'm more interested in that particular human being living in a particular part of Britain, and how they felt, and what they understood, and how they approached their realities. I remember when I was researching

Half of a Yellow Sun, I was reading this book about the war, written by an American, and there was this section about how people were being unreasonable—about how they weren't eating the food brought by the Red Cross. And the writer couldn't understand why the Biafrans did not want to eat the food; they were starving, and they just wouldn't. And talking to people who were there, I realized it was because there was a myth that the Nigerians [the other side in the war] had poisoned the milk. People believed this—it wasn't true, but people believed it. And it deeply affected how they approached their reality, why they chose not to eat the food. It's easy, you know, to sit in your academic chair and say you know, that was quite irrational. But it's what I'm interested in, the little stories, less the generalities than those details.

JJS: *Half of a Yellow Sun,* though, is at least as much about memory as history—less about the history of Biafra than about how Biafra is remembered (or perhaps not remembered). One of the ways you do that is in the structure: the narrative moves back and forth in time—it reads like we remember things, not necessarily in the order they happened.

CNA: I think so, too. Though you know, it's interesting—I spoke at the University of Ife, in Nigeria. And usually when I do these events in Nigeria, I tend to divide the questions in categories. There are those people whose family were Biafran, who are still burning with this kind of neo-nationalist zeal. And there are those who are like me, who are sort of skeptical of things, but who feel strongly that we should talk about it. And there are those who are just furious with me for writing this book, because "let's let the past be the past"—and it was one of these people who was saying: "Why do you insist on bringing up the past, that is gone?" And I remember thinking, For you it's past, but for so many people I know it's living memory. And I think that's the approach I brought to the book.

Talking to my parents, their friends, my relatives, it's still very present. They don't talk about it unless you bring it up. But then you do, and you realize, my god—there's so many things that haven't been dealt with. You know my uncle, he's a farmer, in my village. Things aren't going very well for him, he's poor—and he feels very strongly that this would not have happened if Biafra had won; he wants Biafra to come back. He's projected his hopes on this phantom Biafra, and it's moving, and also funny. But he fiercely believes this. And he'll tell me: "Well, look, I'm very poor, my farm is not going well, and if Biafra had won this wouldn't happen." And my aunt, his wife, who's also a farmer—she's told me that about two years ago, she went to till the farm, and did so in the field, and dug up these bullets from the war. I wish I'd had that story before I wrote the book.

JJS: The book reminds me in some ways of those books by the kids of Holocaust survivors: Art Spiegelman's *Maus,* for example—stories that deal with "remembering" traumatic events your parents lived through, with the ways in which their memories become yours, in a way.

CNA: I think those of us who didn't experience the trauma, but have somehow inherited it—I think we're fortunate to have that. I think one of the reasons that writing about the Holocaust is still coming out, for example, is that the people who experienced it just couldn't write about it. People ask: Why hasn't Chinua Achebe written a novel about Biafra? He was in the thick of it. And I think, Well that's why he couldn't—he was in the thick of it. I listen to what my father went through and think: My god, if all that happened to me, I would be a bitter, bitter person. I'd just be angry with the world, and I wouldn't be able to write anything.

JJS: I heard Amos Oz say recently that he's tried to write of his experience as a soldier, but that he never could; that whatever language he's tried to give those experiences in analogy to everyday life, it doesn't accord with what he remembers—the smell, noise, everything.

CNA: Right, and I understand that.

JJS: People tend to talk about the "historical novel" like it's a unitary form, but of course there are a million ways to tell a story related to a historical event or era. Was it immediately apparent to you how you had to approach Biafra, how you had to write it as an intimate story about sentiment and relationships?

CNA: It's so difficult to have proper answers to questions like that, because when you're doing it, you're not really very consciously analytical, or justifying the choices you make. But the idea of a historical novel—I don't really like the label. Because it evokes for me books I read when I was growing up, about Renaissance Florence, and it was usually really bad romance, with the women in really tight dresses. They were these books called Historical Romance; it was a series. And there's always been something about the label "historical novel" that just puts things in my mind.

I suppose the thing I was most certain about, though, with that book was that I wanted it to be about human beings. There is quite a bit written about the war, of course, but usually it is sort of about battalions and things of that sort. And I don't much care who won this town or commanded this battalion and took that town. I wanted to write about people. And I think there's something always contemporary in that—there are people who have written to me and said, "These people seem like they could be in the year 2000." And I say, "Well, you know people don't really change; people's motivations don't really change." The circumstances change, but people don't really change. People have the same motivations.

II. "I DON'T THINK IT'S SO MUCH ABOUT WHAT SEX ORGANS WE HAVE AS IT IS ABOUT WHAT WE WRITE."

JJS: How do you feel about the distinction that's often made between "female novels" and "male novels"? Both your novels seem in many ways to collapse the way those labels are applied. And you write some very empathetic and fully realized males in *Half of a Yellow Sun*—Ugwu, the houseboy, but also Richard the Englishman.

CNA: Well, you know, I do think *Purple Hibiscus* was sort of a girl book—and *Half of a Yellow Sun* sort of crossed over. [*Laughs*] My friend Binyavanga [Wainaina] said the problem with *Purple Hibiscus* was the cover of the book. That he'd be so embarrassed to have this on the train—that he can't read a book with a flower on the cover. And I thought, Well, you know I understand that. I hated that cover, too.

But the male-female dichotomy is all quite silly when you think about it seriously—though there are writers, both male and female, who are less engaged with emotion. And I'm sort of old-fashioned in my taste—I like emotion, and I like the story, I like humanness. And there are people like Cynthia Ozick, for example, who's a writer I really respect, but I don't really want to curl up and read Cynthia Ozick. It's like I often don't remember Cynthia Ozick after I've read her—you sort of read it, and think, Oh! She's brilliant. But then at the end, or weeks later, I just really don't remember. But then Michael Ondaatje, who's male, I think has that human thing. I read him, and I'm just in love...

JJS: He writes good women, too.

CNA: Yes! And I read him and I'm crying. I remember I was crying when I read *Anil's Ghost*. So, I don't think it's so much about what sex organs we have as it is about what we write.

JJS: Your characters' physical selves play an important part in how we come to know them, their interactions with each other. I wonder if you could talk about the place of bodies in your work.

CNA: I think it's a key part of the way I understand the world. I think people are very physical beings. I was doing a reading in Lagos, and someone said, "You know, for an African book, so much sex in it!" And I said to him, "So Africans don't have sex?" And he said, "No, they do—but for an African book, so much sex!" I suppose it's an expectation that we're supposed to be restrained. But it's just not my vision. And I think particularly, when I was writing *Half of a Yellow Sun,* I remember listening to my parents—who lost everything, had to run from town to town, much like the characters in the book—and realizing that my brother was born during that war. And my parents speak of going to weddings during that time, of laughing. I really loved that, and I hoped that I could show it in the book— the ways in which people can be running for their lives but also laughing. And I was thinking as well about how the way in which you relate to the person you love changes, the way you have sex changes, the way you look at sexuality changes. I don't know, I guess it must be that girl thing, that I'm such a girlie girl...

JJS: But it matters! How do you approach the challenge of writing about bodies—be it sex, or also violence—in a subtle way? How do you approach it in a way that doesn't feel pornographic?

CNA: I think I actually struggled more with the violence. Because I wanted it to be stark. I didn't want to be euphemistic about it; but at the same time I didn't want to be pornographic about it. You don't want your reader—or you—to feel like you're taking advantage somehow. You're writing about this killing that makes no sense, and you just don't want a reader to feel manipulated. And really, the violent scenes—the massacre scene, the rape scene—were so hard. I rewrote them so many times; I was obsessive about them. I was going crazy.

III. "I THINK: LET'S JUST TELL OUR BLOODY STORIES."

JJS: You use bits of Igbo dialogue in your fiction. But most often when your characters are speaking in Igbo, you render their speech in English, with some Igbo words thrown in. I wonder if you could talk about how you've thought about language. There was a time when debates around writing in a "colonial language" were a big deal in Africa—the whole polemic around Ngũgĩ's *Decolonizing the Mind*.

CNA: Well, the first thing for me is that I belong to a generation of Africans, really, who no longer speak only one language— I go back to Nigeria, and I'm speaking Igbo, and I can't speak two sentences in Igbo without throwing English words in there. And that's become the norm for my generation. I'm very sympathetic to Ngugi's argument, but I think it's impractical. And I think it's limiting. The idea that only Gikuyu, for example, can capture the Kenyan experience is just no longer true.

JJS: Language itself is always changing; it's living.

CNA: Right. And you have a great many people, urban Africans, who don't even speak those languages, who speak only English. But again—it's an English, I've often argued, that's ours. It's not British English. It may have come from there, but we've done things with it. I went out recently in Nigeria with a friend of mine who's an Englishman, and we went out with friends, and afterward we got in an argument—not an argument, but Nigerians are very good at shouting at each other more than necessary—and I hadn't realized that we had lapsed into this kind of very Nigerian English. And my friend said to me, "What's going on?" I said, "We're speaking English." And he said, "I don't understand a thing." And I thought, Ohhh, you don't understand. And I felt very pleased at that moment. Ahh, you don't understand, fantastic...

In writing, I just always want to capture that—that living in two languages, the negotiating back and forth. And of course I can't do it as much as I might; I have to think about my readers who don't speak Igbo, which is why I'm constantly doing a back-and-forth with my editors, who say, "Take a little more out." It is always a balancing act, but I can't ever see not doing it.

JJS: Achebe has that line about how it's the price English pays for being a global language—people make it their own.

CNA: Yes—and it's why academics these days talk about "Englishes" rather than English. In Achebe's fiction, I think what Achebe does that I find interesting is that he really uses that Nigerian English—he writes these constructions that are deliberately awkward; and you realize, Oh, he's doing the Nigerian English. I think his generation spoke it more. I think my generation is more likely to actually use Igbo words, or Yoruba, or whatever, in the English itself. So Achebe actually doesn't have so many Igbo words in his work, and I have more—but I think that does reflect a generational change. We're freer in a way; we're fortunate, we don't feel the need to divide them.

JJS: One of those other longstanding debates in African literature is around the place of the novel in so-called "oral cultures." There was that idea that an authentic African novel had to be an "oral novel" in some sense—people speak of Amos Tutuola, for example, that way: that in using pidgin, he wrote *The Palm-Wine Drinkard* in spoken language. One thing I never quite understood about that debate is that good prose is always about writing sentences that sound good—whether we read them aloud or not—wouldn't you say?

CNA: Absolutely. That's exactly my feeling. When people start to talk about the Novel, and the Origin of the Novel... I think: Look, it's just storytelling. And just because it's written down, or somebody's saying it, it's just bloody storytelling. You know, my friend

Binyavanga says, "Anything an African makes is African." And there is still this stupid thing, that people argue: "Is this authentically African?" And Binyavanga, you know, he has a friend in Nairobi—a street artist, who paints only white people. And someone's asking him, "Why do you do this? It's not really African." And the painter says, "I'm Kenyan, this is what I paint, it's Kenyan." And Binyavanga says: "Exactly." Why should we be prescriptive? This African authenticity becomes this really contested thing, and I think: Let's just tell our bloody stories.

JJS: It seems that's in some ways a real generational change.

CNA: I think so, too. But I think of course it's also easy for me to sit here and say that. Because there are people who fought the fights before.

JJS: Are there particular books you go back and read again and again—novels or anything else, before you write or anytime?

CNA: I often go back to *Arrow of God,* Chinua Achebe's book. That's really a book I love. I like Jamaica Kincaid—so I've read *Autobiography of My Mother* a few times. I like her sentences. I like the rhythm of them. I like Philip Roth. I've read *The Counterlife* a few times. I quite like how he deals with… the sociological? [*Laughs*] I just feel that he's very engaged with the world. Sometimes I think there are a lot of writers who hide, in a way, behind the idea of the aesthetic, and art, and don't really grapple with things, and the world. And I think he does. And he's also just a really good writer. I like his sentences.

JJS: One doesn't often hear Kincaid and Roth mentioned together. I suppose there are common themes—memory, family, fictional autobiography. But Kincaid's style is so much more about literary effect—those poetic, visual sentences; Roth is more about character and story, libido—getting the sentences to move. What is it that's important about those two for you? How do they shape your aims as a stylist?

CNA: I like the energy of Roth, the use of repetition, the sense of story without undue self-indulgence. It's a little amusing that his characters speak in improbable blocks of text though. Kincaid is more self-consciously interested in language and I admire that unabashed lyricism because it's done really well.

IV. "I'VE NEVER CONSIDERED MYSELF AN IMMIGRANT."

JJS: You've been going back and forth between Nigeria and the United States for a while. How do you think that's impacted your work? Is it easier to write about a place when you're not there?

CNA: I think that one of the advantages of coming here when I did—I was nineteen, I came for university—was that I had the opportunity to see Nigeria in a way that I never would have. And it had to be America. It had to be this really strange country of extremes, and also this country that gives you space. I mean, if I had gone to England, it would have been so different; England would have been so close, in so many ways. And the U.S. just gives me space. I quite appreciated that, and still do—that I suddenly was looking at Nigeria and could write about things. I think if I hadn't left Nigeria, *Purple Hibiscus* wouldn't have been the book that it is. There's something about it that is both consciously sentimental—and also, it's just the kind of book that one writes looking from the outside. If I'd been in Nigeria, I don't know that I would have been able to have the measure of... love?

JJS: Distance is important.

CNA: Yes, I think so.

JJS: You've written about the actual migrating, the travel back and forth, both in your fiction and nonfiction. You did that op-ed in the *Times* about waiting in line for a visa at the American Embassy in Nigeria; showing up at 4 a.m., the way everyone is treated...

CNA: Yes—you know, I was terrified when I went back. I was convinced I'd be blacklisted and no one was going to give me a visa!

JJS: But it's such a universal experience—at U.S. embassies all over the world.

CNA: In Nigeria now they have special Pentecostal church services entirely for dealing with American visas. But I should say too that in my case, I've never considered myself an immigrant. Because I'm not, you know—I have temporary visas, I go back very often. So I do see myself as sort of a bridge between those real immigrants in America—people like my sister, for example, who moved here fifteen years ago, who made lives here, her kids are American—and people at home. And I'm just fascinated by things like my sister celebrating Thanksgiving; she doesn't even know what Thanksgiving is. She'll go through the thing, she'll cook the turkey—she doesn't even like turkey—and she'll do cranberry sauce. And it's fascinating to watch. And she'll turn to her kids, like immigrants everywhere, to explain the reality of this place to her. And a lot of these immigrants have this vision of: we're going home someday—although I really don't think they will.

JJS: It's interesting, this difference between generations, around going back—whether or not one does return, there is that idea that one could. And that's so different from a couple generations ago, when to emigrate was to emigrate—you went and that was it. The old country was the old country—past.

CNA: I think we were also quite lucky in that way—there isn't that same pressure on my sister and newer immigrants, that pressure many once felt to assimilate immediately—to speak English right away, all that. Now you can speak the older language with your children, you can build communities. You do have that choice, which is good.

V. "I HAPPEN TO LOVE THIS BLOODY COUNTRY I COME FROM."

JJS: You're one of a number of younger African writers who have gained some wonderful visibility in the U.S. recently—Dinaw Mengestu with his book on Washington D.C.'s immigrants; Ishmael Beah and his memoir from Sierra Leone; Chris Abani and his fantastic novels on Lagos and Los Angeles. These seem to be writers who aren't doing stuff overdetermined by the national drama, who are engaging a really wide range of themes and problems.

CNA: I think it's very exciting. And when I talk about this sort of thing with my friend Binyavanga—we're quite close, we have these conversations where we disagree fiercely about these things— I often say to him that I feel that I am one of the younger people in this generation, but also in some ways I'm the most old-fashioned—I'm still very keen on history, on the state of this bloody country I love. But much to my excitement, people like Chris [Abani], he'll do this marvelous book about L.A. And I love that. Or Helen Oyeyemi, she writes of mythology, about Cuba. And I think, Well done! I love that we have this diversity, that African literature no longer means everyone is simply fighting colonialism. Which isn't to say fighting colonialism is still not very legitimate. The idea that we gained independence in 1960 in Nigeria, for example—all you have to do is go there and look at the school curriculum, or watch the Senate, and realize that the whole thing is just deeply messed up. But I really like that—I love the diversity, of approaches, of subjects...

JJS: There seems to be less of that pressure that's existed for "ethnic" or "third-world writers"—the idea that every time out you're meant to write allegory about one's people. But still there's that sense that you don't always have the same license to write "universal" stories, to write of places or cultures not one's own; a pressure that "non-ethnic"—white—writers don't necessarily have.

CNA: I think it has to do simply with the fact that white American remains the norm, so it's never questioned. And then everything else is "ethnic," which is hilarious to me. It becomes the one story that becomes the every story. We can read a white American and not be expected to see it as their white American story. It's sort of like James Baldwin, writing for the race—where some of his work becomes "the African American story," not a story about these characters. And even though I really resent it at times, I think that more and more, as I'm increasingly aware of having an audience, I find myself thinking about things I don't want to be thinking about. Such as: My vision is dark. I like to write about violence; for some reason I'm drawn to horrible things people have done. And then I realize: Am I somehow adding to the stereotype of my continent? Because I'm angry about the stereotype. But on the other hand, I'm also horrified by people killing each other in Lagos, and I want to write about—but if I do… And it's that kind of thing that I wish I didn't have to consider. Like everyone, I want just to be allowed to follow my artistic vision. On the other hand, you do think: I happen to love this bloody country I come from, and I don't want to contribute to it being seen only in horrible ways.

JJS: Biafra's important in this respect too, isn't it—that sense in which Biafra isn't just an Igbo story, or a Nigerian story, but also inaugurated the way Westerners have seen "Africa" since. It was the first time that those images were on TV everywhere—of starving children, of black people from the same country killing each other for no apparent reason.

CNA: It started it all. Part of me wishes someone had kept those photographers and TV cameras away from Biafra! The image of Africa would be different. Because it is the image—it's been modified in some ways, but the thinking behind it has been passed down to the coverage today. It's still Biafra when CNN is covering the Congo. And it's this sort of coverage that doesn't deal with African actors. Which is why I get so depressed when I'm outside Nigeria. I think, My god, we're finished. And then I go back home—and yes, things are messed up. But you see people doing things, and making an effort, and pushing back, which you never see in the way that it's covered outside Nigeria. It's frustrating.

JJS: One of the clichéd questions asked of African writers—in part, I suppose, because so many African writers have felt moved to write on it—is that question about "the future of the African novel." So I won't ask it.

CNA: Good. [*Laughs*]

JJS: But I wanted to mention that essay of Nadine Gordimer's from a few years back where she engages that old concern around having more African readers to read African books. She wrote that "African literature will either make history... or be history."

CNA: Again, it's that discourse of the "future of the novel"; and I'm just not that concerned—we'll always tell stories. People will find ways. If it's not through novels in two hundred years—if it's PowerPoint or whatever—well, well and good. But the point is that people will tell stories. When people call me a novelist, I say, Well, yes. But really I think of myself as a storyteller. ✲

MICHAEL ONDAATJE

TALKS WITH

TOM BARBASH

"I'VE ALWAYS BEEN ANNOYED WHEN
THERE'S A HUGE EMPTY SPACE WHERE I NEED
SOME INFORMATION ABOUT SOMETHING
I'M WRITING ABOUT, BUT IN FACT IT'S ALWAYS
VALUABLE TO ME TO HAVE THAT EMPTINESS
SO I CAN THEN INVENT. THERE'S A DANGER
OF HAVING TOO MUCH RESEARCH."

Revelatory moments for the author during the composition
of his novels:

*A man having his photograph taken and then having him realize he had to
steal it back* (The English Patient)
*A scene where a mother says, "Shoot the dog" and the son
doesn't shoot the dog* (Divisadero)

A *good part of Michael Ondaatje's recent novel*
Divisadero *takes place north of San Francisco, on
a farm near Petaluma where he has been coming
for the last few years to work on the book. That
local landscape inspired him, just as the discovery of
an old villa near Florence, where he wandered around for several hours,
sparked the story of* The English Patient. *All his novels have begun with
a specific landscape—whether an abandoned family home in his native
Sri Lanka, in* Anil's Ghost, *or the discovery of a forgotten writer's house
in the French countryside, while writing the portion of* Divisadero *that*

takes place in France. He says he can get work done anywhere, but that a particular house can ignite his imagination and eventually provide the landscape for a novel.

Ondaatje was born in Sri Lanka, moved to England, where his mother was living, in 1954, and relocated eight years later to Toronto. He began as a poet, and a very good one, twice winning the Governor General's prize. He still writes poetry but has found his home in the novel, for which he's earned an international reputation and has been awarded a long list of major awards including the Booker Prize for The English Patient. Divisadero is his fifth novel; he is also the author of ten books of poetry, two plays, three works of nonfiction, and a memoir.

Ondaatje's books are morally complex and structurally adventurous, in part because he doesn't know the structure going in. His method, he says, is to cast out in the dark. He begins with dreamlike images, slowly build ing his intricate story, but then subjects his work to a lengthy and vigorous editing process that can span years. Ondaatje is a genius with time and place, in part as a result of what he's learned from his other loves: music, film, and photography.

He spent two afternoons with me talking about his influences, meth- ods, and ambitions. He acknowledges that he never knows as he's writing whether he'll be able to pull a book off. Now in his early sixties, Ondaatje has a gentle, welcoming manner, and longish white hair, which rises some- what wildly from his head. He has a soft but resonant speaking voice and laughs easily, often while poking fun at himself.

—Tom Barbash (August 2007)

I. "WHATEVER I LEARN FROM POETRY I WANT TO TAKE INTO MY FICTION AND VICE VERSA."

TOM BARBASH: What started you writing in the first place?

MICHAEL ONDAATJE: I think I was just trying to bring some order into my life. I was nineteen, I was in Canada for the first time.

I was in a new country. I was at a university where I had a great English teacher. So it was a combination of all those things, but there was also a need within me for some kind of self-awareness, something like that. And then there was simply the pleasure of writing. I was a big reader all through my teens.

TB: Was there a single book or author you read that made you want to write?

MO: Not really. My reading was very various and random as a teenager. It ranged from popular thrillers to Forster. But in Canada I began to read poetry: Ted Hughes, Thom Gunn... and other contemporaries. Later I discovered Gary Snyder's book *Earth House Hold,* a book of journals and poems, and I loved the form of it, a book that seemed to allow anything to enter into it. It helped me to imagine how I could create a book that was a portrait of somebody who wasn't me talking, using all the genres. And that led to *The Collected Works of Billy the Kid.*

TB: And what were your first attempts like? Were you showing talent immediately?

MO: I'd be deeply embarrassed if I saw that early work now. I've buried it somewhere. But what really helped me then was being involved with a university magazine. It brought me into a community of people who were also writing and arguing about books and poetry.

TB: You were writing poems at the time. Were you writing fiction at all?

MO: No. I never imagined being a prose writer or doing anything with prose. I wrote poetry. Later on I was approached by Coach House Press in Toronto—and they wanted to do a collection. So

I was lucky. With them—another community—I was exposed to the whole art of making a book, not just the writing, but how you put the book together and how you could design it and bend the rules to suit yourself and make it suit your voice. That whole process was tremendously important to me and still is, even when a book is designed at a place like Knopf. The art of making and designing books is part of the act of writing.

TB: Between prose and poetry, which do you find more difficult?

MO: I find both very difficult. I know that when I finished *The English Patient,* I really wanted to write poetry and I found that I had to reassess how I wanted to write it. For me, a novel allows anything into it, it's like a carpetbag that can take in everything. But with poems there is usually one governing voice and it's important to stay in that voice. The single voice of the lyric, which is still probably the most difficult thing for me to write. But then when I write fiction I find it just as difficult. Whatever I learn from poetry I want to take into my fiction and vice versa.

II. BRINGING IN THE CHESTNUT TREE

TB: How did you come up with the title *Divisadero?*

MO: It began as a working title. Whenever I'd drive in San Francisco I'd cross Divisadero Street and I always liked the sound of the word. And then the book was partly set around here. There's a point where Anna talks about what *divisadero* means: to divide or to look at something from a great distance, which I think fits what happens to her, and her perspective in the story.

TB: In what way does that idea of distance figure into the novel?

MO: Quite a bit. There's a line I use in *Running in the Family;* it's from Denise Levertov—"the mercy of distance." It has a lot to do with this book too. It means forgiving oneself, or recognizing oneself, to see one's story in a different way.

TB: So Anna in essence is finding her own story in the archival work she does in the second half of the book.

MO: Yes. I think that's partly true. There seem to be two different versions of the same tale in a way. It became evident to me as I was writing the book that I was moving between a real life and an imagined life.

TB: Where did the character in the novel of Lucien Segura, the poet, come from? Was he based on a real person?

MO: Not really. I invented the French poet and found a house that he might have lived in. The house became a way of inventing a story about Lucien Segura.

TB: Did you do what you did with *The English Patient* and actually go to that house?

MO: Yes. Finding the place allows me to write about much more than that. There's a house in *Anil's Ghost* that I also found and used in such a way. I seem to need the house before I can write a story.

TB: When you're in these houses does the discovery of plot become a physical thing? Do you walk the rooms of these houses to stimulate your imagination?

MO: If I have the house in my head I can mentally walk from room to room. And the house in the book isn't necessarily a replica of a real house. The site is important. What's outside is very important: how big the garden is, whether there's a river there or a pond, or a hill. Once I have a sense of all that I can write, and bring in a chestnut tree or something like that.

TB: There are several moments in the novel in which a character will think or say something which has to do with the process of writing. I'm thinking of Lucien Segura's lines: "The skill of writing offers little to the viewer. There is only the five-centimetre relationship between your eyes and the pen. Any skill in the living or dreaming is invisible…"

MO: With writing you're always a little underwater. No one's going to know why you're pacing something in a particular way, without commas as opposed to with commas. It's just a hand moving. Film is interesting because all the elements that go into writing are there physically—the sound man, the lighting man, the cutting, the acting, the inventing of the story by the writer. All these things are there in the writer—you're thinking about how loud someone's saying something; are they whispering or yelling? All those elements are there unspoken in the text, but in the writer's mind. No one can see them actively or physically on a stage, but these choices affect a reader. In writing it might be something small while in film that decision might be physically enacted through the soundtrack, or the swell of music.

Think about the choice of where a paragraph breaks. It is such an intricate little thing that happens during the editing process. I was reading *The Curtain* by Kundera. He was talking about how when Flaubert rewrote one of his books he made the paragraphs longer. Three paragraphs became one. It changed everything—pacing, meaning. It's fascinating. And yet who but a writer talks about things like that?

TB: Speaking of stylistic and punctuation choices, I wanted to ask you about dialogue and specifically the absence of quotation marks in the new novel and in sections of the others.

MO: Well, I've gone back and forth on that. I think *Coming Through*

Slaughter didn't have them; it had dashes. And then in *Anil's Ghost* I used single quotation marks, the European style which I rather like; I suppose because it's not so busy. The double quotation mark is like saying something twice as far as I'm concerned. But I'm never quite sure what's the best way to do it.

TB: Do you struggle with dialogue?

MO: I definitely spend a lot of time on it. I've been accused of writing terrible dialogue by some people. [*Laughs*] But I spend a lot of time on it. It often gets written without too much intent when I'm actually writing scenes, and later on I'll go back to it. The dialogue that was most difficult to write in *Divisadero* was where Claire meets Coop after many years, in the restaurant. I went through five or six completely different versions, trying to figure out what to say. You can't say too much, you can't say too little, you can't be too casual. Yet everything there is loaded, even though it might not seem loaded. A lot of the time that's the effect I want. In retrospect, what someone says in a totally innocent-seeming scene can mean a lot. But you don't want to have that feeling of something meaningful and portentous while you're reading it.

TB: You have an ability to create a great deal of emotional and psychological momentum very fast in the summarized sections, when we're not actually in scene.

MO: I'm very interested in how you can build a narrative by going from A to C to E, and between sentences something has happened and the reader has to catch up with you. It's not an intentional thing, but when you're rewriting or re-reading something, you see that you've done that, and you're not in real time. I think it can enliven the action, make it more tense. From the first sentence to the third sentence, so you're now on a wall looking down as opposed to being in the same position.

TB: Which aspects of this book were surprising to you as you were writing?

MO: The character of Roman, for one. He became very interesting to me, but I didn't know he'd be so important and central. There was a while when I didn't know where I was going with him, but in the scene where the mother says, "Shoot the dog," and he doesn't shoot the dog—the minute he doesn't shoot the dog a door opened and he became more interesting and more compassionate. And the whole French section of the book was a surprise. I started writing and I wasn't sure if I could make it part of the story. I thought, Is this something else or is it part of the same book? And I just trusted it. It just seemed very right by the end, but it wasn't something I planned in the beginning. But as I was writing it I knew it was the essential way to continue the first part of the book.

TB: The central story of the two twins, Anna and Claire, who aren't really twins: Was that something you'd heard about? And what interested you about the differences between them?

MO: No, it was all just kind of invented. When it began I think the first thing I wrote was the scene in the barn with the horse, but there was only one woman there. That was literally the first thing I wrote. Then when I came back to it at that point there were two sisters, so when the other sister became part of the scene it had different significance of what was going on there. It was also now about this strange kind of competitiveness that exists between those two. While they were also at times the same person for Coop—so that was interesting.

TB: Is it pleasurable to add another country to those you've written about? Had you written about France before?

MO: It is pleasurable. There's a kind of nomadic motive behind it.

[*Laughs*] As a writer you're fairly solitary, in one room, really, and there's a pleasure to looking over the wall, if you will. After *Anil's Ghost,* I thought I'd write another novel about Sri Lanka. I began something, and I realized I was still in the same wave as the last book. I found I couldn't get out of that. I realized I had to not only find a new vocabulary but a new place, a new note or tone from the last book.

III. "I NEED THE PHYSICAL LOCATION BECAUSE OTHERWISE I FEEL THE BOOK WILL JUST FLOAT AWAY."

TB: Tell me about the genesis of *Billy the Kid.*

MO: My interest in the myth of Billy the Kid goes back to my childhood, in Sri Lanka, which is somewhat absurd. I think in my early twenties I wanted to write a Western and make a movie, a half-thriller, half-adventure film. I wanted to make something bizarre and crazy. And dangerous. It began as a group of poems and then I leapt into prose. It was the first prose I had written—so I found this whole huge field of writing that was possible. I just wrote it—and I think I hardly edited the prose at all.

TB: How long did it take?

MO: About three years. I wrote the poems individually and then, after about a year, I found I wanted a bigger form, and then I was writing prose. It expanded into this huge mongrel thing and I wondered if I might be going crazy when I was writing it. Later I went back and looked at it. I knew I had to find some kind of shape and form for it. That was probably the most difficult thing I had to learn—how to shape the material—place three hundred or two hundred pieces into an organic structure that seemed natural, and still juxtapose a gentle scene with something violent. I think that was when I became interested in how a collage works. That's been a very important thing for me.

TB: It seems like you were learning the principles and skills you would take into your novel writing. How did you fight the uneasiness of wondering before you reached the end, How am I going to shape this? or even, Can it be done?

MO: This is the dark side of my story. [*Laughs*] That sort of tension is there for about four years each time I work on something. I think if I knew everything going in—the structure, the story, how things will get resolved—I probably would not be as interested in it. For me it's much more a process of discovery.

TB: What were the origins of *Coming Through Slaughter?*

MO: Probably a love of jazz more than anything else. The success of *Billy* was, on one level, quite small, but on another level, quite large for me. Suddenly I was almost a public figure. So I was interested in what it would be like to be "the public figure." I went in with that idea of writing about the excitement of jazz—the world of Louis Armstrong and the Hot Five and the Hot Seven—that period of jazz fascinated me. But [Buddy] Bolden came before all that. He was the source.

TB: Was that something you listened to as a kid?

MO: More when I was a teenager in England. I went to a lot of jazz clubs.

TB: On a different subject, there's a wonderful photograph of your parents in *Running in the Family.* And you said that's the only picture of them you have. I wanted to know about their influence on your development as a writer, your mother's tendency to tell hyperbolic, larger-than-life stories, and then your father's humor and reticence. How do you feel each of them in your work?

MO: I guess I didn't really know what their influence was on me. My mother was an excessively dramatic, very gregarious and generous person. The house was always full of people, half of whom she didn't know. When she was in England in the last part of her life, anyone from Sri Lanka would drop in for lunch, so the house was full of people from all ages, which was exciting. My father was much more solitary and quiet. I definitely think those two things are in me. But we were never just a nuclear family; there were always uncles and aunts and a whole complicated community around us.

TB: In *Divisadero,* and in your other books, there's almost always an archivist of sorts who has gone back and dug up the past. We always feel the weight of the past on the present in your novels. I wondered if much of that began with the research for *Running in the Family.* I wondered how the process of learning so much about your family changed you as a writer.

MO: With the earlier books, such as *Coming Through Slaughter*—which was about New Orleans—I had to write that book without going there. I couldn't afford to go there. Even with *Billy the Kid,* I never went to Mexico. It was an imagined world, a mental landscape more than anything else. What I gleaned about it came from random archival things I got hold of. With *Running in the Family,* there were no archives, and that was exciting to me. No one wrote books, they just talked. So when I went there I moved around and had many conversations with uncles and aunts, hearing each story again and again. Half of them were lying [*laughter*]… they were trying to tell a good story more than anything else.

So I was having to deal with that. There was so much material, I had to write everything down very fast. I wrote very, very fast. Usually I'm a fairly slow writer. When I got back to Canada

I had to try and figure out how I was going to shape all this. There were two trips back to Sri Lanka, each about two or three months long, and my time there was quite intense. The book focuses on my father more than my mother because I knew my mother better in England. I knew I had to stay, the book had to stay on the island. That became the rule, one of the shapes of the book for me. What happened also was the book began joyously rather like a restoration comedy of eighty-five people coming in drunk and going off in a car into the country or something.

Then I stopped for a while and began to write the darker half of the book. About my father, which wasn't where I thought the book was going to go. I wanted to capture the way one "talked" a story as opposed to writing a story. That was the tone of the book. It was listening to stories, and believing them. Putting it all down.

TB: After that you wrote *In the Skin of a Lion,* which was another shift in form and subject matter.

MO: There were lots of false starts with that one. I began with the story about Ambrose Small first of all, but after writing a hundred pages he bored the hell out of me. So I went back and started again with a character called Patrick. But I didn't know where I was going with it. I knew nothing about Toronto in 1910, which is when the book took place.

TB: Was there any great text of Toronto in that period?

MO: Nothing. And that was a gift in a way. If there was a major book about the sewers or the tunnels I would have swallowed it up but then thought, Well, we already know that. I've always been annoyed when there's a huge empty space where I need some information about something I'm writing about, but in fact it's always valuable to me to have that emptiness so I can then invent. There's a danger of having too much research.

TB: But clearly you have done some research for quite a few of your novels, especially about processes, like bomb disposal, or gambling in the new book, or the beauty of the desert.

MO: For me the research is much better when it's accidental. I tend to write and research simultaneously, or almost simultaneously. It's like building a bridge and writing about the bridge being built. I don't do that much research, to be honest. Often I'm inventing a very technical detail, or an archival situation that may not be there. But oftentimes these turn out to be true. The stuff about the tunnels underwater in fact is true, but I sort of imagined it before I discovered they had existed.

TB: How essential is the setting to you when you begin each book?

MO: Very. It's not only place, but the time period is very important to me, whether it's the desert in 1938, or Italy at the end of the war, or New Orleans at a certain time, or Toronto a hundred years ago. I need the physical location because otherwise I feel the book will just float away. I need a landscape—it could be partially invented but I want real names of streets and so forth.

TB: Do you tend to use maps and photographs to activate your imagination?

MO: I will look at those, sure, but I will try and go to that place. I often need to find a place, a physical landscape, while I'm writing as opposed to before I'm writing. When I began *The English Patient,* for instance, I had created the house in my mind where all the action takes place. But it wasn't yet a real place. Then about a third of the way through the book I went to Italy and actually found a place that would've worked for the characters and the situations.

TB: You actually went there.

MO: Yes. I tend to need just a little glimpse through the window of a place. I can see a photograph of somebody who is half in the picture, and that person for me can become the central character of a book. Again, if you have too much—if somebody had handed me a book about that place, it would have spoiled it. It would have been too painted already.

TB: How long a time period did you have between *In the Skin of a Lion* and *The English Patient*?

MO: It always takes about a year for me to get over a book. I mean, I can't just leap into the next one. I was writing poems, but I was sort of looking around for what to do next. Six months later I had no idea what I was going to do. And three days before I began *The English Patient* I still had no idea. I had no idea who the patient was, or that there was going to be a Caravaggio again, or these other characters. I have to creep into the book with not too much lighting at first and try to find out what's in there. There were two things that started to emerge: one was the man in the bed, and the other was someone being photographed. I remember that I was at an airport and I was waiting for a plane, and I started writing this very vivid thing about a man having his photograph taken and then having him realize he had to steal it back. Just that little detail—that was it. I think the voice of the patient came in later, after he'd been in the book awhile, and then suddenly it was almost like I hit a spring and somebody would start talking in this grand post-nationalistic way about cultures and nations. Nothing I had ever even thought about, but that's what happens after you've been writing awhile. It was really a matter of waiting around with three or four people in a house, waiting for something to happen.

IV. "THE WAY PEOPLE TALK
IS THE WAY I DON'T TALK."

TB: Time in your novels is always interesting—part of it is the collage effect that you speak of, and how things are ordered, but also there are all the sudden jumps, the flash-forwards and flashbacks you use so seamlessly. I'm remembering the line about Caravaggio and Kip in *The English Patient*: "Years from now on a Toronto street Caravaggio will get out of a taxi..." and he'll hold the door for an East Indian man and think of Kip. You know the line I'm talking about.

MO: Yes. It just seems very natural to me. If Caravaggio is talking about an affection for Kip and imagining that in twenty years' time there is an Indian on the street in Toronto... there's a gesture of graciousness on his part as a result of this moment. It just seems very normal and almost chronological to go there and then leap back. But if it felt "planned," "set up," that would be a problem for me.

TB: Do you consciously create—I was thinking of Kip, the bomb disposal, and other experts—characters who do things that you would have loved to have been able to do?

MO: I think that's one of the pleasures of writing. There is a lot of that. The way people talk is the way I don't talk. It's like putting on Agamemnon's mask, or a costume. So you can behave like them.

TB: How do you get what feels like a comfortable vernacular for the different time periods you write in? Do you read texts or letters from the period?

MO: I think what I said earlier on about waiting a year or so is really to get out of the vocabulary I was using in the last four or five years, because I think there is a vocabulary for each book. I love finding language that is not my own language, some line or phrase that I would never have normally used. I'll think, God, I haven't used that word ever before. The notion of a new vocabulary is very exciting to me.

TB: There's a real music to your writing and I'm wondering if you read your work out loud as you're writing. Or do you just hear the voice in your head?

MO: I sort of hear it in my head, though I never read out loud, but I can imagine it. I can hear the pitch changing or the speed shifting in my head. Music is certainly important to me, I mean, I listen to a lot of music all the time. I don't listen to music while I'm writing. Some of the music probably comes from writing poetry.

TB: What sort of setup do you like to have when you write? Do you need a view, or do you like to close off the outside world?

MO: I can write anywhere, as long as there's no one around that I know. If I'm in a room with friends I know it will be difficult for me to write. In terms of views, I can be working in front of the most beautiful place in the world and not realize it's there. I remember writing the whole scene in the tunnel for *In the Skin of a Lion*. I spent about four days writing the scene with Patrick, the underground, tunnel, water, swimming through the darkness. I was sitting in front of a bright window on a bright summer day in the country, totally unaware of where I was, of the real landscape. The tunnel was what I was focused on.

TB: You talked about how the first time you received attention as a writer was with *Billy the Kid*. I was wondering how that attention changed you as a writer, what sort of confidence it gave you. And then I wanted to ask you about the tremendous reaction to *The English Patient* and what effect that had. It must have been a tough act to follow.

MO: The trouble is I've never been that confident even after something has been a success. Not that I don't feel happy about it, but it doesn't necessarily give me confidence. I think if your first book is accepted and published, that's great, but you know three hundred people read it usually and that's it. With *Billy* there was a larger response in Canada, and then it got published in the States, but it didn't give me any artistic confidence. I've never had that kind of security, even now. The paranoia always steps in. On the other hand, what happened to *The English Patient* was so surreal, it was just crazy.

TB: How so?

MO: The book suddenly took off, and then it won the Booker. And then there was the film. Luckily, while that was all going on I'd begun writing *Anil's Ghost,* so that was what preoccupied me, even during the filming.

TB: Did your success give you a heightened sense of outside expectations, the thought of, This better be good?

MO: Very early on in my writing life I realized that if you're going to write, the last thing you should think about is an audience. Otherwise you're going to give the audience what they want as opposed to what you want to do or discover. The act of writing is so difficult anyway that you don't want to add to it the imagined sense of five hundred people in a theater listening to you, or watching you, waiting to see what you do, like that Monty Python sketch about watching Thomas Hardy write his eleventh novel. "Oh no, he's doodling again."

TB: Are you someone who revises as you go along, or does most of the revision take place after you're done with a draft?

MO: It's both. I discover the story while I'm doing the first draft.

I go back and re-read it and then rewrite it. There will be about four or five drafts that are all handwritten. Some things that don't seem important to me anymore, or don't interest me anymore will drop away, or I'll be reading and realize there's a big hole somewhere. And I'll try and write something for that hole. So I'm adding things, removing things, unearthing things, and then moving stuff around.

TB: Is there anyone you allow to read your work while you're in the midst of a novel?

MO: No one reads it until I've taken it as far as I can go without help. I've pushed it through many, many drafts by that point, and I have no idea if it works or if it's crazy. Then I give it to about three or four people to read, and I get their responses.

TB: What are you looking for?

MO: Anything. I want, you know, cautious praise [*laughter*], or cautious complaints. One of the problems is that by now the characters have become so real to you, you know them so well, you can't see what more has to be said about them. You need to clarify things that seemed obvious to you, because you created the situation.

V. GOING TO EXTREMES

TB: In terms of meaning, are there specific things you want to say in your work? Do you begin knowing what your story is going to mean?

MO: I don't have a clue what the meaning is going to be; I discover it much later on. I'm more concerned with the characters and the evolving story. Have I made this character too obviously this, or that? I want the characters to be as convincing and complicated as possible.

I'm not interested in what it means or what it signifies. When I first came to Canada I was expected to write a Canadian book, and I wrote *Billy the Kid* and *Coming Through Slaughter*. When that stopped, then I was expected to write about Sri Lanka, and I didn't write about Sri Lanka, and then I finally felt like I could write about Sri Lanka and do so properly. It's difficult to say what one should write or what one shouldn't write. I think I'm always interested in trying to write something that I don't think I can do.

TB: What was most challenging about *Anil's Ghost*?

MO: The political situation is so complex and there are so many voices that disagree with each other, so the question was: where do you begin? So I decided I wanted to write about what it was like to live there, not to write about the three opposing parties but just write about what it was like to be a doctor or a nurse or a citizen in general. But it wasn't until I had the two voices that I felt I had what I needed, two differing opinions that represent a much larger group of voices.

TB: Did you worry you'd be criticized for not fully representing one side or the other?

MO: Definitely. I was stricter with myself in that book than I had been before I felt responsible to a political situation. It was a fatal, strict road I was on with *Anil's Ghost* and I had to stay on that fatal road and represent it. I mean, it is a fiction, and an odd kind of fiction, but at the same time it is more faithful to place and time than a book like *Billy the Kid*. So in a way the fact that *Divisadero* jumps all over the place was a relief.

TB: I thought we'd talk a little bit about your interest in film and the art of filmmaking.

MO: I loved film very, very early on in my life; I've always been dazzled. To me it's still pure magic up there, even the most inane movie. Film for me is pure magic, as when I read a wonderful book by Russell Banks or Cormac McCarthy or someone like that, I don't want to know how it ties together or anything like that. That's what I love about film and books. At the same time, as a writer and someone who edits his own work—the act of editing is so important. The reason I did the book with Walter Murch [*The Conversations: Walter Murch and the Art of Editing Film*] was that everything we were talking about there was really about how one edits a book or edits a dance, or an opera, or how you produce a record album. That little tone at the beginning of a song, and then the two tones that appear one minute into a song—all of these careful little devices and so forth. I love the craft. That's what's fascinating for me.

TB: What are some of your favorite films?

MO: This new film *The Lives of Others* is fantastic. And the Italian film *The Best of Youth*. In the back of the Murch book in my biography I just list about ten films that I like. Having said that, I think film is a kind of limited art form, or has been in the West. The limit of two hours, or one and a half, or whatever it is is a big part of that. It's difficult to go to the extremes in a film without losing your audience, whereas I think in a book you can. Hopefully in a book you can.

TB: What is it you love about the novel, specifically? What does a novel offer you as an art form that's made you return to it again and again?

MO: You know, when people think of well-made novels they think of Jane Austen or Robertson Davies or someone like that. Well, they are well-made novels. But what interests me about a novel is that if it's well made it can be two hundred pages long and still

encompass practically everything. Or it could be a huge, sprawl-
ing object. There's a tremendous freedom in the novel, for me,
and mostly because it doesn't have to be written in a certain way.
You can use a variety of different voices, you can change the pace
and tone and the direction of events in a novel. I think I realized I
wanted to write novels when I read Faulkner. Before I read him I
thought that in a novel you wouldn't have the same freedom you
had in a poem, but then I read *Absalom, Absalom!,* and I saw that
you did. ✶

SARAH SCHULMAN

TALKS WITH

ZOE WHITTALL

"TO REMEMBER THAT YOU CAN ACTUALLY WRITE
A BOOK THAT CAN CHANGE PEOPLE'S LIVES
IS SOMETHING I HAD FORGOTTEN."

Consequences of America's sexual regression:

Diminished lesbian content in fiction
False naturalization of AIDS victims
Guys smoking cigars

I n the spring of 2012, Sarah Schulman invited me to her partner's
Toronto home on a rainy Saturday afternoon. The partnership
being somewhat new and long-distance, she moved about the space
a bit awkwardly, claiming she had never spent much time in a
house before, having lived in Manhattan for fifty-three years, and
in the same sixth-floor walk-up in the East Village for the past thirty. "In
New York City, if you want privacy, you just sit in the same room and don't
talk. This house thing is very new to me." She made me a cup of tea and we
sat in the living room with my iPhone recorder between us on the ottoman.

At the time, her fifth nonfiction book, Israel/Palestine and the Queer
International, was the forthcoming lead title from Duke University Press,

and she was in Toronto for the launch of The Gentrification of the Mind: Witness to a Lost Imagination. *Her documentary,* United in Anger: A History of ACT UP, *had just premiered in New York City. But while Schulman is many things—an accomplished political activist, a distinguished professor, filmmaker, playwright, and general cultural agitator—her primary love is writing fiction. When we met, she had just finished writing her tenth literary novel,* The Cosmopolitans, *which she described to me as "an answer book to Baldwin's* Another Country *and a response to Balzac's* Cousin Bette," *set in New York City in 1958.*

A gifted storyteller, Schulman has spent much of her career chronicling queer lives. She approaches fiction with a fearlessness regarding both form and content, and possesses an unflinching ability to create nuanced, emotional characters while simultaneously crafting stories that embody the political and cultural complexity of America at its most unrepresented. Her versatility as a writer is proven with each new story she puts out, whether she's embracing her own imaginative take on literary realism or jumping into satirical speculative fiction, as she did with her latest novel, The Mere Future. *She is best known for her widely praised, groundbreaking 1995 novel,* Rat Bohemia, *which was set in the swirl of the AIDS crisis in New York City.*

While many writers of her generation are content to stay coyly closeted— too many prominent best-selling American writers to mention—Schulman has steadfastly refused. As a result, her status as a cultural pioneer and icon to aspiring queer writers has been cemented, while her literary career has, on occasion, suffered. As the publishing industry has grown more conservative, her last two novels were difficult to place. When recounting the plot of her latest literary manuscript, The Cosmopolitans, *she acknowledges: "It's an opportunity for me to return to mainstream publishing, if they'll have me."*

—Zoe Whittall (February 2013)

I. LOVING MENTOR

ZOE WHITTALL: I want to talk about your experiences trying to publish your novel *The Child.* It seems to me as though America is in a period of deep sexual regression right now. I mean, the right to acquire birth control is actually up for debate. What was the process like, trying to publish it in this climate?

SARAH SCHULMAN: It was a nightmare. First of all, I had been publishing a book almost every two years since forever, and suddenly I was stopped dead. People would stop me on the street and ask, "What's happening with you? I haven't seen any books by you." And I would say, "It exists! They just won't let you have it." I was sending it around as samizdat. I would print it out and give it to people. This was in 1999, before Kindles. It was awful. So many bad things happened. An editor at Beacon read it and really loved the book and told me she was going to buy it. She made an offer, but her editor in chief vetoed it because she said it was supporting child abuse.

Finally, one day I ran into Diamanda Galás in the neighborhood. She asked me why I hadn't published in so long. I explained that I had written a novel about a sexual relationship between a fifteen-year-old boy and a forty-year-old man, from their points of view, and that since I didn't condemn the relationship, it was unpublishable. She took out her cell phone and called Don Weise at Carroll and Graf on the spot. "This is Diamanda Galás," she said. "I'm sending you Sarah Schulman's new novel. Treat this sister with respect." Don ended up publishing the book, but, typically for the book business, Carroll and Graf went out of business the week *The Child* was published. They printed it, but it wasn't reviewed or distributed. Fortunately, Arsenal Pulp Press in Canada published the paperback, but the book never got its moment, which is very sad for me since I love it. I think it would make a great movie.

ZW: Was it hard to inhabit any of the characters creatively, or to have empathy for them? Do you believe writers have to have empathy for their characters?

SS: It wasn't hard to have empathy for the characters. My job is to figure out what is it like for these people to be alive. What is their perspective on their own experience? That's my job because I'm a novelist. But because I did my job, it made the book unpublishable, because I saw that there were positive aspects to the experience for both of them. The kid's parents were so homophobic and awful that the fact that he had a sexual relationship with an adult man was, in a way, an antidote to his relationship with his father. It wasn't a desirable relationship—the man in the book is very childish and can't take responsibility for things, but the kid got many positive things out of it. What caused him pain was not his boyfriend, but his parents and the state. And that's not what the message is supposed to be. The message is supposed to be *the evil, child-abusing predator, blah blah blah*. I had the wrong message. I was in a state of perpetual censorship for almost ten years.

ZW: In a recent interview, the *New York Times* said that you were a loving mentor to many young writers. Do you agree with that?

SS: Yes, I do agree with that. I'm very supportive of young artists. I treat them with respect, especially queer artists. I want them to do well. Because *somebody* has to care.

ZW: Did you have mentors when you were young?

SS: Grace Paley famously helped me by sending me home after my first and only day of an MFA program. That was truly great. But mentor as in sitting down and reading the books and helping me professionally? There wasn't anyone. It wasn't like there was some lesbian writer who had published mainstream books and had access to stuff who could help me. There wasn't such a person. The generation before me is, like, Susan Sontag... they were just in the closet. My generation is the first to be completely out in popular culture. The people before me couldn't and wouldn't help me. The ones who didn't have access, because they were out, *couldn't* help me. The ones who *did* have access, had access because they were in the closet, so they wouldn't. I found out later that *behind the scenes* people do do things. I got into MacDowell in 1986, and years later I found out that Tillie Olsen was one of the people who supported my application. So that's cool. I never met her, but that was nice. Edmund White did me a huge favor by writing that review in the *New York Times* of *Rat Bohemia*. That was extremely supportive and kind of him. Kathy Acker wrote a really nice review of *After Delores* in the *Village Voice,* and I didn't know her. She did it just because she liked the book.

ZW: Tell me about the group of young writers that you host in your apartment.

SS: I did a reading at Bluestockings in New York City about four years ago, and there was a big discussion afterward about how frustrated I was that younger lesbian writers are not having lesbian content in their work. I know why they're not doing it: because you can't have a career if you have it. But unless people keep submitting that material, it's never going to change. What we see is really bad-quality work, because the most talented writers are escaping the content. The literature gets destroyed. I was talking about how MFA programs are a really obstructive force in the development of lesbian fiction, because most of them don't have faculty who actually understand how it works and who can actually give informed support to their students. I mean, you know this. There are all kinds of representational and aesthetic questions in writing lesbian fiction that are very specific. The English language is constructed around a male-female dichotomy, so just having two *she*s in one sentence is something that has to be finessed, right? Then there is the balance of characters. When I wrote *People in Trouble,* I had a straight male protagonist and I had a lesbian protagonist. Balancing them was almost impossible, because anything she did, she would be seen as pathological, but anything he did, the reader could excuse. Having them in the same scene was so hard because he could do anything and she couldn't do anything. All that stuff—you need people who can understand that. MFA programs don't provide that. Lesbian writers who go into them end up producing material that doesn't have any primary lesbian content. Ellis Avery was my graduate student. You can actually trace who the exceptions are, and see who they studied with.

So I was talking about that, how upsetting it was, and the audience was quite young. Someone said, "You should start a group!" or, "Put your money where your mouth is!" I said OK. I passed around a sign-up sheet and I called everyone who signed up and invited them over to my house. I live in a very small apartment. About ten girls came over to my apartment. I didn't know any of these people. They crammed into my living room. I didn't do any screening. It's turned out to be a wonderful experience for me.

ZW: What do you get out of the experience?

SS: They're very interesting. I love to watch the ways they help each other. They're quite smart. They're very different. Their work is very engaging. They struggle. They rewrite. One of the rules is that once we agree on a date and time, no one is allowed to cancel. You can't come late and you can't cancel—no matter what. I got a free trip to China and I came home early because I had promised the date. If you keep all your promises, you can be very productive. If you say that you're going to come here on this time and this day and bring a work that is four to ten pages—and you do it because you said you would—you will produce work.

II. "SO WE GOT A CAMERA."

ZW: Can you describe for me how the ACT UP Oral History Project and the documentary *United in Anger: A History of ACT UP* came to be?

136

SS: It was 2001. I was in L.A. trying to get a job in television or movies. That's already funny. I was in a white rental car, and I can barely drive. It was the twentieth anniversary of AIDS. NPR was talking about it, and somebody said, "At first, America had trouble with people with AIDS, but then they came around." And I just thought, That is *not* what happened. There's this American tendency to falsely naturalize change that people fight for and earn with their last drop of blood. America pretends that we just naturally evolved. We've always been that way. But in this case, because so many of our friends are dead, and they're not here to speak for themselves, we do have a special responsibility. It's one thing if everyone who participates in a social transformation somehow collectively decides not to contest the historicization, but when the people who did are not here, and they don't have that option, there is a special responsibility. I remember thinking, They're going to do this to AIDS. They're going to pretend that all these thousands of people who fought until their death never suffered, never coalesced, and that it was by the graces of the beautiful dominant culture that suddenly we were all so understanding. I couldn't bear the thought of it. I called Jim Hubbard. We had been collaborators since 1987, and we decided we would start an oral history project. At that point, no one remembered ACT UP, except for the people who'd been part of it. There was no discussion about AIDS; AIDS was over. AIDS activism was barely mentioned. I mean, Benjamin Shepard had written a book called *From ACT UP to the WTO*—I think that was the only modern engagement with ACT UP. So we got a camera and we wrote a grant to try to get software to start interviewing people. Lo and behold, Urvashi Vaid was at the Ford Foundation. Years ago, she had been the head of the National Gay and Lesbian Task Force. At that time, it was considered to be the most conservative gay organization. It was to the left of the Democratic Party. There were no right-wing gay people at that time. Being in the Democratic Party was considered conservative.

ZW: This was pre–Log Cabin Republicans...

SS: It was pre-*everything*. It's pre–Human Rights Campaign, pre–Don't Ask, Don't Tell. We were the street-politic people. They were the policy people. We weren't that far apart, but we felt like we were. So she helped us write the grant proposal, and we were able to get three hundred thousand dollars. It was her vision. She knew that we could do this huge thing. To date, we've interviewed 128 people. Long-form interviews. Everything is available for free online at the website *actuporalhistory.org*. We've sold the archive to Harvard. The agreement is they will make it available for free in perpetuity in all future formats, so let's say everything switches to HD; they're going to have to switch it to HD. This is the kind of thing we could not do. Before that, all the tapes were in Jim's office. He's sixty-three. I'm fifty-three. If we got hit by a bus, that would be it. It was too much responsibility. This turns out to be the perfect solution. That's how it started. We couldn't take it. We couldn't take that thought of it being falsely historicized. Now there is a little moment going on where other people are making it work. That's really what cultural activism is: you take the void and transform it into a context. It's not carpetbagging, where you look for a context and jump on it. It's starting from nothing. We did the same thing with the MIX festival. There was no venue for gay, experimental film in 1987, so we invented one. Twenty-five years later, we have people showing work in our festival who were not born when we started it. What we learned is that creating a venue creates artists, because people see the venue and think, Oh, I can make something for that. Then they become artists. That's really what cultural activism is. It's not exploiting other people's work. It's doing the labor from the ground up.

III. THE GHOST WORLD
AND THE WORLD

ZW: I want to talk about the idea of deaths that matter and deaths that don't, which you write about so eloquently in *The Gentrification of the Mind*. You said, "The deaths of these 81,542 New Yorkers, who were despised and abandoned, who did not have rights or representation, who died because of the neglect of their government and families, has been ignored. This gaping hole of silence has been filled by the deaths of 2,752 people murdered by outside forces. The disallowed grief of twenty years of AIDS deaths was replaced by ritualized and institutionalized mourning of the acceptable dead. In this way, 9/11 is the gentrification of AIDS. The replacement of deaths that don't matter with deaths that do." How did you come to this conclusion? Have you taken any heat for it, or any of the other things you say in the book?

SS: No heat, except *Publishers Weekly* said I was vitriolically against motherhood. Women who question parenting are always the witch. [*Laughs*] I live on Ninth Street. I saw the World Trade Center thing happen from my roof. When the building went down, I got on my bike and I went to St. Vincent's Hospital to give blood. On my way there, I was watching these people in business suits walking up from Wall Street covered in ash. When I got to St. Vincent's, there was a line around the block. So many people had had the same thought and just ran there. But there was no need to give blood, because everyone was dead. It was a weird, ghostly thing. Then they closed off the city at Fourteenth Street. We had free access, if you lived downtown. I biked to the World Trade Center. You could watch. Everything was burning. Everyone was so shocked. It was so strange. The first thing I thought was—this was when we were bombing Bosnia—I remember thinking that Americans were finally going to understand what it's like; what we do to other people. That was my first thought. *This will be an incredible wake-up.* The next day, people came looking for the corpses. And because most of the people who died were either cops or firefighters or traders, the people who came to Manhattan to look for their dead people were from Queens and Staten Island and New Jersey. They were bringing these American flags, they were putting up signs: HAVE YOU SEEN MY PERSON? And it just suddenly turned. It could have been this moment of compassion, understanding, and revelation, and it became this patriotic nightmare. Bush went on TV and said, "They are evil and we are good." Everyone was stunned and in shock. I thought, This is *so* how I felt during AIDS, emotionally, and now everyone is feeling it. That thought stayed with me the whole time. Later, I found out that only two people I knew had died. One was the mother of a friend from ACT UP, and one was the husband of an actress I knew. So in all of those thousands of people who died, it didn't reach my people. It was like AIDS in reverse. Back then, I knew all these people who were sick and dying, and then I'd meet some straight person and they didn't know anybody. I started to think about these two things as like, the ghost world and the world: two sides of the same situation, but infecting entirely different populations. As the whole schtick around 9/11 evolved, and the war in Iraq, I always kept that in mind. AIDS was one version and 9/11 was the other.

IV. THE APPARATUS

ZW: I read *The Gentrification of the Mind* within months of reading *Just Kids* by Patti Smith and *Inferno* by Eileen Myles. They feel like excellent companion pieces to yours. My experience of New York City is limited—I have spent only a total of seventy-two hours there, as a tourist. But reading these books and yours in succession felt like I was taking a course in what it was like to be an artist in the New York City of the 1970s to the 1990s. What did you think of those books?

SS: I loved *Inferno*. I think it's her best book. I love her work. It's funny, sexy, it's got a history of the New York School, it draws its own literary genealogy. I hated *Just Kids*. I felt it was very disingenuous. She made herself very clean. She's a good person because she was understanding that her boyfriend was gay. Yet he ended up being pimped by a rich guy, whom she kind of pimped off also. She doesn't like women at all. Every man she dates ends up being incredibly connected and powerful, and propels her professionally. She has a high ick factor around lesbians. The only woman she mentions is Sandy Daley, an experimental filmmaker who made the film *Robert Having His Nipple Pierced,* which we showed at MIX. She seems to have instinctively stayed away from women who don't have any power, and gone with men who had enormous amounts of power. I was shocked to discover that, because Patti Smith was my hero!

ZW: Feminists love Patti!

SS: She wrote all that great lesbian stuff in her songs, apparently none of which is real. I quote it in *After Delores*. None of it was true. I was crushed when I read that book. But I loved Eileen's book.

ZW: Your style is not stagnant, and it changes often, but it was quite a switch to speculative fiction with your dystopian novel, *The Mere Future*. The villain, Harrison Bond, is a parody of a depressed celebrity author, and he's writing a book called *My Sperm*. Was he based on anyone?

SS: When I was writing this, I was at Yaddo. When I arrived, there were five male writers there: Tom Beller, Donald Antrim, Rick Moody, Jeffrey Eugenides—and was it Jonathan Franzen? No, I can't remember. It was of that ilk. I arrived with my suitcase and they were sitting on the porch and smoking cigars. I said, "I can't believe you guys are smoking cigars." And the guys said, "Paul Auster showed us how."

I spent the summer with them. At that point, I had published maybe eight books, and they each had one or two. And they had no interest in me. They had no respect for me. The worst of the lot became Harrison Bond. He's a type.

Gish Jen was there, too. She's an Asian American writer who at one point had a lot of currency and success. At that time, she was really up there. We were at dinner, and it was me and this gay Filipino guy, and we asked her, "What's it like to be up there with all the guys?" She said, pointing to us three, "We are the center of the culture, but they have the apparatus." And that's true.

ZW: There was a period of time in the 1990s when queer writers were embraced by the mainstream publishing industry. Do you agree?

SS: It was caused by AIDS. AIDS made it impossible for people to deny that homosexuality exists. There were a couple of women editors—at Penguin, at Avon—there were a couple of lesbian editors who started publishing lesbian books in the mainstream. That went on from '85 to '92. In 1992, you started to get the niche marketing going on. That's when Barnes & Noble starts its gay and lesbian section, which is the worst thing that ever happened to us. That's when companies started hiring gay people to niche-market gay books to gay audiences. We were removed from mainstream literature. Then it was a self-fulfilling prophecy, because you could never get the sales. Instead of selling the books as American literature, they started to niche them as gay literature, and that killed it. That was the end of that little seven-year period. The end of that was the publication of *Bastard Out of Carolina,* because it was a book that had no lesbian content but had an openly lesbian author. That was something that the industry could handle. But they could not promote and reward and have a great American success be a novel with a lesbian protagonist. The editors stopped being willing to publish those books. There was a time when seven to ten lesbian novels a year would be coming out of mainstream publishing houses. Now there are zero, or maybe two. It's the inability of the reading public to universalize to a lesbian protagonist. The industry has such a high ick factor that it's been unwilling to do what's necessary to help readers make that connection. But in Britain, lesbian writers are human beings. Their books are considered books, and regular people read them.

ZW: I want to ask you about your book *Ties That Bind: Familial Homophobia and Its Consequences.* What was its reception like?

SS: It got a very divided reception. In terms of regular queer people, I got two to six contacts per day from readers on Facebook, or email, or people leaving messages on my phone, letters, stopping me on the street; they were reading it in their church group in Iowa. I hadn't had that experience since *Rat Bohemia,* when people with AIDS would stop me on the street and say, "You really got it." To remember that you can actually write a book that can change people's lives is something I had forgotten. But I did not get a single review, or one mainstream review. It was this transformative book for all these people, and yet it doesn't exist.

ZW: Your novels are political because you're a political person, and your characters reflect that, but your fiction isn't didactic, and it doesn't seem as though the authorial voice has a political agenda. But when I read criticisms of your work, I feel that critics take your characters as political ideas. Yet books where characters talk about ideas that are considered politically mainstream are not critiqued this way. It reminded me of what the poet Sina Queyras tweeted a few months back: "Don't judge a book by your limitations." What do you think of that statement and how it might apply to your work?

SS: The problem is that novels that reinforce dominant culture values are considered to be neutral, but actually they are political. So they're like, why can't you be neutral like these really right-wing novels? That's the problem. In terms of reading reviews, I've only ever had one review that taught me something, and it was a negative review, and it was by Vivian Gornick; she's a genius, an older feminist woman. She reviewed *Rat Bohemia*. She said that these characters are not bohemians, because bohemians are refuseniks—they step out of their class position, but my characters had been thrown out. And I was like, *You're right*. That's it. All the other reviews, whether they rave, rave, rave, or hate, hate, hate, I never feel like they *get* it.

ZW: Do you feel that way when you talk to readers who give you feedback?

SS: Usually when people talk to me about the book, the benefit I get is I understand that it was meaningful to them, even if they hated it, because they were invested on some level. That is important information for me. But what I almost never get is that they read something that then gives them a deeper idea that they can bring back to me, and then we're actually in a dynamic conversation, so that I now think about something differently than I thought about it before. That almost never happens.

The problem is that it takes a lot to really meet someone on the level of everything that they are offering in a novel. It's very easy to read superficially and to project. Most people read just to find out about themselves, and it's interesting to me what readers have found out about themselves by reading my books, but it's not that helpful to me as a person.

I also want to say that I've been very lucky that I've had a very high level of interaction with readers for my entire career, since 1984. I often walk into a room and there are people there who have read many of my books. Some of them I've aged with, as audiences or as readers. They're very engaged and very invested. If they hate something, they hate it, hate it, hate it. I've never had this experience of passive readers. I've gone to the readings of yuppie writers and I feel like their audience is completely unengaged. So I'm lucky. I'm writing for people who don't have any representation, and so they're happy to have something, and they want to interact with it. ✱

BRUCE JAY FRIEDMAN

TALKS WITH

AMY SOHN

"WHEN A WRITER CAME TO SCHOOL WHEN
I WAS A KID I WASN'T EVEN LISTENING TO HIM.
I WANTED TO SEE THE WAY HE SMOKED."

Why Jews don't become junkies:

They have to have fresh orange juice in the morning
They have to read the New York Times
They have to get eight hours of sleep

I got turned on to Bruce Jay Friedman a few years ago when a
novelist friend referred to him as "one of the lost writers of the
'70s" and recommended his novel About Harry Towns, about
divorce and cocaine. I loved the spare, mordant style, and quickly
devoured his novel A Mother's Kisses (about a mother who
accompanies her son to college). Later I read Stern, his first novel, while
struggling with my third, and told my husband that there was no point
finishing it because I would never be as good as Friedman.

Stern (1962) is about a man who comes undone when he learns that
his neighbor may have referred to his wife as a "kike" and also may have
noticed that she wasn't wearing underwear. Friedman has published five

other novels, five collections of short stories, three plays, and several works of nonfiction, including Even the Rhinos Were Nymphos. *His latest story collection,* Three Balconies, *has just been published by Biblioasis.*

His short story "A Change of Plan" was adapted by Neil Simon and Elaine May into the movie The Heartbreak Kid. *He wrote* Doctor Detroit, Stir Crazy, *and* Splash, *for which he received an Oscar nomination. The Steve Martin film* The Lonely Guy *was based on Friedman's book.*

Friedman suggested we meet at the Century Club, a private club for men and women in the arts and letters on West Forty-third Street that is surrounded by an aura of secrecy. I arrived at six o'clock on a chilly spring night, fifteen minutes early. There was a board on one side of the entryway with all the members' names—J. Galassi, W. Zinsser, and J. Feiffer were a few that I recognized—and colored pegs indicating whether the members were in. A few minutes later Friedman arrived, wearing a tweed coat and hat, strongly built and dapper. "Are you early or am I late?" he asked in a melodious, lightly Bronx-accented voice, putting his hand on my arm. He took me upstairs and we talked in the library over wine, and then in the dining room over clams, veal, and lamb, until we were the last guests to leave the club.

—Amy Sohn (October 2008)

I. "BED WETTERS SAY, 'NICE HORSEY.'"

AMY SOHN: Your characters suffer from a heightened self-consciousness. They see the way others act and want to be like them but can't. Do you feel self-conscious?

BRUCE JAY FRIEDMAN: Like any other young person that didn't have a trust fund and came from the Bronx, I did. It has waned somewhat.

AS: Did you grow more confident when you became successful as a writer?

BJF: A writer is never successful.

AS: I was going to ask you about that, about money and success.

BJF: I could use a little of both, actually. I was rich for a while, when I had all that screenwriting money. I was living alone and didn't know what to do with it. But now I've paid for that a little bit, like that English soccer player who said, "I spent a lot of money on booze, birds, and fast cars. The rest I just squandered."

AS: You've said that you spend literary money and Hollywood money in different ways.

BJF: A check for ten dollars a page from the *Antioch Review* had to be treated very carefully. You'd spend it to listen to Mozart or get a subscription to the *New York Review of Books,* whereas a check for a couple hundred grand for a script—well, that's play money, that's a joke.

AS: In the '60s, if a novelist made money in Hollywood, was it seen as selling out?

BJF: There were girls in the Village who refused to roll around with you if you sold your book to Hollywood. I fell into that way of thinking. The gods were Hemingway, Faulkner, and Fitzgerald to me, that was what you aspired to be—

AS: But they all worked in Hollywood.

BJF: That's true, but everyone denies working in Hollywood. I never met a writer who didn't have secret screenplays he was trying to get produced. There's a truly celebrated writer who always scolded me about Hollywood: "Why are you wasting your time? How could you do that?" Then I met a Czech director who said, "Are you crazy? I was locked up in a room with him for six months trying to crack a screenplay." Bellow and Malamud probably tried to get screenplays produced.

I started to get pretty good at screenwriting but what I didn't like is that it's the only form where the work is being shot down as you're writing. You could be writing the shooting script for *All About Eve* and it would be just a first draft.

AS: How did *The Heartbreak Kid* come about?

BJF: I was living in Great Neck with my first wife. She had just read a story in the *Reader's Digest* and she said, "I think this is terrific." I said, "You think you liked it but you didn't really like it because the author wasn't playing fair and the ending didn't grow indigenously from what the reader knows. Sit here and I'll show you what I mean," because I always had a dozen stories percolating in the back of my head. I still do.

I went upstairs to the attic and wrote "A Change of Plan." I came down and she was fast asleep. I sent it to [my agent] Candida Donadio and *Esquire* bought it within thirty-six hours. The second it was published I got film offers. It was two hours' work and out of that came the first movie—I haven't watched the remake—and now Neil Simon is working on a musical-comedy version. It could be an opera before we're finished.

There is so much luck involved in getting something made in Hollywood—like with *Stir Crazy*. Richard Pryor owed the producer a favor because she had bailed him out when he was struggling. She had the idea to do a movie about a prison rodeo in Texas. They approached me and I said, "Why not?" but I was so snobbish that it was a nuisance. "I'm a novelist, don't bother me with this." Then I get a call from the head of Columbia Pictures saying there's an empty lot at the studio and they need to put something on it.

I saw something happen at a bank where they had people lining up to make deposits and two people were putting on a little show while you were standing on line, entertaining. That became them dressing up and having a bank robbery, which landed them in prison. All of a sudden it comes together.

AS: Do you have any Richard Pryor stories?

BJF: When I went out to the set the one time I visited, he was a wonderful person. They have the artificial bull and Gene Wilder is about to get on it and Gene says, "Nice horsey." That's something that I would never in a million years write. Bed wetters say, "Nice horsey." And they had brought in somebody to pump up the dialogue so I was a little offended. If I were going to write a story about that whole experience I would call it "Nice Horsey." I was starting to leave. Richard saw what was going on in my head and said, "I never met a writer like you: take the money, don't take any shit. I have fifty in cash. I believe I'll do the same." Sure enough, he disappeared for three days soon after that.

We walked out together, and on the way to his trailer, he said, "You ever get high?" Joking, I said, "Once, in the spring of '63." Then I said, "Here's why Jews don't become junkies: a Jew has to have fresh orange juice in the morning, has to read the *New York Times,* and has to get eight hours of sleep. Ergo, no junkie." We went into his trailer and there were all kinds of pipes and African things with wicks. Soon after that is when he blew himself up.

It's terrifying when I think of how close I've come to being busted, to getting shot. It's a miracle I'm sitting here. It's a miracle anybody my age is sitting here.

II. "DARK TRIANGLE"

AS: From 1954 to 1966 you worked at the Magazine Management Company, editing *Men, Male, True Action,* and *Man's World.* What kind of stories did you publish?

BJF: They were adventure stories with the thinnest layer of sex. The strongest phrase we were allowed to use was *dark triangle.* When a woman showed up in a negligee it was a "dark triangle." It was pretty hot, actually. The publisher thought *nympho* was a good word so we used that a lot: "The G.I. King of Nympho Island." There were a few pictures of women, not even in bikinis, but bathing suits, and a lot of war stories about Anzio and all the famous battles. When we ran out of battles I told Mario Puzo, who was one of my writers at the time, to make some up. I'd say, "It wasn't Anzio but a few cities over. Nobody knows about it."

I was annoyed by this James Frey story and I had forgotten what we used to do. There was a story about a Jewish prisoner and a Nazi commandant, and the stock photos we had bought to illustrate it didn't look right. The Jewish guy looked like a Nazi and the reverse. I said, "Just switch them." It was a little bit like reality television. The stories were sort of true.

Once in a while we would take a few liberties and somebody would bring a lawsuit. We ran a story about a Canadian who had died in the wilderness, but we had him involved with nymphos. It turned out the guy was alive and a chaplain in Canada. We were afraid he would sue. So I called a Toronto newspaper and we found out he had gone off to hunt bears and was believed to have died. We were relieved.

AS: How were you able to write *Stern* while working a nine-to-five job?

BJF: I had a two-hour commute to Long Island each way and I used the time on the train. My kids remember seeing me slumped over the table in the morning when they got up to go to school. Somehow you make use of the time when you have very little of it.

AS: Was *Stern* the first novel you wrote?

BJF: No, I had written one novel that Candida, to her dying day, said she would get published. It was about a Martha Stewart–type character that went to different air-force bases buoying up the spirits of wives of air-force officers. She would say, "Don't worry about preparing wonderful hors d'oeuvres. You are your own hors d'oeuvre." That was the title, *You Are Your Own Hors d'Oeuvre*. It got a few rejections and I lost confidence in it. But I learned how to write a novel from doing it badly. It was awful, working for four years to get it finished, like pushing a stone up a hill. Back then, if you hadn't published a book by thirty it was all over.

As my thirtieth birthday was approaching, I had a very brief nervous breakdown, like Stern. I wasn't allowed to have a real nervous breakdown, because I had kids and a mortgage. But in that period I wrote four stories of a different kind. They weren't science fiction but they were fantasy stories of a kind I never tried before. I sent them to Candida and she called back and said she'd sold all four of them to *Playboy*. I got a check for around six thousand dollars. The best thing about the experience was that I had passed thirty and hadn't even noticed it. I bought a baby blue MG with the money. All of a sudden I was OK.

AS: How did *Stern* get published?

BJF: When Candida read *Stern*—she later denied this—she said, "You have written a very ugly book." That cost me a week of sleep. I was really ill over that. A week later she called and said, "There's one person I know who might respond to this book. His name is Robert Gottlieb." She sent it to him and he bought it but there was this long period, like the Sitzkrieg—after Hitler invaded Poland, and France and Germany were officially at war with Hitler but nothing happened—when my manuscript was accepted but it was unofficial.

Bob Gottlieb was the best editor I ever had. He would say, "Do something here." He was always right. Or he'd say, "You didn't write that," about this one line in *Stern*. I knew exactly what he meant.

AS: What was it?

BJF: This is so embarrassing. In a dramatic moment, it said, "Stern reeled as he had never reeled before." That's promotional copy. He was absolutely dead-on.

AS: Did he change anything else?

BJF: The book ended another way initially and Robert found it disagreeable. I still think I was right. Stern and his son are on a Ferris wheel and Stern climbs down, leaving his child at the top, goes back to his own mother, and gets into bed. Bob didn't want anything bad to happen to a child—it was a personal thing for him—and I changed it.

He edited six or seven of my novels. In *The Dick* I had an extended section that really didn't need to be in the book. Bob called it the "flying down to Rio" section. You're not quite ready to end the book so you fly people down to Rio. It really stuck with me.

AS: How did you get started as a fiction writer?

BJF: I had an experience in the air force that I didn't know how to deal with so I wrote a story about it called "The Man They Threw Out of Jets." I sent it to the *New Yorker*. A guy named Hollis Alpert was charged with what they called unsolicited manuscripts, the slush pile. His job was to pull two stories a month out of the mass of material and work with those two writers. I got pulled out, along with a writer named John Sack, who went on and had a decent career.

Hollis Alpert read the story and said, "We can't publish this. What else do you have?" In my mother's kitchen I wrote another story, "Wonderful Golden Rule Days" and they bought it. "The Man They Threw Out of Jets" was subsequently published in the *Antioch Review*. I never published in the *A.R.* again until fifty years later to the day. Some impulse told me to send a story to them and a woman pulled me out of the slush pile, again.

AS: Christopher Buckley wrote that your stories, "with their whammo endings, tend to divide into two kinds: the first leave you whispering, 'Wow'; the second go whistling over your head like an artillery round and leave you muttering, 'Huh.'" Do you know the ending of a short story when you sit down to write it?

BJF: I learned not to begin a story until I knew the approximate last line, if not the actual last line. That has saved me a few times over the years. To me a story is like a bow and arrow. It has to go straight to the target and hit it in the center. There are a couple occasions when I really didn't know where I was going, like in "Black Angels," where the story bailed me out and the ending revealed itself to me. In a novel I don't think it's quite required.

III. "I CANNOT READ A PEDESTRIAN SENTENCE."

AS: *Stern* drew comparisons to Nathanael West, Hieronymus Bosch, and Marc Chagall. Who were your influences when you started writing?

BJF: When I was in the air force, I had a commanding officer named George B. Leonard, who later became a major counter-culture figure on the West Coast. He gave me three books to read: *Of Time and the River* by Thomas Wolfe, *From Here to Eternity* by James Jones, and *Catcher in the Rye*. I read the books in close to one weekend and it was my only epiphany: a Jewish guy can have an epiphany. I thought, Wouldn't it be wonderful to try something like that? This was particularly true with *Catcher in the Rye*. I had an image of literature as being something I simply couldn't do, having to do with life and the cosmos and the universe and the rolling hills of South Carolina. When I read Salinger it was the first time I thought, This is my world; I could try something like that.

I was influenced by radio—I listened to a lot of radio, there was no television—and the street. The way young people admire rock stars, I had a thing about writers. When a writer came to school when I was a kid I wasn't even listening to him. I wanted to see the way he smoked.

Someone reviewing one of my early books said, "Obviously Mr. Friedman has been influenced by Céline." I had never read Céline but then I read Céline and they were right, meaning you could be influenced by someone whose influence is so widespread that you get influenced without reading it.

Later I started to get influenced only insofar as I enjoyed someone, like Evelyn Waugh. He's written some novels that I can actually prove were perfect, like *Decline and Fall.*

I read *The Day of the Locust* for the first time recently. I really loved it, except there's a lot of unnecessary "he said" and "she said" where you don't know who the speaker is. It could have used a good edit. It wouldn't have lost any literary value.

I'm really, really touchy about this, maybe more so than others, but I cannot read a pedestrian sentence.

AS: What's an example of a pedestrian sentence?

BJF: I like to know what's going on and what pop culture is once in a while, so I read *The Da Vinci Code.* I was reading along and I came to a sentence where the hero is in a hotel room and he dons a bathrobe. There's no particular reason but I said, "OK, let him don a bathrobe." It was like a king donning his raiment. Then twenty pages later he dons another bathrobe. I said, "If he dons one more fucking bathrobe I'm out of here."

AS: In the late '60s you had a hit play Off Broadway called *Scuba Duba,* about a man who goes on vacation with his wife to the south of France only to have her run off with a black scuba diver. How did you get interested in playwriting?

BJF: One thing I am proud of is that I've been able to have things work out as a novelist and a playwright and even in Hollywood. There's always that "they." *They* say, "OK, you've written a short story but you can't write a novel." Then you write a novel. "Terrific, but you can't write for the theater." And you write for the theater and it works out. After *Scuba Duba* was a hit I was in the locker room at Vic Tanny's gym, naked, and this guy said, "I haven't seen your name on the big screen."

I did have some background in theater to the extent that I had seen a lot as a kid. My aunt worked for the Shuberts in the box office. From the time I was five years old whenever they had a flop that was going to close I would be rushed down to see it, so I learned what terrible plays were like.

AS: There is an absurdist sensibility in your play and I wonder if you saw anything that influenced you.

BJF: I don't know if I saw this play before or after but there was a play called *Outward Bound* by Sutton Vane—great name, the guy's real name was probably Ginsburg—and it really haunted me. It was about some people that were on a steamer, a vacation cruise, and they realize that they're dead. In 1962 I went to see Arthur Kopit's play *Oh Dad, Poor Dad, Mamma's Hung You in the Closet and I'm Feeling So Sad*—and I was really taken with it. Ionesco was being shown and Beckett and Edward Albee. It was upside-down theater. It didn't have a formal structure. I thought, I ought to try something like that. At that time in my life everything I touched worked out.

AS: Then what happened?

BJF: The first time I had a ten-car collision was when I got a lousy review in the *Times*. The review troubled me. It was written in a personal way and I was upset by it. It was written by Anatole Broyard at a time when we didn't know he was black. The book was *The Dick* and I'm writing about a Chicago homicide bureau, which is racist from the second you walk in. So the implication was that I was racist. I resented that. It really was wounding. He had been a big fan of mine, sought me out, and had invited me down to the Village to have dinner and meet Ralph Ellison. Ellison, I still remember, irritatingly kept calling me "Mr. Stern" throughout the evening.

Broyard was one of those guys who had published one short story, about his father. Called "What the Cystoscope Said." It got some attention and would seem to be the beginning of a big career as a writer. The night I came to dinner Broyard showed me his desk. It was the most beautiful desk I'd ever seen, with the finest bookshelves, all neatly organized. He said, "This is my in-box, and this is my out-box," but I knew no books would be written there.

IV. "CAN I WASH SOME GLASSES?"

AS: There are certain writers who don't want to admit that any of their fiction comes from life, because they worry that the admission would denigrate their craft. Do you feel that way?

BJF: I know exactly what you're saying, because there's a feeling very often by the questioner that if all you're doing is reporting on your life that's a lesser achievement. My answer is: try it. If I were to describe what my actual days are like it would put everybody to sleep.

I think all writing is autobiographical. If you write about Venus and Mars it's your view of Venus and Mars. But to me the great fun is "Write what you don't know." That's more exciting.

AS: Do you consider yourself a Jewish writer? Do you find the question irritating?

BJF: I'm not so easily irritated, but I'm not sure how to deal with it. I wrote one play that dealt with Jewish issues, called *Have You Spoken to Any Jews Lately?* In my new collection there's a story about a guy who moves to the country and he's on the alert for anti-Semitism and he can't find any. He feels deprived. What's the point of being a Jew? So he creates some.

AS: Your new collection has some stories that seem influenced by I. B. Singer. I wonder if your stories are getting more Jewish as you get older.

BJF: Lately I've been flooded with memories of old Yiddish expressions from my childhood. It's wonderful. Hitler would have been more successful if he'd attacked the language rather than the Jews. The language is so powerful. When Hitler told von Manstein his plan about invading the Soviet Union and opening up a two-front war, if von Manstein had said, "This is a *farshtunkeneh* plan," he could have called off the whole thing.

AS: Your novel *A Mother's Kisses,* about an overbearing Jewish mother, came out five years before *Portnoy's Complaint.* Did you ever feel competitive with Roth?

BJF: Not at that time. I admired him tremendously. I'm sure it's provable that there was a similarity between the two mothers but I simply didn't feel any connection.

The rule with me is if I'm happy with the work I'm doing I admire everyone else and wish everyone well. When my work is going poorly, that's when I get envious and resentful.

AS: Did you know Philip Roth?

BJF: I met him a few times. In the early '60s *Mademoiselle* magazine did a feature—a wonderful idea—in which they paired up new writers with Swedish models. There were different teams and I was on one with Norman Podhoretz, Jack Richardson, who became a lifelong friend, and George Plimpton. I got to chatting with George. I had a bumpy marriage, I was living out there in the suburbs, and I thought, I could use a new friend.

He invited me to a party. So I show up to his party and apparently I was early and his house was empty. I called up to him, "This is Bruce. You remember, *Mademoiselle.* Can I help out? Can I wash some glasses?" He said, "Oh no no no, dear boy, don't worry about a thing." So I walked around the block, came back, and suddenly the entire Western world walked through his door: Jules Feiffer, Jacqueline Onassis, Truman Capote. Philip Roth was there that night, I believe Norman Mailer was there. I said, "This is some friend." I knew Philip Roth's stories in the *New Yorker* but to actually meet him, and Jules Feiffer? I couldn't believe I was actually talking to these people.

V. "YOU CAN GET THE WHOLE STORY IN FIVE MINUTES IF YOU'RE GOOD."

AS: Did you invent the phrase *black humor?*

BJF: All that meant was that someone approached me from New American Library and said, "How about doing this anthology?" It was a way to pick up five grand and read some people I had never heard of: Thomas Pynchon, Nabokov, a fellow that belongs to this club named Charles Simmons. I wrote an introduction about black humor, which was published everywhere. For some reason that idea caught fire. They started teaching college courses on black humor.

AS: You've written so well about shrinks. In your story "Mr. Prinzo's Breakthrough" Prinzo murders his shrink's wife to test his shrink's contention that he's there to help his patient any way he can. Have you had any luck with therapy?

BJF: At one point I had my first writer's block so I went to see an ancient Viennese guy, who I think had studied at Freud's knee. He was a hundred years old. I told him, "I had a flamboyant mother, a reserved father." He stopped me after five minutes and said, "OK, Mr. Friedman, you are obviously bipolar. You're not crazy bipolar but you're in a decent range and I would advise you to take some medication for that." Then he puts his arm around me and says, "I wouldn't concern myself too much because art wouldn't exist without you manic depressives." I said, "Wait a minute. I started out bipolar a few minutes ago and now you've promoted me to manic depressive?"

Joe Heller got a big kick out of that—I told him the story—but what he fastened on was the fact that the guy knew the whole story after five minutes. You can get the whole story in five minutes if you're good.

AS: It seems half the people in therapy complain because their parents overestimated them and the other half complain because their parents underestimated them. Which is worse?

BJF: In the case of my mother, it was both. In some ways I could do no wrong, but when I called her after she had seen *Scuba Duba* and it got a rave review in the *Times* I said, "Ma, what did you think?" She said, "I could not take my eyes off that boy," meaning Jerry Orbach. I said, "He wasn't reading the phone book."

VI. ON NOT GOING
TO JAPAN

AS: Can you describe a typical day?

BJF: It's to put off writing as long as possible. I walk the dog. There's the laundry. There's the garbage. I have to read three newspapers in the morning. I'm a news junkie. I can work my way up to noon, one o'clock before I have to face this. Then I work.

I was reading an interview with Alice Munro. I like her stories. One thing she said I really responded to, about the need to work every day. If she doesn't, god forbid, and misses a day, she's really impossible to be with and irritable. I'm the same way.

AS: Do you go on the internet?

BJF: Most of the time at the computer I'm staring at it in wonder of all the time it could have saved me. I wrote this book called *Tokyo Woes* about a guy who goes to Japan. I had never been to Japan. My wife was pregnant and I thought I'd wait till we delivered the baby and then go to Japan. I started to write it and I had a little cottage near the house where I worked and it was filled from floor to ceiling with books about Japan, Japanese culture, and Japanese art. All that stuff would have been available with two clicks and it would have enriched the book.

AS: Didn't you wind up publishing it without having gone to Japan?

BJF: I figured I could get the character over Mount Fuji, which I had read a lot about. I knew what a Japanese apartment would look like, so I could get him into an apartment. Before I knew it I was finished with the book, never having gone to Japan. There were a lot of reviews and there wasn't a soul who guessed that I had never been to Japan, including Michiko Kakutani. Later a magazine found out that I had written a whole book about Japan and never been there, and they sent me. I thought my version was more accurate.

AS: What are you working on now?

BJF: With God's help, as we say in our religion, I should have a draft of a novel in a month or so if life doesn't overinterfere. I've never written a multiviewpoint book. One of the viewpoints is a woman's, but in this work that I'm struggling with it's the easiest part. I'm having trouble writing about the male.

You would think someone who had been at this for so long would be able to solve any problem, and yet every work creates new challenges. Isaac Singer said, "Just because you've written ten wonderful novels doesn't mean the next one is going to be any good." You would think I knew what I was doing by this point but I don't. I get sidetracked. I'm really impressed by how little I know. ✶

JOY WILLIAMS

TALKS WITH

LENI ZUMAS

"I DON'T FEEL WRITERS
SHOULD FEEL COMFORTABLE IN REGARD
TO THEIR WORK."

Ways that cats are like humans:
They are indulged and indulgent killers
There are too many of them

Joy Williams doesn't use email (or even own a computer) *and prefers the U.S. mail to the telephone. The following interview was arranged by postcard and conducted by letter. Williams is the author of four novels, including* The Quick and the Dead, *which was a finalist for the Pulitzer Prize, two collections of stories, and a collection of essays,* Ill Nature, *which was a finalist for the National Book Critics Circle Award. She has received many other honors and has taught writing at the Universities of Arizona, Florida, Houston, Iowa, and Wyoming.*

Joy Williams writes some of the best sentences in American fiction. Her uncanny sense of rhythm and her eye for frictive symmetries dig up the deep strangeness of the ordinary. A child's vagina is "beardless as a bun." The light in the Florida Keys is "a sort of blandly insistent urban light—feathery and bemused—not insistent but resigned." Everywhere in her work, the ghoulish interlocks gorgeously with the comic. She writes about people who have come to the ends of ropes that weren't too strong in the first place, and about the hilarity that blooms in disaster. From grief to feverishness to black humor and back again, Williams nails the discomfort of being alive. "This was no place to be tonight for any of them," says the narrator of The Quick and the Dead, *"but this was the place they were."*

—Leni Zumas

I. "ONE OF THE NOISIEST CITIES IN AMERICA."

LENI ZUMAS: Your sentences are so beautifully built that although they move swiftly—sometimes even deliriously—I imagine they must have been made slowly. I've heard you say that you don't revise much, if at all, but I wonder if a kind of re-seeing is happening as you compose. What is the role, in your writing process, of excision, second-guessing, refusal, and scraping away?

JOY WILLIAMS: The latest fad in paperback editions is to place a reader's guide at the end, often with an interview with the writer concerning the work's composition. These things always amaze me. How can the writer analyze her own work with such aplomb? Once you usher a story into existence it gets to possess its own secrets, and one of them, it seems to me, is how you managed to usher it into existence in the first place. No, I don't revise much. My head is messy but once I get down to it, the page is pretty clean.

LZ: Do you harbor any superstitions about writing?

JW: All my work harbors a dog. Got to have the dog.

LZ: You don't use email or the internet; you work on a typewriter. What are the rewards of this arrangement? And do you have a favorite brand of typewriter?

JW: I have several Smith-Corona Super Sterlings and a Galaxie Twelve. A few little Royals with no cases. Very low-tech. Pretty much everything I have is low-tech. Clotheslines, swamp coolers, water tanks, broom. And of course we all know vinegar can do just about anything except make a good martini.

LZ: Don DeLillo once told David Foster Wallace, "The reason I use a manual typewriter concerns the sculptural quality I find in words on paper, the architecture of the letters individually and in combination, a sensation advanced (for me) by the mechanical nature of the process—finger striking key, hammer striking page. Electronic intervention would dull the sensuous gratification I get from this process—a gratification I try to soak my prose in." What's your relationship to the sculptural quality of words and to the sensations of typing?

JW: Don DeLillo is the finest writer writing today, no question, and I'm thrilled we share this preference. In that same letter, he also, I believe, speaks of the pleasure a finely crafted sentence brings, how with care the work becomes more gift than product. I like the sound a typewriter makes. Yaddo is such a different place these days.

LZ: What about acoustics? How much do sound and rhythm affect your decisions?

JW: I always try to live in quiet places. Key West drove me nuts. And people would just walk in the door. Key West has to be one of the noisiest cities in America.

II. "ANY READER
WITH A HEART IS APPALLED."

LZ: What is the importance of surrealism to your work, and to fiction generally?

JW: It's of enormous importance. It's freedom, a way of thinking, a way of getting beyond and beneath appearances. When it works, it's involving, untranslatable. But most artists shy away from the word. It's no badge of honor to them. Surrealism at its worst produces an empty, indulgent mannerism. But in the right hands it's absolutely fearless and fabulous. Lucy Corin is a young writer whose surrealistic approach to her materials makes for riveting reading. Another young woman, a poet, Matthea Harvey, is one of my favorites, too.

LZ: In your 1998 essay "Uncanny the Singing That Comes from Certain Husks," you say: "The writer doesn't want to disclose or instruct or advocate, he wants to transmute and disturb." Do you still agree?

JW: I do. And yet when I read a story that was truly truly disturbing in the most soul-sickening way, I was furious at the author. My reaction was quite similar to that of Elizabeth Costello, J. M. Coetzee's fictional author, when she reads Paul West's novel *The Very Rich Hours of Count von Stauffenberg*. She dins the chapters detailing the execution of Hitler's would-be assassins *obscene,* causing her to deliver a rambling lecture on evil and the writer's responsibility in bringing it to our attention. Her conclusion is that certain things are not good to write or to read and she is baffled by the incoherence of her thought. "What had she said? *I do not want to read this.* But what right had she to refuse? What right had she not to know what, in all too clear a sense, she already knew?"

I had a violent reaction to "93990," a story by George Saunders in his collection *In Persuasion Nation*. Saunders uses the arid

JOY WILLIAMS & LENI ZUMAS

emotionless language of a lab report in an animal-experimentation project. Monkeys are given higher and higher doses of a dangerous drug until they die. But one, 93990, does not die. The experimenters are frustrated and amused by this but they patiently, coolly, systematically persist until their goal—death to all their subjects—is accomplished. It is a placid and grotesque piece of writing. Any reader with a heart is appalled, but because of the manner in which it is told there is no way to enter the story or (probably more accurately) to exit when finished. It's smut. It demeans us. It provides no outlet for understanding or outrage. Of course, these cruelties and useless investigations are inflicted on animals many many hundreds of times a day in laboratories. We pretend we have the right not to know what we already know. Saunders makes us implicit in perpetuating this horror by reading about it. And no judgment befalls us. George Saunders is a smart, playful, and ironic guy, but "93990" has released a black and noxious cloud over the powers and employments of "story." Maybe we should put together a panel or some damn thing to discuss it.

LZ: Your collection of essays, *Ill Nature,* bears brilliant and savage witness to various ways that nonhuman life forms are destroyed by human self-interest. A sickening recent example is, of course, the BP oil spill in the Gulf of Mexico. Have you written anything in response to this disaster, or might you in future?

JW: Robinson Jeffers saw humankind as a vast, spreading fungus of slime-threads and spores, an evolutionary mischance in which ego-consciousness, our distinctive trait, pits us against the harmonious integrity of natural processes. This was not appreciated in his time, and this fine, angry poet of the sublime was marginalized. Today he'd be investigated by the FBI. We need more environmental writers, not the soft squishy kind but the great loud preachers and advocates.

It's ironic that American officials fault the Japanese government for being evasive about the nuclear meltdowns after the tsunami,

169

deferring instead to the incommunicative electric companies that run the plants. But the Obama administration behaved in the same manner after the BP blow out. The oil company had complete control of the narrative and the cosmetic solution. BP and the Coast Guard prevented any real inspection of the Gulf after this ecological tragedy. Now we have infant dolphins washing up dead ashore and the discovery of an oily mucus covering the sea floor, creating a vast graveyard. The nightmare is ongoing but we hear mostly the whining of businesses who were "affected" by the spill, the car dealers and waitresses in cheesy restaurants and so on. We seem to have no guilt and no leaders. We're greedy and destructive and indifferent.

Certainly I'll write something, but I can't imagine it changing a thing. We know we're being lied to. We know we eat too much and want too much and breed too many babies. We've swapped green space for cyberspace. And we don't care.

LZ: Animals are everywhere in your work. What kind of contact or communion with animals do you have in the non-writing parts of your life?

JW: I do not communicate with cats nor would I ever, ever wish to. But I would say that they're indulged and indulgent killers, just like us. And there are too many of them as well, just like us.

III. "MORE OR LESS
THE BAGGY MONSTER."

LZ: Your second novel, *The Changeling,* was reissued in 2008 by Fairy Tale Review Press. How did it feel to watch the book take on a second life? And how did the critical reception this time around differ from thirty years ago?

JW: It has a much nicer cover. Goya's *El Perro.* But I am not familiar with the critical reception of which you speak. I just remember the first reception, which was horrible, horrible…

LZ: You're the author of four novels, three story collections, a book of essays, and a Florida travel guide, so clearly your powers play in multiple genres; but is there one form that enthralls you most, or in which you feel most at home?

JW: When I start an essay, I think: Wow. I can go anywhere I want with this! And: It's so nice to use your mind and stir things up! Then, finished at last, I turn to a story. I think: I know exactly what to do here! What a pleasure to work with these cool clear images, this bright dialogue. And then, failure firmly in hand, I conclude, and perhaps turn to the novel. Now here's the open range, I think, I can really run with this. But novels are minefields and nerve-racking because they take so long. Nor are they as indulgent or elastic as you might think. I'm not at home in any of these forms, actually. But I don't feel writers should feel comfortable in regard to their work.

LZ: Why do you suppose the short story has become such a stepchild in mainstream American publishing?—by this I mean the perception among many agents, editors, and marketing departments that a collection won't sell well and should therefore only be tolerated from a new author if a novel is close on its heels.

JW: Is that still the case? I know very little about the wiles and stratagems of publishing, although I do hear that beginning, middle, and end are back in fashion. The short story tends to be a literary and comely creature, the novel remains more or less the baggy monster. Hundreds of university programs produce many hundreds of these collections each year, and summer writing programs pound and prune even more stories into shape. Thinking about this is sort of disheartening, actually. Writing workshops are big business now and the teachers are more and more expected to have some clout in getting their students published. Connections. At least an introduction to an agent. Otherwise… what use is a divine story? I find, too, that graduates are becoming more and more loath to leave the institution and are applying to PhD programs in creative writing. Which means more critics and teachers and jobs. God help us if it all comes down to jobs. But I didn't answer your question.

LZ: How do you feel about "schools" of writing? I'm not talking about MFA programs, but rather aesthetic cliques, coteries, gangs. People sometimes associate you with the minimalism camp, but your fiction unfailingly resists, it seems to me, being corralled.

JW: It seems to me just a way of trying to nail down the future in its perception of the past. Writers certainly like to be mentioned, but are probably less joyous about some of the affinities critics come up with. There seems to be a lot of droll fabulousness going around lately. But who wants to be corralled? We want to be Queen of the Broncos. We ladies of course. The men probably want to be King of the Broncos. It's only reasonable.

IV. "THE SOOTHING POUNDING OF THE SEA."

LZ: Many of your fictions contain absent, ambivalent, afflicted, or substitute mothers. How has the figure of the maternal changed shape in your work over the years?

JW: With the exception of a story or two and several essays, my writing is consciously unbiographical. I adored my mother. My fictional mothers bear no relationship to her. Still, the idea of mother—powerful, lost, absent, unfathomable, closer to our very existence than breath—is of limitless fascination to me.

LZ: I see a real affinity between your work and W. G. Sebald's—the quietly ruthless vision you both have, and the nimbleness of your sentences, and your talent for stitching together the chilling and the hilarious. There's a sentence in *The Rings of Saturn* that makes me think of your books: "The astonishing monsters that we know to be properly part of the natural world leave us with a suspicion that even the most fantastical beasts might not be mere inventions." Do you consider Sebald a kindred writer?

JW: What a tragedy he's gone. And yet it really was a death foretold in everything he wrote. In my home I have the painter Tess Jaray's beautiful abstractions accompanying a Sebald fragment from *The Rings of Saturn*:

> I was watching the sand martins darting to and fro over the sea. Ceaselessly emitting their tiny cries, they sped along their flight-paths faster than my eyes could follow them. At earlier times, in the summer evenings during my childhood when I had watched from the valley as swallows circled in the last light, still in great numbers in those days, I would imagine that the world was held together by the courses they flew through the air.

He was a great hymnist of man's relentless ecological destruction. I would love to have met him. Naturally I would have been speechless.

LZ: Have you recently read anything that made you feel (to paraphrase Emily Dickinson) as if the top of your head were taken off?

JW: I like Mark Richard's memoir *House of Prayer No. 2* a whole lot.

LZ: How would you describe a typical Joy Williams writing day?

JW: Tea and fruit in the morning, then four or five hours of solid work, a salad for lunch. A nap, in which my lost loved ones come to me and tell me they're happy and still love me, a walk through bird-songed woods, followed by several more hours of oxygenated work. Drinks with friends, each more accomplished and interesting than the other, then bed, windows flung open to the soothing pounding of the sea, turning rock over rock, all messages which will fuel the morrow's pages coming to me in friendly and artful dreams... Yup... Oh, sometimes it's a little different.

LZ: What are you working on at the moment?

JW: Not succumbing to the despair of having a broken foot. I never realized how much I had to move around to think. ✶

STANLEY CRAWFORD

TALKS WITH

NOY HOLLAND

"WE HAVE ALL KNOWN WRITERS
WHOSE BOOKS HAVE GONE UP
IN THE SMOKE OF TALK."

Stanley Crawford's yield:

Five novels
Three works of nonfiction
Five hundred pounds of garlic (per year)

I have a wooden box, a small chest, really, covered in ragged leather, in which I keep years of letters, starting with Donna Gardner's ("it is super fun here without you") back in the fourth grade. Another box sits on my bookshelf, every letter in it written by the same lovely man, same fellow who made the box and gave it to me. My husband hoards the letters I wrote to him, and I hoard the letters he wrote to me, in our drawers beside our bed. Messy, mixed in, but we know we are there—those greenhorns we used to be. Who do you know heartless enough to throw a careful letter carelessly away?

I liked writing to Stanley Crawford. I liked that the days were warm when we started, and when we stopped, that winter was closing in. I liked *making up a new person who turned out not to be him.*

I met Stan and his wife, Rose Mary, on the eastern seaboard, in the lobby of a B&B too dolled up for any of us. I knew his work—the novels, starting with Gascoyne, Some Instructions to My Wife, *the splendid* Log of the S.S. the Mrs. Unguentine, *and, more recently,* Petroleum Man. *I knew he had lived and farmed in the Embudo Valley of northern New Mexico for going on forty years, and written three books of nonfiction there. He and Rose Mary built the house they raised their children in: built it from the clay it stands on, made every brick. I was smitten with them both.*

Crawford is tall, even sitting down. He is serious, and boyish, and straightaway I could picture him with his dog in his arms fording a swollen river. He isn't Unguentine, not that cranky, brash, seafaring tyrant, but quiet, and maybe inward, a man accustomed to fixing things, to living in the wind in open country. —Noy Holland (February 2010)

Dear Stanley Crawford,

I have been trying with no success to know why it is I have waited so long to write to you—waited years, really, since I read you first—and now these many weeks. I could not get over the hurdle of knowing how strange it might be, for you, to write in this now-relatively-intimate manner to a stranger. I know something of your life and you know nothing of mine; it seems a little uncivil, this imbalance, as though I've spooked around in your house and fields. I know garlic-planting season is upon you. I know the wind you speak of that blows from March until May. I grew up in New Mexico, a good ways from you, in an old adobe, in what used to be the outskirts of Albuquerque, on ground we irrigated from a wide ditch that drew water from the Rio Grande. We grew grass, little more, for horses, and for one highly obstinate cow.

I live in western Massachusetts now, where anything grows except okra and green chile. What is life without green chile? Without posole on a cold day? We had frost this morning in the shadows. Time to plant fall bulbs, dig gladiolas, harvest the green knots of brussel sprouts. I grow a little, nothing like your annual yield of five hundred pounds of garlic a year. I live in the hills, but haven't, as you have, headed for the hills to make a new life, to build a house with bricks you made by hand, one at a time, for the first time. I guess I won't likely be finished being amazed by such a feat until I have embarked on such a life or left this one.

Did you consider, in your twenties and thirties, settling down in South America and farming there, at a similar elevation, in those rich volcanic soils? What drew you (besides *Easy Rider*) back to the states from abroad? You write about your place, your life there in New Mexico, in three books of nonfiction—but has building a house and garlic farming and plunging into the wind in Dixon also changed the way you write fiction? Would the peripatetic Stanley Crawford have written different books? (Am reminded here of Sebald and the long purposeful outings of his novels, the walking tours to discover and dispel, of the body's desire for motion.)

Please feel free to ignore any question that strikes you as silly or meddlesome. I'm curious, and feel unsettled by this unsettling world.

Noy

Dear Noy—

It is agreeable of course to write to someone who has a good sense, through the actual experience of it, of the gardening and farming life, and of the landscape hereabouts. Just last night, we had a downpour and all the arroyos were running—three of them to ford on our way home through the village, axle-deep in muddy brown water, the roof leaking in its three predictable places.

The rain and the sopping fields means that this morning I actually can take the time to answer your thoughtful letter. I've spent all of two months, on two separate occasions, in New England, mostly at the MacDowell Colony, with a few excursions a ways north and to western Massachusetts—whose occasional patches of openness were a relief from the enclosedness of the landscape—and always with a sense of disjunction between what I imagined it should be like from my youthful reading of American literature—in effect, New England literature—and what I was actually seeing twenty and thirty years later. I finally walked around Walden Pond only in November of 2001, but I still keep that other one, my own private one, in reserve. And, to stray a little, I chose to set my most recent novel in Connecticut on the strength of what I absorbed from the backseat of a small BMW racing back to Manhattan on the interstate.

You ask an interesting question about South America. I was twenty-two or -three when I started teaching English as a foreign language in Cali, Colombia, a beautiful city at three thousand feet in the Cauca Valley, with topsoil seventy feet deep—on which they grazed cattle! One of my classes was an advanced English class, and some of my students were so good that we spent time trading, you might say, English for Spanish. I left Colombia with a fluency I was never quite able to attain either in French, which I read better, or Greek, now mostly gone. I was intrigued by the thought of staying on for more than a year, but I had begun to take note of the melancholy fate of longtime expatriates, particularly those of an artistic bent. There was an old Belgian pianist (and probably composer) who had fled to Colombia in the late 1940s out of the fear that the Cold War would heat up in Europe into World War III. He was too old to return, at least in his eyes, and his life seemed consumed by fretting about termites eating their way into his pianos. Yes, I entertained fantasies, if briefly, of homesteading over the mountains in the Putumayo—but as a spoiled American, I too much missed the abundance and ease of my native California, and returned there in late 1960 and enrolled in the UC Berkeley graduate program in English lit.

That first two-year session abroad, Paris and then Cali, was followed in 1963 with a five-year expatriation consisting of four years in Greece (Piraeus, Lesbos, Crete) and a second year in Paris. When I think about it now, there were two conflicting pulls in my life. One, the literary thing. At the time that meant exploring oneself through tramping around the world, experiencing the extremes, in effect creating through a chaotic-seeming life the material about which one could then write. Learning other languages, learning to invent and play new personas through new languages, seemed very much a part of this. The ethos, if you will, was not something I picked up from my academic studies so much as from my fellow students, writers-to-be and filmmakers whose alternative canon had not yet been sanctified by the academy. Rose Mary and I met on Crete in 1967 not long after the April 21 Colonels' Coup, at a time when I was becoming disillusioned with the expatriate life and longing for something literally hands-on. My father had been a high-school wood- and electric-shop teacher; I grew up in a house where I knew you could build or fix anything, but this was of no interest to me until after fifteen years of living as a student and then as a writer I began to feel too helpless in a world that seemed to be about to crash. We returned to the States in December 1968 into a very unsettled country, to the Bay Area, one of the epicenters of anti-Vietnam protest. Ten months later we took refuge in rural northern New Mexico.

It took me fifteen years of building the house, learning to garden and then farm, to figure out how to write about the life I was trying to live. It was not my intention to do so; that came when all other possibilities had withered away. In my fiction, *Log* foreshadowed our agrarian life, and *Some Instructions,* in a convoluted way, was in its time a wry summing up. After that, the void for about ten years. The way I have put it elsewhere is that my life had become more interesting than anything I could invent. Had I remained the peripatetic novelist I started out as? I tremble at the thought. Within a few years of publishing my first novel I knew but did not acknowledge that from then on books were more likely to come to me in slow, indirect ways, rather than in the lightning flashes of the first four novels. A year's study of the Los Alamos National Laboratory atomic weapons work finally crystallized into a short chapter in the garlic book—ten years later. Another long study of the basic processes of industrial civilization ended up in exasperation—at my own limitations, as well as the political situation of the time—as *Petroleum Man*.

Tomorrow morning snow is predicted, rather earlier than usual. I had the luck or foresight to harvest all of the acorn and butternut squash last week, a good three thousand pounds. There's nothing like a big pile of winter squash to give comfort in these strange, shifting times.

All best,
Stan

Dear Stan,

With great pleasure I received your letter, which speaks with more eloquence than I can summon of the conflicting needs and desires a person faces most any day, between the pragmatic and the literary, the want to move and the want to stay put. I'm restless, and feel often that I ought to have grown through it. Funny, too, at this time of year, even living in the center of town on little more than an acre, how strong my want is to draw in, shore up, have a little store of fruits and nuts to carry us through the cold months ahead. Maybe this is a form of restlessness, too. We still have apples on the trees—a record harvest, the limbs breaking they have been so heavy with fruit—and cider to press with the neighbors. Not a leaf on a tree. Even the tamaracks, gone yellow, are losing their fine needles.

This morning I finished your *Garlic Testament* and felt fortified, exhorted, by its quiet loveliness, by your optimism and good sense. Honest work, self-sufficiency, staying put. A neighbor of mine once insisted that no matter how brief a person expects his residency to be, he ought always to live in a place as though he expected to stay forever. I used to plant flowers I never saw bloom—I had to imagine them blooming: a lesser satisfaction, but a satisfaction nonetheless. It occurs to me that this is a bit like having a book out in the world: you write the book, and you know it is out there, but you will never track its dispersal, or its effect on those who come across it.

I wonder about the role of the political in your work. You speak of politics overtly in *Testament,* and in your recent novel, *Petroleum Man.* In a book like *Log of the S. S. the Mrs. Unguentine,* the role of the political—maybe I mean simply casting a lens on the contemporary and the public—is, on the surface, scant. The Unguentines cast off; it's a domestic drama set on the high seas, an adventure in which there is neither an element of pursuit, nor of questing (unless it's the questing for the perfect climate to improve what grows onboard.) I think it's brilliant, to fuse these two traditions, to graft a new animal altogether. Everything is marvelously out of whack. I wonder about the evolution of the book: did it arise from your qualms about the restless, expatriate life, from a divided desire? Unguentine can fix or invent just about anything; he is scientist, artist, carpenter, gardener, tyrant, wizard, husband, father. (He is maybe some version of your able father?) He is dead when the book begins, and yet he lives. Lives to father a child who "matured a genius at five, became an excellent swimmer, grew modest and swam away one day, no doubt having had his fill of us, the barge, these seas"—surely one of the swiftest childhoods on record. Unguentine builds a biodome and takes it down again, in what strikes me as a premonitory frenzy (perhaps he needed that good heap of winter squash to settle him down). Maybe Unguentine didn't inhabit a "world about to crash" but, arguably, we do. Were you, do you remember, seeing forward fearfully into the mess we're in now? Were you looking back, say, to Melville, when you wrote that first irascible line: "The name is Mrs. Unguentine"?

I remember Grace Paley saying that she was afraid some of the literary life; she worried that hanging out with writers would draw her away from mothering, from the political activism so central to her life. So many of us wear so many hats, for better and for worse, and perhaps it's unreasonable to expect that we'll ever stop negotiating and measuring and assessing the various ways we spend ourselves. Where to march, what to write, what to grow. How to be. It's refreshing to hear you speak with such clarity and pleasure of the choices you have made. "I like to do one thing slowly," a musician friend said, and I thought of you bending and stooping and picking up again and again: a brick, a squash, a bundle of garlic. A word.

I hope your planting has gone well.

All best,

Noy

Dear Noy—

Both rooted and restless, yes. You put it well.

We finished garlic and shallot planting ten days ago, and I'll finish up the field this afternoon by shaping the beds—smoothing out the planting ridges with a bed shaper, which makes it easier to manure, mulch, and lay down the drip lines in the spring. This is a terribly beautiful time of year, skies clear beyond belief, the shadows long, the hours of midday warmth of an urgent preciousness, with so much less to do in the field that I can now and then take time to sit and muse.

You touch, perhaps indirectly, on something else. Rose Mary and I live, to many eyes, a commendable life in a beautiful place, and though we often tire of it, we're always anxious to return here from a day in town. To a certain extent it is the gaze of others that renders this life beautiful, if only because those quieter perceptions or more miniscule ones, the glint and texture of things, cannot quite survive the relatively clumsy business of speech or even pointing. You can tell when another wordlessly perceives the minutiae on a walk, say, but we also have visitors in whose presence the sky grows dull and the colors fade, those who don't know why they are here and who wish to be elsewhere. Readers are like visitors, only of a different kind. I've met quite a few of my readers. A few have told me that one or another of my books have changed their lives. I don't know quite what to think; that isn't what I had in mind.

But I was going to say something else. I'm always drawn back to Frost's aphorism, perhaps incorrectly remembered: "To socialize is to forgive." The implication here is that alone, working in solitude, we tend to become self-obsessed, become envious or superior, grind axes, refine feuds. I have known the occasional soul who seems to live the good life without having to be constantly battling his or her inner demons. I'm not one of them. Perhaps this is why I also write fiction. Which is or can be an exploration of all the uncontrollable in one's nature. This is not necessarily negative: some of us are uncontrollably hopeful, at least some of the time. I used to think that writing fiction was also a way to defend oneself, one's psyche, against the predations of mainstream culture, but this seems to have become somewhat more complicated than it was; and perhaps that's what I'm trying to do with my nonfiction now.

At the time of writing *Log* I wasn't anticipating the grand mess we're now collectively in; I was responding to the relatively minor mess, minor compared to now, we were in in the late 1960s. (Until recently I thought of it as an apocalyptic novel; the reality, as I now see, is more ambiguous.) I bought deeply into the myth of self-sufficiency (which had not yet become survivalism, but no doubt was on the way) in which one attempts to free oneself from all the "corrupting" dependencies exacted by industrial and postindustrial society, which we all "knew" would crash somehow, sooner or later. If one were to have taken Stewart Brand's *Whole Earth Catalog: Access to Tools* seriously, which I certainly did in 1969, a fictional result would have been something like *Log*. I think even my father was startled in the end by the number of tools and amount of agricultural equipment I amassed over the decades. These days, I feel that the book was written by someone quite different, a younger self I would now feel uneasy being around. And of course it was.

I don't spend a lot of time with fellow writers; I'm much more interested in small-scale agriculture, local economies, and the social-justice issues connected to them. Farming didn't make me a better fiction writer; it enabled me to become a nonfiction writer.

You mentioned Melville. A weight, more than an influence. A good friend loved his work but I could never get there.

To get back to rooted and restless. While going through Thoreau some years back to try and pin him down on his attitude toward the emerging technologies of the day, the railroad, mainly, about which he was critical and enthusiastic both, I was intrigued at his late fantasies of going west: the rooted man, dreaming of Chicago... Maybe we're all incurably split down the middle. The curse—and gift—of the imagination?

Stan

Dear Stan,

Thank you for your letter, and for your patience with my ridiculous delay in responding to it. I have the usual excuses, the veiled complaining about the hectic that is so much a part of the fabric of social exchange. Even complaining is likely a form of seeking forgiveness, as the quote you offer from Frost suggests, an expression of the want to feel not-alone, an assertion of the doing for others we do in part to take the teeth from the possibility that we will ourselves be (alive still) forgotten.

Here in our region, we've had a small healthy dose of knowing what it might take to survive here, should the scientists and writers of the end-of-everything be right: a massive, gorgeous ice storm that snapped power lines and hardwoods, gathered on every twig and blade of grass and fattened around the seed pods until the fields looked to be embellished by thousands of vodka lollipops that broke musically as we walked. (We harvested these and melted them for drink and wash water on the woodstove.) The good life you live and speak so candidly of surely prepares you for disaster, hopefully allows you better than most of us to enjoy hardship of this kind. We were fairly un-Unguentine about it, adept at fixing nearly nothing. Cheerful and inept. For our tribe, the storm was more adventure than hardship.

By now I hope you have settled in to the simpler months of winter, your writing months, a different sort of pleasure and complication. My husband is a writer, too, and I always know by his mood how well and how hard he is writing: the better the work is going, the harder it is to come up from under it and be with others. Tricky business—finding solitude, or privacy, in the unrest of the domestic. I wonder if you reserve the winter months for writing to avoid the messy difficulty of juggling too much at once. How do you think it affects your writing, the long dormancy through the farming months, the intense months of work when the ground sets? Can you say at all how raising children affected, and affects, your writing life? To what extent did *Some Instructions* arise from lived experience, the want to make order from (natural) disorder? (You say in your letter that fiction "is or can be an exploration of all the uncontrollable in one's nature"… this seems right to me. But does external disorder—the uncontrollability of others, say—also compel an orderly rendering in fiction? A record of flux? Fixity and flux; rooted and restless. I see I am back to my old pairings.)

A student of mine (I typed *a student of mind*) recently made use of the common phrase "he thought to himself." It struck me that we seldom think "to ourselves," that our thoughts are predominantly a running conversation with others—alive or dead, near or distant—and that it would be truer to say "he thought to his mother, to his brother" and so on. We don't say so. But your novels—I'm thinking particularly of *Some Instructions* and *Petroleum Man*—posit a speaker and a listener: they address, explicitly, a wife, children. Would you talk a little, please, about how this restriction enabled and complicated the writing of those books? And (I ask this sheepishly) would you be willing to say more about what you are working on now?

Noy

Dear Noy—

After your account, I can have no complaints about our weeklong run of merely cloudy and snowy weather.

When I first started writing I didn't have to worry about "the unrest of the domestic," as you put it so well. I lived alone, but in a convivial seaside village on Lesbos and then a small town on Crete;

when I finished my solitary writing day, I stepped out the door and inevitably found someone to talk to on the street, at a café, a restaurant, or out on the beach. Even better: there was always a feast of languages. When Rose Mary and I got together, our first year and a half were the most difficult. I was writing my head off, but not well, and was no doubt moody and difficult. I was a new writer and was supposed to write all the time, wasn't I? I had not yet discovered that there are times when one can't write, one shouldn't write, times for thought, for deepening, or just reading, or simply living.

Camus said that what prevents you from doing your work becomes your work. This is how I regard talking about writing, at least before the lonely work of writing is completed. Writers are probably unhappy or discontented much of the time about what they're trying to write, but if you actually give voice to such complaints, or even to your hopes, then that, not the writing, can become your work. Talk is the cuckoo egg that hatches and eventually nudges the authentic fledglings out of the nest. We have all known writers whose books have gone up in the smoke of talk.

The genesis of *Some Instructions* is something of a puzzle. I don't know where the obsessive voice came from. I had been given an apartment for a month in Santa Fe and was re-reading everything by Chekhov I could get my hands on. But the voice came. I was delighted, appalled. Perhaps this is a reliable sign that something is interesting: I am at first appalled. Add, perhaps, that I have always delighted in Molière's obsessives. Finally, the strange satisfaction of bottling up, you might say, the chaotic. The novel has been widely misunderstood, especially by men.

But perhaps all of the novels posit a speaker addressing a listener, not just *Some Instructions,* as you have said. The wife there is of course no Mrs. Unguentine, who would have talked back; she's a cipher, a nonentity, a projection, an ideal, whatever, as are the son and daughter. By *Petroleum Man* they are "real" characters and they talk back. I have never thought of this in quite this way, but perhaps as I writer I need an implied or explicit overarching dialogue, that in effect my nonfiction persona or fictional narrator is in fact addressing someone, a someone who voices objections, asks questions, irritates, stimulates, attracts, someone in the past, someone in the future. Perhaps the hardest thing is to find that pairing, that speaker, that listener, and that tie or issue that binds them. Perhaps as a reader I'm most satisfied when I feel I am overhearing, or even participating in, a conversation.

I'll leave it at that. Always good to hear from you, your musings and thoughtful questions, which will soon (I suspect) exhaust the small matter of this particular self.

All best,

Stan ✷

GARY LUTZ

TALKS WITH

ROSS SIMONINI

"FOR ALL I KNOW, THE AGE OF THE COMMA
IS OVER. BUT IT WAS A BEAUTIFUL TIME
TO BE ALIVE AND TO BE FINGERING WORDS."

Words used in this interview rejected by Microsoft Word's spell-check:

Lish, affixationally, replenishings, Barthes, Michelet, blunderheaded,
disrupture, overthrowal, fussbudgetry, Fellini's, Cabiria, punctuational,
suss, undire, writing-programmese, paragraphic, sequentiality, vocality,
limital, paginal, tenantry, writerly, DeLillo, Lipsyte, perishability,
peculiarizing, manifestoish, upcroppings, unignorable, chorings

Gary Lutz's past is a bit vague, which is how he likes
it. He grew up in Allentown, Pennsylvania, and has
lived much of his life outside Pittsburgh, where he
builds tight, unusual stories in an unfurnished apartment. He studied with the highly respected editor
and educator Gordon Lish "for twenty-six days between June 1992 and
June 1997" and considers himself "fortunate just to have been present."
Under Lish, he developed a unique voice, using compression and aphorism
to cohere narrative fragments into untraditionally beautiful shapes. His characters spend their time enduring the weight of everyday life, dwelling on the
minutiae of their own neuroses. In a story titled "Slops," a college professor

with colitis maps out all the campus bathrooms in a small notebook. In another, a man passes out pamphlets and gives forty-five-minute presentations (with charts) in search of a prospective wife. Lutz labors at each meticulous sentence, word by word, to create a language of striking insight, peripheral emotions, and reinvented vocabulary.

*Lutz has published two short-story collections—*Stories in the Worst Way *and* I Looked Alive*—both of which will intrigue anyone even mildly interested in the capacity of language. He also edits fiction for the online experimental journal 5_Trope.*

This conversation took place over the summer of 2005, with the help of many computers. —*Ross Simonini (February 2006)*

I. "THERE ARE BOOKS I'VE ENJOYED PAGE BY PAGE WITHOUT HAVING ANY IDEA OF WHAT THEY WERE ABOUT."

ROSS SIMONINI: I've heard you use some unusual methods for generating prose—something to do with crossword-puzzle dictionaries.

GARY LUTZ: Well, I've never done crossword puzzles, but early on, in my impatience with thesauruses, none of which are very generous, I chanced upon a book called *The Master Crossword Puzzle Dictionary,* which houses the largest stockpile of words to be found outside of the best unabridged dictionaries, and I've recommended it here and there to people who are interested in precision. The problem is that it's out of print, and secondhand copies are priced as high as $750. I think you have to know what's available in the language, because a lot of our words rarely make an appearance in print anymore, so a book like that can have real utility. I find it helpful to have lots of words passing before my eyes as much as possible when I am trying to write, because the one word I feel I need the most might just be somewhere in the stream, though I might have to chop part of it away or twist it a little or elongate it affixationally.

RS: When you manipulate words like this, is it a technical process? Are you using many reference materials? Or is it mostly intuitive?

GL: I think that a lot of what I seem to be doing when I try to get from one end of a sentence to the other—a crossing that can take hours, days, weeks—is introducing words to each other that in ordinary circumstance would never meet. I might pair them off because they share a throbbing interior vowel or the same consonantal shell, or because I have some other hunch that they belong together, even though anyone else might write them off as entirely incompatible. I guess I work my way through a sentence by instigating these relationships—a perverse sort of matchmaking, apparently—and then to keep the words from getting too cozy, I might reach for an uncustomary preposition that plunges the sentence into some queasy depths. The whole undertaking seems to be largely intuitive and probably unnatural. I never have any ideas.

RS: In general, what do you want to accomplish with your sentences? What, exactly, should a sentence do?

GL: I guess I would define "sentence" as "a quasi-independent unit of tended language, deliberate in every syllable" or something close to that. Ideally, as I see things, every sentence should bestow a fresh verbal bounty on the reader. A writer needs to give in every sentence—a writer is someone who is forever bearing gifts. A paragraph should be a sequence of replenishings. Judged by this standard—which I of course fall short of every time—a lot of writing might seem costive, unsatisfying, maddeningly ungenerous. But maybe readers shouldn't have to wait out half a paragraph or entire pages just to get something they haven't had before.

RS: Because your sentences do have a sense of fullness and density, they obviously ask more of the reader than most sentences.
  Something like "There was no need to even come face to face to be stuck in failing familiarity forever" has a simple enough sen-

timent but an intense, thick delivery. Do you think there's a "right" way to read one of your sentences?

GL: Reading, like writing, is a private, intimate, and unnatural act. I wouldn't want to tell anybody how to go about doing it. As a reader, I find that I like sentences that make me stop and stare into them, or at least gawk.

RS: But isn't grammar basically just a way of telling someone how to read—how to think, when to breathe? And considering how interested you are in precision and grammar, I would expect you to be less easygoing about the reading process.

GL: If a sentence of mine finally finds its way out into the world, readers who move their eyes over it are free to make of it whatever they want. If a reader sees something I intended, that's fine by me, and if a reader sticks with a story and sees something entirely different or is completely baffled, I'm OK with that, too. There are books I've enjoyed page by page without having any idea of what they were about.

RS: Which ones?

GL: Some of the books by Roland Barthes (in translation). The one about fashion, the one about Michelet, the one called S/Z— I savored them without comprehending them. But I am lousy at managing abstractions and am blunderheaded in general. Until a couple of years ago, I'd thought the expression "No news is good news" meant that all news is necessarily bad. Punch lines can take weeks, months, to clobber me correctly. I was late to learn the facts of life, and they were something of a letdown.

RS: Your acceptance of ambiguity seems more on the experimental side, while your interest in grammar seems more traditional. Would you ever call yourself a traditionalist?

GL: I think it helps somehow if prose that on the surface might seem vivid in its disrupture or overthrowal of the conventional is ultimately discovered to be pure grammatical fussbudgetry underneath. (A friend tells me I'm a Victorian at heart.) I probably would not have had a long-enduring, even morbid fascination with prescriptive grammar and punctuation if I weren't convinced that exactitude in such matters was a lost cause. As a teacher of English composition and business writing, I am guilty of talking a lot about the comma.

RS: Any comma wisdom to impart?

GL: For all I know, the Age of the Comma is over. But it was a beautiful time to be alive and to be fingering words. Sentences had precision. These days, you see a theater critic in a prominent magazine describing the Broadway show *Sweet Charity* as "Neil Simon's sanitized musical version of Fellini's *Nights of Cabiria*." Without a comma separating "sanitized" from "musical," the phrasing implies, unhelpfully, that there are at least two stage musical adaptations of the Fellini picture, that the versions differ in their degree of sanitization, and that the sanitized version is the one under review. A few weeks later, in the same magazine, a film reviewer refers to "a new movie version of *Bewitched*"—implying, misleadingly, that there was at least one previous movie version of the sitcom (there wasn't). Prescriptive grammarians would say that, in each case, a pair of coordinate adjectives (adjectives individually modifying a noun) have been erroneously presented as if they were cumulative adjectives (adjectival pairs in which the first adjective modifies the duo formed by the second adjective and the noun), with the unhappy result that the first adjective has been thrown into a restrictive role—distinguishing one "musical version" or "movie version" from another—even though that is violently at odds with each writer's purpose.

RS: What about the hyphen? No one ever gives straight answers about hyphens. I love them and yet I feel somehow seedy when I use them. Is this normal?

GL: A little book needs to be written about the hyphen—it would be a very consoling book, at least to me—because the hyphen is the most neglected punctuational device we've got. I went a little nuts when I first took notice of it, back in third grade. I started putting hyphens between all of the words in my sentences. I thought that was a way to keep things from falling apart, but the teacher made me stop. (That year I also bought a vocabulary-improving book. The first chapter offered the adjectives "eldritch" and "gelid." I tucked them into a paragraph I had to write in class, and the teacher told me to quit making up words.) The hyphen, though, is the sweetest of punctuation marks, because it unites words into couples (and sometimes threesomes and foursomes). It's an embracer. It does most of its most important business in front of nouns, and its business is to make things clearer. If somebody were teaching a workshop devoted to short fiction, for instance, too many people would describe it as a "short fiction workshop." But that would mean it was a fiction workshop of brief duration. A hyphen between "short" and "fiction" would formalize the union of the two words, and they would together serve, in conjugal fashion, as a single adjective. But not all of the words in adjectival compounds preceding nouns should be hitched together with hyphens. You should never force a hyphen into the space between an adverb ending in "ly" and an adjective or a participle ("a nicely-turned phrase" is always wrong), but if the word ending in "ly" is an adjective, a hyphen is required ("a sickly-looking dog"). Things get very, very complicated when a noun is preceded by an adjectival compound whose first word is an adverb not ending in "ly." Do you write "a once popular singer" or "a once-popular singer"? A few years ago, trying to recover from a traumatic breakup, I made a study of hyphenation patterns in the *New Yorker* magazine back when William Shawn was in charge. I made the hyphen my lifeline, and I put my trust in William Shawn and his grammar genius, Eleanor Gould Packard. I noticed that the *New Yorker* would publish a formation like "a not too pleasant afternoon" but also "a not-quite-pleasant afternoon." A phrase like "a once-happy child" would sport a hyphen, but "a once promising student" would not, so I concluded that you put a hyphen after "once" if it's followed by an adjective, but you leave the phrase unhyphenated if "once" is followed by a participle. I tried my best to suss out all of the underlying patterns (I was really, really grieving, and may have been missing all the obvious points), and I compiled a biggish list. But I started finding inconsistencies: something like "an ever so delicate girl" would show up in one issue and "an ever-so-prissy girl" in another; something like "a much recorded song" in one article and "a much-visited city" in another. A further source of big trouble for me was whether to hyphenate an adjectival compound that follows a linking verb. Do you write "She is well thought of" or "She is well-thought-of"? None of the manuals addressed this matter to my satisfaction, so I again turned to the *New Yorker* for guidance. I eventually fell in love with somebody else and slept deeply for a while.

RS: How did you develop your knowledge of punctuation? Any good books you could recommend?

GL: I learned commas by making a study of the punctuational splendor of the *New Yorker* during the final decade of the William Shawn regime. The *New Yorker* seems to have been the only magazine to see the gorgeous fitness of inserting a comma in a sentence like "He lived in Trenton until his death, in 1999" or "I visited her at her house, in Newark." Virtually every other publisher would run those sentences without commas and thus fuddle things by implying that the man died more than once and the woman owned more than one house at the time. There's no one book, unfortunately, that covers all this stuff.

RS: At what age did you first become involved with language?

GL: I was nineteen or twenty. I was in college, and had been changing my major every semester until I ended up in English, which, it turned out, was the one field of study in which the very thing that gave it its name was the one thing that was almost never taught. That might have been a good thing, because I'd never learned how to study. I went to a counselor at the college, and he gravely counseled me to buy a book called *How to Study.* The book advocated a method called SQ3R, which I never got the hang of and which was rendered obsolete anyway by the arrival of the highlighting marker. Reading was transformed into an activity whose desired outcome was the yellowing of certain regions of the page. I had one professor, fortunately, who threw many salutary scares into me—he was the only person from whom I ever learned anything in a collegiate setting—and then I happened upon a book called *Modern American Usage,* by Wilson Follett, which offered a magisterial consideration of sentences and their sicknesses. I had to overcome the inclination to color the book instead of reading it, but read it I did, many times. I eventually graduated and then packed myself off to an M.A. program in creative writing, and after graduating from that, I gave up writing for a little over a decade.

RS: Did you have a negative reaction to your graduate program?

GL: The stories of mine that met with approval in graduate school were stories that I knew were shallow and completely fake and not worth the reader's moment. I became confused and lost interest in writing. I found a job and went to work, and after work, I just walked around stores until they closed.

RS: What was so shallow and fake about them?

GL: My stories were drowsily lyrical ordeals. There was a lot of catty, undire dialogue involving lovelorn youths of ornamental sensitivity. It was all writing-programmese of the most inconsequent sort. I didn't know any better, and nobody told me to stop. Eventually, I must have leveled with myself.

II. "I REGRET THE SPECIFICITY."

RS: You have called film "the perfect storytelling medium" and have said that you "don't read fiction for the story." In a certain sense, I completely understand your point. But in another sense I wonder: if language is the only driving force behind fiction, why not just abandon fiction for something purely language-driven, like poetry?

GL: I think that movies are the ideal medium for getting characters from one place to another without making a big deal out of routine movement, and at the same time you can get the colors of the rooms or the neighborhoods, the weather, and emotionally convenient music on the soundtrack. Nobody has to come out with dulling declarations of "Then she got into the car" or "There he goes to the bathroom again." How-to books on the short story instruct writers to block out scenes as plays in miniature. Something in me wants to counter: Then why not just write a play or movie script instead? Why not try to do in a sentence or paragraph what can't be done in a shot or filmic sequence? Anyway, I am not one for plots—I think I recall somebody having remarked that the word "plot" itself gives off a whiff of burial dirt—and I find the concept of "cause and effect" to be tediously overrated.

As for fiction versus poetry, the border between the two seems less secure than ever. A lot of writing passes back and forth without anyone summoning the authorities. Some people have told me that what I write is poetry, that it could be laid out as such. But I am a sucker for the old notions of poetry and would never think of my paragraphic jitter in that light. Besides, regarding my stuff as prose is a much more cost-efficient use of paper. The reader gets a full page.

RS: How exactly do you write outside of "cause and effect"?

GL: Well, for one thing, I never ask Why? or What next? There's got to be more to life than logic, sequentiality, psychology. The only question I put to myself when writing is: Anything else? I'm interested only in whatever's beside the point.

RS: Does that mean you avoid unifying ideas or themes in your writing?

GL: Sometimes I think we don't give words enough credit for knowing where they truly belong. You'd be surprised by how quick certain words can be at giving up their seats in a snug lexicon and throwing themselves at the first perfectly rotten mood that comes along in somebody with a pencil. Sometimes the words just seem to come and claim their places. So the unity of a story might then be evident in the peculiar scope of the overall vocality. There might even turn out to be a kind of acoustical daisy chain discernible from one end of a story to the other. Or the language might be steeped in a single, unspecified grief and take on that tint or coloration through and through. Or there might be a limital tilt or pitch to a narrator's leanings. Or the verbal matter might give the impression of having been spewed exclusively from a tiny, ramshackle elevation somewhere out of the reader's sight.

Another way of looking at this, maybe, is that the motions of even the most centrifugally active mind or heart have a circumference, and the writer of a story should probably respect or even celebrate the fixity of that circumference. But within those limits, anything should be welcome to clamor on behalf of itself or rise to an occasion or veer off into ultimately pertinent digression.

RS: Can you talk more about acoustical daisy chains? Are you saying that, sometimes, pure phonetics might be your unifying theme (like sound translations)?

GL: Nothing I ever do is that methodical or scientific. It's just that in the most favorable of circumstances, a sentence-starting word at long last presents itself, and the language at large gets wind of this little instigation, and then whichever word in particular is feeling itself to be the most acoustically sympathetic to the first word will eventually throw itself at it, and then a third word arrives on the scene and senses an affinity with what the first two are doing and figures itself into the emerging pattern. If you can keep this up, if every word has such deep attraction to its neighbors to the left and to the right, the prose coheres and takes on a distinct character or tonality. This is part of what Gordon Lish taught me, if I understood correctly.

RS: Do you think it's important that writing can sound fluid when spoken? Or are you more interested with the visual, on-the-page aesthetic?

GL: Both, actually. A sentence, at least as I see it, has to come out of the mouth in a plausible, presentable way. But I try to be mindful as well of its paginal life, its typographical predicament.

RS: So, despite the burial plots, do you still enjoy films?

GL: I do. Every couple of years or so, I seem to find one movie and then watch the thing over and over—sometimes every night for weeks. I was like that with *Requiem for a Dream,* and then *Ghost World,* and *The Last Days of Disco,* and, just recently, *Before Sunset.* I always watch with the closed-caption function on, because I like the dialogue to come at me doubly.

RS: What sort of effect do you suppose film has had on your writing?

GL: I was five or six when I saw *Breakfast at Tiffany's* at a drive-in theater. That movie filled my head with every radiantly wrong idea about New York City and its tenantry, all in a single, potent, life-lasting dose. The only TV series I ever took to heart was *The Honeymooners.* But I've spent most of my life listening to screwball talk radio and pop music in its more pathological forms. Those, I know, have taken various tolls on me.

RS: Your stories almost never reference pop culture. Is this purposeful?

GL: It is. I mentioned McDonald's in one story in my first book, and Coca-Cola in one story in my second book. Although that seems to be the extent of it, I regret the specificity. But, for that matter, I don't mention place names or decades, either.

RS: I rarely see writers reference specific movements in pop culture without being insulting or at least sarcastic. In fact, it almost seems impolite if there isn't some sort of cynicism, as if pop culture and literature are eternal enemies.

GL: I'm often moved to tears by pop music and movies, and I don't turn defensive or ironic when I talk about what I love. But I've never felt any desire to include pop culture in my stories. Maybe it's because whenever I'm reading a piece of fiction that mentions, say, a particular song I like, I start hearing the song in my head, or I start longing to hear the record, and I feel as if I'm being seduced away from the story. And the sentential setting of the song title often turns out to be less enchanting than the song, and more often than not, there's no attempt to describe the song; its title is most likely just there on the page as a kind of shorthand or prompt, which the writer obviously hopes will be evocative. I just don't see what's gained by directing a susceptible reader's attention outside of the frame of a story. I love it, though, when fiction writers go out of their way to invent performers, song titles, even lyrics, and then, through sheer writerly brilliance, make you hear the music. Don DeLillo has done that. Sam Lipsyte has done that. They keep the reader entirely inside the story. As for the wider use of popular culture, I realize that there's a type of contemporary fiction that borders on journalism and might be subject to similar perishability, and I also realize that decades from now, that sort of fiction can acquire a kind of time-capsule value. And it can be enormous fun to read right now. But if you look back at a writer like John O'Hara, who, it's often been said, stocked his fiction with loads of social-class-signifying details, you won't find the kinds of brand-name particularity and "name checking" that are all over the place in some of today's fiction.

III. "AS FOR GENDER, SEXUAL ORIENTATION, THAT SORT OF THING SEEMS TO COME AND GO WITH THESE PEOPLE."

RS: Fiction can seemingly bend time in ways that film could never do. It can almost exist outside time.

GL: I think so. One feels less beholden to the chronological, and freer to enter the inner space of a character.

RS: A lot of your stories experiment with the ambiguity of a character's "inner space." Sometimes large things like sexuality and gender are obscured while other, more nuanced aspects of character are attended to with very deep precision. In this sense, why do your characters have such difficulty understanding themselves?

GL: I venture that I belong to the school of thought holding that human beings are vividly unknowable, even to themselves. My narrators and characters seem to amass lots of peculiarizing data about the spaces and bodies they inhabit, or the routine transactions they manage during the course of a day, or any other person they might blunder up against eventually in an antic calamity of attraction. But they seem to be stumped when it comes to forming any kind of big, reliable picture of themselves. It's not that they can't generalize—they make pronouncements and judgments left and right; they come out with strictures and formulations of an almost manifestoish vehemence—but their generalizations seem to carry them further and further away from themselves; they seem expelled from any lasting sense they might be trying to make. They can't even apply the first-person pronouns to themselves without sounding at once evasive and self-aggrandizing. I don't claim to know who these narrators or characters really are. In most cases, I don't even know their names, and if I stuck names on them, I would feel that I was violating them. As for gender, sexual orientation, that sort of thing seems to come and go with these people.

RS: It sounds like you distance yourself from your characters about as much as you acquaint yourself with them. That's pretty unusual to hear from a writer. On the other hand, maybe it's more normal, more like the unrefined and clumsy interactions between real, flesh-and-blood people.

GL: Well, I think of my characters less as figures in case histories than as upcroppings of language, as syntactic commotions coming suddenly to a head. The characters aren't reductions or enlargements or composites of persons I might have run across in daily, unshapely life. So I don't have any dealings with them, really, other than as specimens of phrasing.

RS: So if the characters and the plot are only a consequence of your prose, what do you write from? Sam Lipsyte has said he usually starts stories from abnormal phrases that catch his ear, like: "You could touch for a couple of bucks." Do you sympathize with that? Is language itself your impetus?

GL: It's with me sort of the way it is with Sam, one of my all-time favorite writers. Every once in a while, a word or a phrase—in my case, an ordinary-looking citizen of our language, more often than not—will just seem to be harassing me, even stalking me. It'll start showing up wherever I go. Eventually I'll find I have to do something about it.

IV. "I'VE LIVED MY ENTIRE ADULT LIFE WITHOUT FURNITURE, SO MY DOMESTIC POSTURES AND POSITIONS ARE LIMITED."

RS: Do you have any intention to work in any mediums outside the short story?

GL: I guess that, even as a reader, I just prefer the intimate enclosures of very short fiction. When I was growing up, some packages of potato chips used to carry, on their backside, a rather defensive notation along the lines of "This package is sold by weight, not by volume. Contents may have settled during shipment." That puts me in mind of most of my favorite books, which may not consume very much space but nevertheless have an unignorable density and heft, at least to me.

RS: What will your new stories be like, in comparison with your previous work?

GL: I'd like to write longer short stories or shorter ones, instead of more of the medium-length ones I seem to have been writing in the last half-decade. Writing something long would be very difficult for me, because I evict almost everything from the little structures that somehow get themselves erected. But writing something very, very short would be even more terrifying, I imagine.

RS: I would expect someone who writes such compact, tight stories as yours to be avid about revising. Do you throw away much work?

GL: I trash almost everything I write. And then I go through the trash. I'm slow.

RS: Besides massive editing, what constitutes your work schedule, your writing habits, your self-imposed rules? What is a typical Lutz day?

GL: I listen to the radio. My weekdays begin with Howard Stern and end with Phil Hendrie. In between, I have my job eight and a half months of the year and my spells at my laptop during the summers. Some of the pieces in my first book were written in pencil on sheets of paper taped to the wall above my bathtub while I soaked for hours and hours, and parts of others were written right after I woke up. But that was before I seemed to know what I was doing. These days, I can write only on a keyboard. I try to stay alert. I usually listen to music for an hour or so in the evening. Saturdays I walk around Pittsburgh or ride a light-rail car to the end of the not very long line, then ride back. Sundays are for choring. I've lived my entire adult life without furniture, so my domestic postures and positions are limited. But I do a lot of laundry.

RS: What's the best thing you've written, in your opinion?

GL: All of my stories are disappointments to me. They gall.

RS: Then how do you keep yourself interested?

GL: There is the possibility, maybe, that I might one day not disappoint myself. Anyway, I can't think of anything else to do. ✶

DANY LAFERRIÈRE

TALKS WITH

ALAIN MABANCKOU

"TRAVEL IS A WINDOW ONTO THE WORLD; IT'S LIKE
LETTING FRESH AIR INTO THE HOUSE, LEAVING
THE LIBRARY BEHIND, FREEING OURSELVES
OF LITERARY AND INTELLECTUAL REFERENCES
IN ORDER TO MAKE WAY FOR NEW REFERENCES,
THUS INTRODUCING INTO YOUR BOOK
THE NOISE OF THE WORLD."

Lingering questions about writers:
Did Léopold Sédar Senghor like dancing in nightclubs?
Did Léon-Gontran Damas smoke cigars?
Did Aimé Césaire favor silk neckties?

The past dozen years have been good to Congolese writer *Alain Mabanckou, who has garnered critical and popular success in France with novels such as* Broken Glass *and* Memoirs of a Porcupine; *earlier this year he won the Grand Prix de Littérature Henri Gal (awarded by L'Institut de France by recommendation of the hallowed Académie Française), in recognition of a body of work that includes nine novels, a half-dozen volumes of poetry, and four essay collections; and though his best-selling-author status, charisma, flamboyant personality, and trademark gavroche cap have made Mabanckou a natural media darling and poster boy of French integration-through-writing-in-French, the author is fond* *of paraphrasing Frantz Fanon and his resistance to the notion of being hemmed in by "the fact of blackness."*

Mabanckou lives in Santa Monica, and teaches at UCLA, but he is often on the road, attending literary festivals and events the world over (his work has been translated into over a dozen languages). Early this year in Port-au-Prince he crossed paths with his old friend Dany Laferrière, the Haitian writer (and former TV weatherman!), whom he has known since the '90s, when Mabanckou was starting out and Laferrière was already well known. Laferrière, who is a (baker's) dozen years older than Mabanckou, published his first novel, How to Make Love to a Negro Without Getting Tired, *in Canada in 1985. He has since published over twenty books of fiction and nonfiction, and has also enjoyed critical as well as popular success in France, where, in 2009, he was awarded the Prix Médicis for* L'Énigme du retour. *Though he currently lives in Montreal, Laferrière spent most of the '90s in Miami, and subsequently wrote with great passion about the United States, going so far as to say that he considers himself American, having lived since 1976 in North America (he returned to Montreal in 2002).*

While at the Festival Étonnants Voyageurs in Port-au-Prince, in the early days of February 2012—two years after the horrific earthquake that devastated Haiti, on January 12, 2010—Dany Laferrière and Alain Mabanckou stayed at the Karibe Hotel, a two-tone building nestled in the hills of the city, with gabled roofs, a majestic marble lobby, and an outdoor courtyard lush with foliage. As the two literary friends set up shop in the courtyard's open-air gazebo, under a shady tangle of cedar, pine, and mango—and throughout their conversation—workmen could be heard rebuilding the partially demolished hotel. —Philippe Aronson (January 2013)

I. TRAVEL

DANY LAFERRIÈRE: Over the last two decades or so, I have noticed that third-world writers—that is to say, African and Caribbean writers—have been traveling more and more extensively. They get invited hither and thither because they write in French. Some of these writers meet at various book festivals and literary gatherings, and become friends, and when writers become friends, they emulate each other. If your buddy publishes a book, it motivates you to write another book. You feel glad for your pal, but you don't want to get left behind. I wonder how you feel about that.

ALAIN MABANCKOU: I agree. I, too, have seen how travel motivates, stimulates, or makes us emulate one another, but I have also noticed writers from whose books the element of travel is entirely absent. The characters don't go anywhere and the books don't, either—when in fact a book is an entity equipped with feet, which can walk, and the book of a writer who travels has the breath of life, which comes from movement. Paradoxically enough, many of these French-language writers who obtain travel grants and get invited here and there are high priests of inertia. You get the impression that they have never been anywhere; or maybe they leave their imagination behind while traveling, when they should probably take it with them in order to create living and breathing characters. I cannot imagine a book of mine devoid of travel. Otherwise it might as well be a boat moored somewhere forever.

DL: Very true. If you travel—broadening the scope of your knowledge and experience—and this does not come out in your books, you've got to wonder about your stance as a writer, and your vision of literature: is it fixed? Does it contain exclusively literary influences? Are we simply reenacting ancient codes, or are we truly striving to bring movement both to ourselves and to the books we carry within us? It is true that there are writers who travel the world while remaining inert, in the sense that travel doesn't appear anywhere in their writing. I'm not saying that a novel should be a succession of cities—not at all. But travel is a window onto the world; it's like letting fresh air into the house, leaving the library behind, freeing ourselves of literary and intellectual references in order to make way for new references, thus introducing into your book the noise of the world. How does this idea fit into your work, Alain?

AM: I think it's very important. Travel poses the same question as James Baldwin did when he spoke of "experience," that is to say: is the novel no more than the sum of the people you've met? How does a novelist manage to take into account all the people whose paths he has crossed in the course of his life, to transform them and set the stage, so to speak, to make something happen, with the sound you were mentioning earlier—and the fury, too? And of course there are writers who travel solely through their imagination without ever actually going anywhere. Many of the writers who have written about traveling around the world have never actually done it; some can describe an invented city so well that the reader believes he is visiting a real place. In fact, I have heard tell of certain writers who prefer to write about a city before actually going there, which they do once the writing part is over in order to see if their imagination was truly faithful to the reality of the place, and maybe also to experience firsthand the difference between dream and reality—which is the basis of fiction.

DL: It is true that dreaming is a form of travel. A taste for dreaming is what made us all read those adventure novels that have always had such a tremendous effect on teenagers. Tagging along with Dumas on his travels through France in *The Three Musketeers*... when they had to stop at an "inn," even if you didn't know the word, you still understood what was going on. The Musketeers would arrive at an inn and they would call out to the innkeeper and ask if they could eat, and if their horses could be fed, etc. This taste for travel in literature made many of us want to travel, too. So it's normal that this should find its way into our literature, that we might enable a reader on the other side of the planet to go places. For me, travel is intrinsic to literature. In the greatest novels—*Ulysses, The Odyssey, Don Quixote, Jacques the Fatalist and His Master*—you always have movement, this idea of setting out to destinations unknown, with the narrator describing everything he sees as he goes along. And, of course, we mustn't forget that life itself has often been compared to a journey.

AM: That's very interesting. And how about a novel in which the journey, for the writer, would be a way of describing things he did not see—that is to say, what was lacking in his imagination when he tried, for example, to create a wholly invented space? It would make for a strange kind of accounting: a novel in which absence, the void, or some other thing we thought existed did not in fact exist. When I think of different types of travel, I also think of fantasy writing, like in *One Hundred Years of Solitude,* when Melquíades enters the village of Macondo on a flying carpet. It's like all of a sudden you're in the middle of *The Thousand and One Nights.* It's magical—even if one should always be wary of seeing things through a tourist's eyes, because a tourist goes somewhere for the experience, whereas a writer travels in order to make sure things are as he imagined them; and since he can never be certain of that, there could perhaps blossom, from his fingers, a novel of disillusionment, a novel as reverie, as a sort of solitary walk, as Jean-Jacques Rousseau put it. And it may very well be that writing and traveling are essentially the same thing.

DL: Absolutely. Even if you look at this idea on a concrete, physical level, we all know that in certain countries where people live in great misery or are suffering at the hands of dictators, more and more often when these young writers get grants to travel and go to festivals, it's like a little breathing room for them, an escape from their daily hell. I have seen many writers who were at their wits' end—they couldn't take it anymore, they thought they were experiencing writer's block, when in fact it was life block they were in the throes of. The life they were leading was suffocating them, and they didn't have the energy to create. But then, all alone in rooms on the other side of the planet, far from the strife they experienced daily in their countries, they found they could write. Prison might have played that same kind of role in hard-boiled black American fiction of the '50s. Prison got those guys off the street and prolonged their life spans. I'm not saying I'm in favor of locking people up, but there is something to be said for the fact that, once off the streets, many of these kids started frequenting the prison library, and some of them became writers. I'm thinking of Chester Himes, for example. In the prewar years, hospitals fulfilled a similar function for European writers, such as Moravia and Thomas Mann; they all began to write because they got sick and had to convalesce in these hospitals, which is where they were able to write. Therefore, the notion of travel must also include a smattering of inertia; after all, there is something to be said for embarking on a journey in one's own head.

AM: Yes. I believe interiority is also essential as far as traveling is concerned, since the internal journey may well be the deepest one of all. For example, I like the idea of imagining someone who is actually traveling—everything that is roiling inside of him—and when he finally reaches his destination, when he finally sees the reality of where he is, the trip itself gets mixed up in various happenings and adventures. I'm thinking of all the great texts of literary history, such as *The Odyssey,* and I think that we have now come to the very heart of literature—though that's always a delicate thing to try to define.

DL: Absolutely. And I would like to point out one of the most important things about travel: the return. We all remember *The Odyssey,* when after having been all over the world and seen all the things he has seen, the sight of Ithaca makes Odysseus break down and cry. Which is a way of saying that the ultimate goal when one travels is to come back home; the return is always enigmatic, since there can be no journey without it. The return reveals how profoundly our interior landscape has changed.

II. FRIENDSHIP

AM: Meeting people, connecting, becoming one with one another; I believe that courtesy owes its existence to the fact that people

DANY LAFERRIÈRE & ALAIN MABANCKOU

meet. Derek Walcott called it "the courtesy of exchange." It may well be the most extraordinary invention of all time. In the past, communicating was difficult; if you wanted to meet someone who lived far away from you, it was a hassle. There was no "crossroads." This state of affairs made certain connections impossible. When I think of meeting people, I think of geography. Geography brings people together, mixes things up. And then there is another kind of meeting, that of the cultures that define us—meeting a person who is different from you. When this happens, something new appears on the scene, and it's called an exchange. I believe this world is based on exchanges. Everything hinges on who oversees these exchanges, culturally speaking; that is perhaps why smaller nations may very well dominate future cultural exchanges, for I am sure we still have many things to contribute to a civilization that believes that it has already invented and understood everything, and that everybody else has to more or less conform to its definitions.

DL: There is another sort of meeting: the encounter of two individuals. This is a very moving thing, and it can happen anywhere. Let's say, for example, you go to a dinner party with friends, and all of a sudden you find yourself having this magical conversation with someone who understands and shares your vision of the world; the encounter is so spontaneous and so vibrant that neither of you wants it to end. This kind of connection can last for years. It's thrilling, and it reminds me of ours—though I can no longer remember when we first met. What I do remember is the joy I feel when my friend is around, and to know that even more than the long, satisfying conversations, the truly magical thing is to share secrets.

AM: And I would also add, my friend, that the most fulfilling encounters are often the most unexpected. I am referring to when we met for the first time in the flesh. It was the '90s, and I was far from thinking then that a few years later we would be so in tune with one another in terms of art and aesthetics... We form a sort of literary family, and we nourish our friendship through the creative process, since a friendship that is not nourished—that is not watered if you will, and well watered indeed—dries up and withers. Many friendships are like a fruit that was ripe but wasn't picked at the right moment to savor all it had to offer, and therefore yielded nothing.

DL: I like your use of the word *yield*. The idea that there must be a fruit, a flowering, a promise of sorts—these are moving moments, the beginnings of something, the joy of being together. When we met for the first time, we realized that we had a lot in common, an emotional connection. There was something unsaid here—and all of a sudden I realized how deeply important your mother was to you. I wonder if this idea of the enigmatic return from a journey is not, in fact, less important than talking about your mother. Your source of strength. By the way, someone once said that I understand you better than most because I grasp how deeply solitary you are. It's not just about sharing the same opinions, be they practical or political; there has to be some subterranean thing, this sympathy of feeling. This exchange of ideas has found its way into our books, and has perhaps even created a common goal. Our friendship has produced this literary flowering.

AM: I would like to add that some friendships start off with a certain imbalance. When I think back on the first time we met, you were already a successful author, whereas I had just begun writing little poems nobody read. I had maybe thirty-five or forty readers, at least twenty-five of whom were friends I would force to buy my poetry. But the fact remains that when I saw you, I saw myself and thought, Here is the example I would like to follow. And when you saw me, you remembered starting out as a writer, paying your dues, when you were typing up the first pages of novels the reading public would get to know later. You saw a budding writer, and it was like in a relay race: you turned around and handed me the baton, which I grabbed, and you effectively said, "Listen, you can run as fast as me, and in fact you are going to overtake me, but I'll catch up over there and you can hand me back the baton." And that's what we are doing now: we're winning together through our friendship, laying down foundations for the future. Friendships such as ours rarely occur in the world of French-language letters, which is so rife with jealousy and antagonism; there is a definite uneasiness between writers in France. But we keep on moving on, like in the fable by the French author Florian—the friendship between the quadriplegic and the blind man—that is to say that I, as the quadriplegic, lend you my eyes, and you walk for me. Together, we are slowly making headway.

DL: Absolutely, and the moment I met you, your behavior revealed to me the kind of young man you were. Because for me, a writer is not solely what he writes. The thing that strikes me first and foremost is his posture, how he holds himself in the world, and you were being discreet, off to yourself, yet ready to pounce; I could see that the sound and the fury was not your thing, and I said to myself, He is hiding something that will one day explode into light. For instance, when I started out, I didn't want to go to my own book launches. I thought I should remain invisible. I didn't ask people for advice. There was something in me that I wanted to protect— this boundless energy I barely managed to contain when I was in public. I could hardly hold my horses, keep them from jumping and galloping all over the place, so I protected them to make them stronger, and I could see that even if you were present that day at the book fair, you were also absent. The other thing that struck me and made me believe that you might actually be a real person was that you seemed lucid. Many of the African and Caribbean writers I used to know were egomaniacs: it was as if they had triumphed before even beginning, and if you think you've made it when in fact you have not even started, you won't go far. But you, you said, "Listen, I've published a book, and RFI [Radio France Internationale] hasn't even asked me for an interview." You said this openly, whereas everybody else was dissembling, walking tall, talking about all the interviews they had given, and here was someone who was saying, "Oh, no, this is not working out for me; I'm not getting anywhere." And I thought, This is exactly what I used to feel: a sort of dissatisfaction—neither resentment nor bitterness, rather a voracious appetite for life.

AM: And you know, Dany, I believe that friendship has been at the heart of many great things: for example, Aimé Césaire and André Breton got to know each other in Martinique, which is why *Cahier d'un retour au pays natal* became so widely read. And for example, the fact that the three major figures in black francophone literature—Léopold Sédar Senghor, Aimé Césaire, and Léon-Gontran Damas—all met in Paris is not a fluke, just as you and I meeting in Paris is not a fluke. We didn't meet in your country, we didn't meet in mine; we met on neutral ground, as it were. You come from the island of Haiti, I from the continent of Africa. Our meeting encapsulated not only the history of the black world, but also added to the mix a country with a somber African colonial past. In any case, I believe that our literature suffers from a lack of these kinds of encounters. They are all too rare.

III. CORRESPONDENCE

DL: We don't have a large body of correspondence between African writers, or Caribbean writers; we haven't given a lot of space or thought to what I might call a certain "parallel literature," that is to say, correspondence, travel narratives, diaries. For me, these kinds of things are the very foundation of a society's literature. A literary tree cannot grow without fertilizer. Our literature, our books, need to be nourished from below, as it were, from some subterranean source. Correspondence not only sheds light for critics and scholars, it also allows writers to develop and express the goals they have set and their vision of literature, and through the responses and criticism they get, to see themselves more clearly and find the resources to carry on.

AM: Yes, Dany, I also believe that correspondence is a part of literature that is often overlooked. Writers write, though rarely to each other, so initiating a correspondence will allow us to further examine our common artistic aims. I have always loved getting to know writers through their letters, because the intimacy of a letter allows you to witness a writer's days and ways; he is writing, he is walking, he is digressing; one finds, in correspondence, things one never sees in a novel, quite simply because the letter writer is addressing himself to a specific person. When I write to you, Dany, I know now that once our correspondence is published, others who will read our letters will be able to walk in our shoes: the reader will be Dany Laferrière and Alain Mabanckou, and vice-versa; that is the playful side of correspondence that I really like. It seems like a forgotten art, in a way. And it's true that our correspondence will be a kind of innovation in our French-language literature; there is nary a book of correspondence between the founders of the negritude movement: Senghor, Césaire, and Damas. It would have been great for the current generation of readers to be able to read what those three were saying to each other, to hear their voices outside of the poetry they published. What did they do on this or that Monday? Did Senghor like dancing in nightclubs? Did Damas smoke cigars? Did—I don't know— did Césaire favor silk neckties? For me, these kinds of details make correspondence one of the essential parts of a writer's work—even if we're living in a time when messages are getting shorter and shorter, almost telegraphic. Well, our correspondence will allow us to flesh things out some, and show a little humanity.

DL: Correspondence is intimate, as you said; it allows entry to the very heart of a person; you get to see the writer up close and personal. Humanity is very important, because for me, a writer is not simply a machine that writes books. A writer is a human being. It's a shame that Senghor's human side will forever elude us. The only things we know about him, we know through the biographical slivers in his poems. The interesting thing in correspondence is the tone, which is very different from a writer's official, public tone; it's intimate, it's someone talking to a friend and confidant, with day-to-day stuff inevitably seeping in, because writers talk about what they do, the people they meet, the literary festivals to which they are invited. And sometimes the writer is in a hotel room in this or that town, and he is cold or hasn't yet had breakfast or lunch, or is having problems writing his latest book. Here and there precious information can be gleaned. And not just for scholars—the reader is granted access to the core of a human being, unlike in the author's "official" books. So I think that embarking on this correspondence with you will be a groundbreaking initiative in our literature: an active correspondence between two writers, which will allow the young people who follow our careers and who are passionate about literature and who read us—and who perhaps dream of becoming writers—to see the people behind the words.

AM: I also believe that this correspondence has something of a testament-like value. It's strange: each time I write a letter I have the impression I'm sharing my "last wishes." I believe certain writers can be understood only through their correspondence. For example, Montesquieu, Rousseau, and Diderot—you almost get the impression that they wrote their letters with a smile on their faces, thinking, I will be in heaven when you read this. I love it when I get a letter from you. I love it when you describe the reality in which you find yourself at the time of writing, and I am always struck by the way you manage to describe the world as a whole through the minutiae of your daily existence. I also believe that a body of work without a correspondence lacks something essential: the writer's humanity. The confessional parts of a novel are not necessarily a confession, whereas a letter is always a confession, a hand held out to a friend. I would also like to add that our correspondence will help future generations understand where we were coming from.

DL: Much like in painting, correspondence gives you depth of field, a linear perspective: you have the foreground, the background, the middle distance, and these details allow you to see the big picture, as it were. In correspondence, it's the same thing: you see that the writer is not only a person who writes novels or poems but also someone who writes about what he is writing—this depth of field reveals all the work that goes into our craft. It's often in letters that a writer will talk about his pain, his anguish, the difficulties he has been coming up against in his writing... All this is well known in the Western world, but it hasn't yet been integrated into our culture. Correspondence gives the reader a first-row seat in the literary arena. A writer can write all sorts of things; if for whatever reason he needs to take a break from his novel, he can correspond with a friend, or keep a journal, thus continuing the writing process—and no writer's block! He can write all sorts of things that are peripheral to literature itself, and that may, in time, blossom into novels and poems and essays; so I believe it's important that we who come from faraway lands understand what lies behind us, and what informs our temperaments. It is also important to interact about everyday life, because I believe that you don't write through remembering alone. It's important to describe this courtyard, for instance, at the Karibe Hotel, where we are sitting under tall trees; and we know with utmost certainty that two years ago, January 12, 2010, the earthquake hit while I was sitting right here; everything was shaking, and from your location you kept posting information about me, and when I got back to Montreal I was in a haze for a few days, and then I wrote you a long letter, the first in which I discussed what I had experienced during the quake.

AM: Whenever I think of Haiti, I think of our friendship, our mutual understanding. If I feel as close to Haiti as I do, it is thanks to literature first and foremost. I always had two island nations in mind whenever I searched for Africa outside of Africa: Haiti, of course, and then, by ricochet, Guadeloupe—since my firstborn son is also part Guadeloupean. I discovered Haiti through writers such as Rodney

Saint-Éloi, who lives in Montreal, and Louis-Philippe Dalembert, who lives in Paris, and other writers, such as Jean Métellus, who have become my friends. All of these guys give off a kind of African vibe. In Congo-Brazzaville, we used to listen to a Haitian singer called Coupé Cloué. He was really popular. He had this song called *"Allez vous-en"* ("Go Away"), and in the bars of Congo-Brazzaville this was the song they would play at closing time. In Congo, people knew this song better than the national anthem. Everybody was convinced that Coupé Cloué was Congolese. And then there was a time when Claudette et Ti Pierre were in vogue; they had a song called *"Camionette"* that was super popular. The whole country was amazed by the extent to which Claudette et Ti Pierre resembled our own bands. I finally decided to come here, to Haiti. So I did. This is my third visit, and I now understand why Haitians sometimes consider me as a brother. Coming here humbles me, it's sobering; I keep searching for any hidden scrap of Africa, though I needn't, since Africa is everywhere. Every time I come to Haiti I feel like I'm coming home.

DL: You know, when I went to Bamako—on my first trip to Africa—I was captivated. I didn't know where I was; the resemblance between Bamako and certain neighborhoods of Port-au-Prince was so strong. I could see it in the streets, in the way people walked… everything in Bamako reminded me of Haiti, despite the ocean and the intervening centuries that separate the two places. I was very moved by my time in Africa. I didn't want to succumb to admiration—I had hoped to view Africa with an unsentimental eye. I was invited there as a writer, so I was curious to see if I would have anything in common with the African writers I met. And I did, not only with the writers, but also with the students; everything was so congenial to me: the scenery, the sounds and smells of the city. And I remember the first time I walked out in the courtyard of the hotel—it was the Hôtel Liberté or something—a mango fell at my feet. And I thought, Wow, the thud of a mango: I could be in Haiti.

AM: When I came here to Haiti for the first time, my head was so full of myths and clichés, because in truth, all that Africans know about Haiti is voodoo, animism, music—that's it. But what I've been discovering about this country, which I have been getting to know better and better, is its cultural power. You sense that people here have a great thirst for culture, which for me means that the country can only move forward. Arguments break out here over nothing, and it's the nothing part that makes this country exceptional. You see it in the poverty, but this country has modified the definition of riches; a nation's riches are no longer quantified through property and real estate, but rather through its cultural baggage. To come to a country where heroes fought such important battles... The world's first black-led republic: that's what Africans see in Haiti. When Africans come here, it's like they're on a pilgrimage. The thing that struck me the most in Haiti was the idea that Africa was no longer Africa—since we Africans have stopped loving Africa and no longer feel joy at having a continent with deep roots. In order to find that lost Africa, nowadays you have to go to other parts of the world. I come to Haiti to recoup. When I return to Africa, I look closely at what we have lost. If one day we decide to reclaim all that, perhaps we'll have to go to Haiti, to Guadeloupe, to French Guiana, and those countries that are all mini Africas, each with its own individual qualities.

DL: I left Haiti in 1976, when I was twenty-three, and have been living in Montreal for over thirty-five years. My first book came out in 1985, and I have traveled extensively ever since. I have met all sorts of people from all sorts of backgrounds, with all sorts of sensibilities. And now I know that Haiti has given me a real gift. It's in my DNA: there's not a drop of despair in my blood. Haiti is a land of devastation, sadness, and pain, yet the music here is joyous. That paradox is deeply embedded in me. I sometimes find myself forced to console people I meet all over the world who are saddened by the situation in Haiti. I want to say to them, "Don't worry about the

Haitian people: they are very tough." Haitians have a kind of wild, unbridled optimism, a death-defying energy. Haiti will never die. These are not merely words. I have never felt this way about any other country. Despite military dictatorships, coups d'état, floods, hurricanes, misery, poverty, chronic illnesses, when you come to Haiti, the thing you notice is the incredible energy that emanates from the people. Nobody looks at you with that total despair you see in the eyes of the people living in the black neighborhoods of the American South. There might be reasons for that: racism, the KKK, the impossibility of climbing up the social ladder; young people are hindered, the system keeps them in a bind. But like I say, I don't see that despair in the eyes of my countrymen; whereas other people from the West, you talk to them for an hour and get a sense of a bottomless anguish, and you think, What is going on? How can a society that is so successful collectively be such a failure on the individual level? And how can Haiti—a society that has failed collectively, but that individually is a total success story—be exactly the opposite? After the earthquake, the entire world was able to see how quickly Haiti got back on its feet and carried on with life. I am not saying things aren't bad. People are still living in tents, the situation is in many ways worse than before, but the apocalyptic predictions bandied about in the Western press after the quake have simply not come to pass. One only need come here to see that despite the tragedy, life has indeed gone on in Haiti. ✶

Translated by Philippe Aronson
With special thanks to Richard Nash

CHRISTINE SCHUTT

TALKS WITH

DEB OLIN UNFERTH

"NOVELS DO NOT GET EASIER TO WRITE."

Adjectives that sound and look great on the page:

Lurid

Rapid

Garish

Grouped

Born and raised in Wisconsin, Christine Schutt came to New York over thirty years ago to write, first as an MFA student at Columbia and then on her own. She met Diane Williams in a Gordon Lish class, from which they emerged the best of friends. They talked NOON *into existence. Schutt gave the literary annual its name, the word being one of Emily Dickinson's favorites, and Dickinson, the poet, one of Schutt's favorites.*

Schutt is the author of two books of stories, A Day, A Night, Another Day, Summer *and* Nightwork, *and two novels, the recently published* All Souls *and* Florida, *a finalist for a National Book Award in a controversial year: five novels by largely unknown women writers, all from New York, and only one in her thirties.*

What characterizes her work for me—the way that I immediately know a Christine Schutt sentence—is the striking repetition of sounds, both vowels and consonants, and the prominent rhythms that make the prose seem as though it is being sung. On the face it sounds "pretty," and she indeed uses many pretty words, but underneath there is a tremendous amount of dark energy: "Jean had lifted the wisps of hair from off their baby scalps, marked as the moon, with their stitched plates of bone yet visible, the boys; how often she had thought to break them."

Depending on the book, the emotion that fuels this darkness shifts between anger, fear, scorn, shame, and rebellious independence: "I was dumbed to saying nothing, to calling him nothing but a cock, a very big cock. What else could you call that red trumpeting thing he slapped across my face?" This work springs from a woman who will dare to disobey any law and violate any custom, in fiction if not outside of it.

This conversation was conducted by many lengthy email exchanges while Schutt was living in Virginia as a writer-in-residence at Hollins University.

—Deb Olin Unferth (May 2009)

I. "YOU MUST BE DESPERATE OR SOMETHING."

DEB OLIN UNFERTH: It's impossible for me to ignore the sound of your sentences. Sometimes I feel as if the entire thrust of the story is based on an exploration of a set of phonemes, or as if you allow sound to determine the direction of the sentence and the story, the content even. Is that true? How do you do that? Why do you do that?

CHRISTINE SCHUTT: I was taught to read poetry this way in high school: to consider the sounds the poet was making and how those sounds could inform us of what the poem was about. "Snake," a D. H. Lawrence poem, was the lesson at the time, and it made a big impression on me. Sound has its own weather, and I respond to it. One night I saw these preposterously large cherry blossoms outside our bedroom window. This happens every spring, of course, the blossoms, but on this night they seemed lit up from below and floating, an absurd efflorescence, and the sentence in response to what I saw and felt about the spring show came out like this: "The preposterous blossoms, candy pink and stupidly profuse, were in the night light strangely come as from another planet." So many *p*'s— the stupidness of it all. That sentence has a mood; it was my mood at the time. *Absurd efflorescence* makes a different sound, has a different mood, different weather; in a story such a phrase would direct me. I am generally uncertain of purpose and have few opinions, no ideas. But sound.

I read poetry this way: I hear meaning long before I decode it. As a writer, I find that sound can give me meaning, narrative direction. Produce a sentence with any sound and respond to it.

DOU: Do you think your interest in narrative is primarily sound and secondarily story? What I mean is, do you feel more like you have a noise to make than a story to tell? And was it always that way for you or did your idea of narrative shift at some point? (It must have been long ago, if it did, since your first book shows a lot of interest in sound.) I guess I'm asking how you became the writer you are.

CS: I like story; I want story. I have characters but they are dimly perceived and what they will do is a mystery to me. I once wrote a version of a John Cheever story in which an attractive young couple who would seem to possess all are yet unhappily married, and then a greater sorrow befalls them while on vacation. This story, "The Hedges," is the only story I have ever written with a plot and the luxury of knowing the plot beforehand; all the others have come forward on sounds and sensations, memories and exaggerations.

DOU: Cheever's stories have a sort of old-fashioned wordiness. Backgrounds are explained. Backdrops are drawn. It is so unlike the spare style of so many of our contemporaries. His work is very sad and feels, to me, urgent, even. I feel like he was writing to save his life. Many of your stories feel that way too. Was that what it was like when you wrote your first book of stories, *Nightwork*? I remember you told me once that during that time you felt that if you could write one sentence a day you would stay alive. What was that about? Why would writing a sentence save you? Did it feel the same way to write your later books or did the experience change? Do you believe fiction can save or change lives? And I love the way you said, "I hear meaning long before I decode it." What on earth does that mean? I know what you are saying, I think. But how does a sound contain meaning? What does meaning mean in this case?

CS: "An awe came on the trinket." What does that mean? When you first encounter Dickinson you have to decode a lot, but a way to enjoy her in the beginning is to enjoy the sounds she makes and often from these you can extract meaning. I trust in the ear to detect feeling before struggling over why the voice sounds so. I should also add that I am charmed by symmetrical sentences and catalog sentences and sentences with bunched-up groups of adjectives that sound great and look great on the page: "lurid, rapid, garish, grouped." Robert Lowell is famous for gathering adjectives that are visually pleasing as well as full of sound and apt. His late wife, Elizabeth Hardwick, was also deft when it came to adjectives. She wrote prose, of course, but Hardwick's sentences are as worked as a poet's. I happen to be teaching her very great novel, *Sleepless Nights*, and so have it here before me. Hardwick has a gift for catalog sentences: "Old English wallpaper, carpets, Venetian mirrors, decorated vases, marble mantelpieces, buzzers under the rug around the dining-room table, needlepoint seats: Alex was making an inventory of Sarah's Philadelphia house before her mother died." Simply to write this sentence—forget the labor of over a hundred pages of them—must have been a strain, but finishing only one such sentence was surely bracing.

I'm trying to clarify whatever it was I said to you about the life-saving properties of a sentence a day. Certainly the idea of its sufficiency has consoled. There is a Ray Carver story, "Why Don't You Dance?," that explains how I felt when I was writing *Nightwork*. You know the story: a man has arranged all of the furniture from inside his house on the front lawn; everything on the lawn looks just as it did inside—bed, bedside tables. "His side, her side." A boy and a girl come along and think it's a yard sale. The crucial sentences are toward the end when the man, having sold the young couple some of the furniture, dances in his driveway with the girl. "They thought they'd seen everything over here," he says, and she answers, "but they haven't seen this." Then, in the story's only tender moment, the girl whispers, "You must be desperate or something." Well, I felt that man's kind of desperation when I was writing *Nightwork*. I was beyond caring what other people thought of me. The first story in the book, about a daughter's failed seduction of her father, was one I had tried to write since graduate school. Now, when it seemed I was ready to put everything out on the lawn, when I had hit on how to, I was beset by difficult, crowded days; often there was only time to write one sentence. Most of *Nightwork* was written, as have been so many books, when everyone else was asleep. When was Hardwick writing *Sleepless Nights*, I wonder?

II. "SORE AFRAID OF
THE DARK PRINCE."

DOU: What was it like for you to write your novels, *Florida* and *All Souls*? The two books seem to me to be so different from each other. What was the essential element in each of them that made you able to visualize the book? Was it a sound like the "preposterous blossoms" that inspired the whole concept? Or an idea? Or a little piece of story line?

CS: *Jane Eyre,* a novel I have read many times, inspired the way *Florida* is put together. In an orphan's novel the ambition is always to find a home: the orphan moves outward from house to house. With the new novel, *All Souls,* I had in mind David Malouf's *Remembering Babylon,* where in the first chapter, Gemmy Fairley, an English castaway raised by aborigines, suddenly appears in his countrymen's settlement in Queensland, Australia. Is Gemmy a white man or a black man? This is the community's question, and the rest of the novel is spent tracking their responses to the frightening half-and-half figure of Gemmy. Everyone is changed by this character, some for the better, some for the worse.

All Souls comes straight out of teaching at an all-girls' private school in Manhattan and my wonderment at the ways in which such a school community works. I wrote the first half of *All Souls* several years ago, put it aside because it was too easy to write, then took the manuscript up again while a visiting writer at UC Irvine. I wanted to prove that given enough free time I could finish a novel in short order—and I did. I have been working on another novel since 1998. Stories have provided respite from the messy, longer work, which has been balked by the characters themselves. They keep changing and other minor figures enter the scene and distract me. Novels do not get easier to write.

DOU: What do you think the writer's obligation is to the literary community? George Saunders comes to mind. I have seen that man stand before a crowd and say, without a trace of irony, that writing can change the world. His writing probably does change the world. What do you think is important for the writer to do? What do you think is the job of fiction? Why do you write?

CS: I make modest donations to writer-good causes; otherwise, I hoard what time there is to write when I am not teaching. Writers who give over time to support writers around the world, who call attention to writers in peril, who believe and promote worthy writers not yet recognized or translated, such writers are heroic. As to what is important to do as a writer, I'd say most importantly, do the very best work you can, then if there is more of you to spare, help other writers any way you can. The niftiest answer I ever heard to the question "Why do you write?" was "Why not?" Why not? This may be the only possible way to answer why anyone would elect to sit for hours, sometimes blankly, to write a few hundred words that most often do not hold up under scrutiny for longer than twenty-four hours.

DOU: You teach a lot. How do you balance teaching and writing? What does your day look like when you're teaching? How about when you're not teaching?

CS: I read your question "What does your day look like when you're teaching?" as "What does your *work* look like when you're teaching?" And I thought it looked pitifully small—unreal, really. I don't dare look at any fiction in progress while sitting on the floor of the upper school. The outdoors in general is dangerous for reading, but it must be done: new work printed out, eyed in full sun. But what does the day look like when I am sitting on that floor? Legs, skirts, girls up close of all ages, some old girls, too, stooped and so long at the school they're known by initials. Miss B! Family!

A starker presentation is every day beginning at 8:15, four classes. Three different preparations. A Tuesday might be Emily Dickinson to seniors, *Macbeth* in the tenth grade, and for the writers in eleventh, Harold Brodkey, "Verona: a Young Woman Speaks." I am free to choose whatever fiction or poetry interests me. The only demand now is for more nonfiction, but the choice is still mine. Last year students read Charles d'Ambrosio's essay "Orphans." Then again, a lot of high-school reading has not changed for decades. George Orwell's 1931 essay "A Hanging" is yet read—for style as well as subject: "When I saw the prisoner step aside to avoid the puddle I saw the mystery, the unspeakable wrongness, of cutting a life short when it is in full tide." Simplicity and moral authority at once. Yearly re-encounters with such literature as I have loved and learned from is no hardship, but like many teachers at every level, I feel beset with committees, meetings, small duties, new goals, and too often I wake up angry at having to go to school at all.

DOU: I find that as a fiction writer I teach differently than many of my colleagues who studied English literature and criticism. I am interested in different things than they are. Do you find that to be the case as well? What do you emphasize in teaching literature and writing?

CS: I like to take the story or novel or poem apart to see how it is made—consider the work as bone art, new-skeletal. The writer's body (freakish) is in every part of the book. Whitman's long-armed, wide-open lines bespeak the man himself and how he felt about the world, but his insistent optimism about mortality—"to die is different from what any one supposed, and luckier"—suggests he was sore afraid of the dark prince. Dickinson's short, gnomic lines and all those dashes are as hesitant as much as musical and reveal the woman herself or at least as she was reported: a figure often out of sight but listening in at the top of the stairs, an almost-invisible at the second-floor window sending down a sweet in a basket to little children. I fail at providing much historical context when teaching literature except to note the Civil War and its appearance or absence in the work of the aforementioned poets. That conflict, that "World's Departure from a Hinge… 'Twas not so large" as to distract Miss Dickinson from doing her work.

III. "LET THE PERFORMANCE BE INSANE!"

DOU: Do you feel that there is anything significant about the fact that the editor and associate editor of *NOON* are women? That is, do you ever feel as though you are working in a male-dominated sphere, that female writers have a harder road than men? I ask because I have heard you make reference to this in the past and I think it's important.

CS: If you go by some numbers for prizes and reviews, the men win, hands down. Since its inception, the PEN/Faulkner has been awarded to a man twenty-four times and to a woman, four. Susan Stamberg, a founder of the PEN/Faulkner, explains the imbalance as the consequences of women deferring to men in judging contests. Stamberg spoke at Word of Mouth, an all-women writers' group, which, as its name suggests, serves to spread word of new books and readings and anything to do with writing by its membership. Katha Pollitt, a hero of mine, was in attendance at my first meeting with Word of Mouth. Would she were here to eloquently articulate my conviction that men have the last word on most literary matters. Ironically, most of the best reviews of my work have been written by men: John Ashbery, Brian Evenson, Ben Lytal, Irving Malin, Bryan Scott Wilson.

DOU: If you could choose an ideal life for yourself, what would it include? You may imagine anything you like: that you are independently wealthy, that you have skills you don't in fact have, that you can fly. What would you like to do best and what from your current life would you retain?

CS: There is a photograph of Elizabeth Hardwick supine on a long sofa. Behind her are bookshelves that extend to the top of a twelve-foot ceiling and the shelves are lined with books, and there are books stacked on a long table pressed against the back of the sofa, and on that same table is a bust of a young man, a Keatsian head, melancholy or sanguine expression. It's Hardwick's expression in the photograph. Her arm is gracefully outstretched; she holds a book. She is a lady of letters in a dark pleated skirt and violet sweater, a writer in a prewar city apartment. I would like to lie as she does on just such a sofa assured of my place in the world of letters. An idealized circumstance, surely, but to be a writer in anticipation of the day's mail and inevitable good news—life's lurid imperfections quite out of sight—would be my first choice for perfect life.

Failing this, I would like not to write at all, not to read with any more purpose than to know the ingredients to a recipe; I would like to be a successful small-time farmer with a garden, horses, goats, sheep, chickens of all sorts, ducks, dogs, cats. My garden, too, would not be confined to produce but would include flowers, climbers especially, honeysuckle, and all varieties of clematis.

DOU: I find I can't help but ask you to talk a little bit about working with Gordon Lish. Could you describe one class you had with him, one specific event—or two or three—that you feel might illuminate what it was like to work with him for those of us who never had the chance to?

CS: Those classes! They fell apart when Gordon's wife died in the early '90s and he left Knopf and lost funding for *The Quarterly,* but for two years the classes were held in my apartment. My apartment is very small, less than a thousand square feet, and yet we packed in upward of twenty-six adults when classes started in the fall of 1988. People sat on the floor or out of sight in the hallway or in the kitchen; some sat at Gordon's feet; some were brave enough to sit near on the sofa although how could anyone approach him without fear of catching fire—he was a performer, a high priest, a sermonizer. Quoting James Joyce—"I imagined that I bore my chalice safely through a throng of foes"—he implored us to carry our stories aloft, to expect the marketplace's jeers, and to write heedless of the marketplace, to resist its corrupting calculations and safeguard our work. It was all very high-minded and grand, and I found it inspiring. Once a week I heard new fiction or advances on new fiction from such writers as Katherine Arnoldi, Noy

Holland, Sheila Kohler, Sam Michel, Yannick Murphy, Dawn Raffel, Victoria Redel, Pam Ryder, Lily Tuck, Rick Whitaker, and Diane Williams. Amy Hempel, Ben Marcus, Mark Richard, and Kate Walbert made appearances from time to time. Dana Spiotta worked at *The Quarterly*. Gary Lutz was talked about, and so were Will Eno and Timothy Liu. Quite simply a lot of what Gordon said about writing made immediate and complete sense to me, and my own interest in poetry, in sound, my arduous effort to compose so much as a sentence, meant I shared his aesthetic: a delight in language and an ambition to make something uncanny.

I value no one's opinion more than Gordon's when it comes to assessment of fiction and while in his class I took notes I have profited from reading again. I try to live by many of his phrases: Stay open for business. Be Emersonian: say what no one else has the courage to say and you will be embraced. Reveal what you would keep secret. You will stay awake when writing such a story; you will also write very, very carefully with so much at stake. Each sentence is extruded from the previous sentence; look behind you when writing, not ahead. Your obligation is to know your objects and to steadily, inexorably darken and deepen them. To be in Gordon's company when he was talking about fiction was to be in full-out writer mode. Let the performance be insane!

DOU: Can you explain what you mean by "look behind you when writing, not ahead"?

CS: He meant this quite literally as a means of composition. Query the preceding sentence for what might most profitably be used in composing the next sentence. He contended that with this method no writer could ever again be legitimately blocked. The sentence that follows is always in response to the sentence that came before.

DOU: Does writing still have the initial urgency that it had when you were writing your first book? If yes, how do you think you manage to maintain that urgency? If not, what has replaced it to drive you to write—since you are more prolific now than at any other time in your life (or so it seems to me)?

CS: The constant has not been a sense of urgency, but the terrors felt with every composition: no you cannot; no you will not; no you should not. To be balked at every turn in the effort with *never* and *no* makes for slow composition, and it dismays me not to have more gift stories, more sentences that rise up alchemical and deserved. Composing for me is largely a dispiriting venture, and the urgency and flushed condition ascribed to the experience may be something I've imagined after the fact of publication, a fictive sentiment necessary to sustain myself as a writer. ✶

LAWRENCE SCHILLER

TALKS WITH

SUZANNE SNIDER

"I SAID, 'FUCK YOU, O. J.'"

Authors who have written books based on Schiller's research and ideas:

Norman Mailer

Many other unnamed, well-known writers

Five days before I interviewed Lawrence Schiller, I re-read *the last six hundred pages of* The Executioner's Song, *the "true-life novel" by Norman Mailer. The book spins a 1,072-page yarn about the life and death of Gary Gilmore, a now-infamous criminal who murdered two* men in Utah in 1976 and received a death sentence by firing squad in 1977. The outcome effectively reinstated the death penalty after a ten-year moratorium on capital punishment in the US.

Most people are familiar with Gilmore's story because it was national news, or because they read The Executioner's Song *(which won the Pulitzer Prize in 1980) or the 1994 book by Gary Gilmore's brother*

(Rolling Stone *journalist Mikal Gilmore),* Shot in the Heart. *A few people may have seen Matthew Barney's take on the Gary Gilmore story,* Cremaster 2, *in which Norman Mailer plays Harry Houdini.*

I chose to re-read the last six hundred pages because Lawrence Schiller is a major character in the second half of the book. What many people don't know is that Schiller is also the man who chased the story, bought Gilmore's life rights, and hired Norman Mailer as the writer. Schiller spent hundreds of hours interviewing everyone who appears in the book—but he couldn't write it, he says, "because of my lack of education and writer's vocabulary." A negative review of an earlier book made him doubt that he could effectively intuit the emotional lives and spiritual nuances of the people in his stories. This didn't stop him from flying out to Utah, pounding around Provo, buying confidence, and witnessing Gilmore's execution.

Norman Mailer never spoke to or met Gary Gilmore before Gilmore was executed. Instead he worked from more than fifteen thousand pages of transcriptions, and later traveled to Utah to study the landscape and interview the mothers of the victims. As a result of this unorthodox arrangement, Lawrence Schiller holds half the copyright to the book.

The Lawrence Schiller I met in the pages of The Executioner's Song *was a barracuda and a hustler—at least as cast in the "true-life novel," which was the new genre Norman Mailer settled upon for his book. Would the Real-Life Schiller be different?*

Schiller was present at Ethel and Julius Rosenberg's death march, Gary Gilmore's execution, and Marilyn Monroe's nude float in the pool. He received advice from Bette Davis and Otto Preminger. He lived across the street from O. J. Simpson. I met the writer-researcher-photographer– film director in Provincetown, Massachusetts, where he serves as director of the Norman Mailer Writers Colony, at the home Mailer shared with his wife, Norris.   *—Suzanne Snider (May 2010)*

I. "I'VE BEEN TOLD BY ALMOST EVERYONE I'VE INTERVIEWED THAT I'M NOT THEIR SHRINK."

SUZANNE SNIDER: I read that you first conceived of Joan Didion as the potential writer for *The Executioner's Song*.

LAWRENCE SCHILLER: Joan was my first writer, but I never approached her. I had hired a "corner man" named Barry Farrell, a friend of mine. In the book, Barry is somebody that I reach out to because I feel I might be missing something in my interview process. Everything is becoming so intense. Am I missing something because of my lack of education? Being an intellectual—I'm not. So I hire him as a corner man, like a boxer; he watches me and tells me what I do wrong before I go in for the next round. Barry thought he was going to write what became *Executioner's Song,* and I told him he wasn't going to. And Barry's closest friend was Joan Didion.

I realized I couldn't go to Joan, because Barry would assassinate me. So I went to Norman. Because Norman had stabbed his wife, I felt he understood knee-jerk reactions to violence and what precipitates that kind of violence. That was a very basic, childish thought. You may not remember that Norman had stabbed one of his wives. As you know, Norman wrote *Executioner's Song* based primarily on my work and his own…

SS: I know Joan Didion ended up reviewing it in the *New York Times*. Did she ever know that she was in your mind as the potential writer?

LS: She eventually knew.

SS: What do you think of Norman's characterization of you in the book? Do you think it's close?

LS: I've had worse done of me.

SS: But do you recognize yourself?

LS: Of course. All is fair in love and war.

SS: Did Norman have free rein to write about anything as he wished?

LS: Yes. We disagreed about things greatly, when he put a thought into the head of a character I interviewed… and when I objected, we didn't speak for almost a year, as I said at his memorial service. Then he sent me a fax one day that said, "If I knew I would have to kiss your ass, I would never have shaved," and I called him up and said, "Hello, lover." And we started to talk again…

SS: And how would you describe your relationship after that?

LS: By the time *Executioner's Song* is over, we were as in sync as two guys rowing a canoe. We interviewed the two widows of the [murder victims] and survived that experience. The oars were in sync. By the time *E.S.* was over, we understood the purposes that we each had and how we served each other greatly.

SS: How do you feel when you're in the field, doing fieldwork, in a town with which you're not familiar, like Provo? Do you feel energized? Do you feel lonely?

LS: I don't feel lonely. No no no. I feel like I'm jumping in a well that has no bottom, and at some point I know I'll hit bottom. I never put a time limit on it. I'm oblivious to anything except that which I'm doing.

SS: I want to know exactly what you handed over, in physical form, when you handed over your research to Norman Mailer.

LS: I didn't "hand over" anything, first of all; I *shared* with him. Isn't that a better word? I shared with him twenty-four thousand pages of transcripts from interviews I conducted. And then continued to do more interviews. And then after reading those interviews, he saw a uniqueness in my interview process that he had not experienced before. He saw the material that a novelist normally has to dream up or invent or create, but here it was: real. He understood every one of the characters.

I never come with a list of questions when I interview. It's organic. Sometimes they'll go for hours or weeks or months. Sometimes I'm very, very bold. Very bold. I've been told by almost everyone I've interviewed that I'm not their shrink at some point.

There are times when I challenge people. In the end of *E.S.*, it ends with my interview with Nicole [Baker, the object of Gary's tortured love] where I'm trying to get her to tell me what got her to go out in Midway and fuck all these guys. What did [her ex-husband Jim] Barrett say to her? And she doesn't want to, and I'm pushing her, and I hand her a piece of paper and I say, "If you can't say it, write it."

Her full answer is not in those pages. Norman agreed to leave out part of the answer because I wanted to keep it for my biography, and it was a great, great line. She said, "Barret told me fucking me was like fucking the wind." Even a novelist reading that line has a whole character there. That line told you everything about Barrett and women… Everything!

How do you get people to spend that time with you? Very simple! You have to convince them that they owe it to history! Sometimes they look at me and say, "Fuck you."

II. "MY CAMERA WAS A SPONGE."

I n between his work on The Executioner's Song *and his charge as director of the Norman Mailer Writers Colony, Schiller wrote several best sellers, and his film* The Man Who Skied Down Everest *(1975) won an Academy Award. Before that, he had a career as a photographer, selling one of his nude photos of Marilyn Monroe to Hugh Hefner in 1962 for the then-highest price ever paid for a single photograph. He worked with the great W. Eugene Smith on Minamata, a book of photos related to mercury poisoning in Japan.*

SS: In *Executioner's Song,* Norman Mailer wrote that you had one eye that doesn't work—I don't see that.

LS: My left eye: I'm almost totally blind. I'm legally blind, in my left eye, since I was seven. They saved the pupil. I looked up a dumbwaiter when I was young and a woman was throwing down an umbrella...

SS: But then you became a photographer...

LS: But that was because I couldn't read. I grew up not knowing I was very seriously dyslexic (I grew out of it a little bit). I was unable to read properly as a young child. I was unable to read at all. I ran away from classes because I didn't want to be embarrassed. At the same time, my father was in the retail end of selling sporting goods, appliances, and cameras. He was a portrait photographer prior to that, during World War II. So about the tenth grade, he gave me an East German camera called an Exakta.

My brother and I were accomplished tennis players at a very young age (I was skinny at the time). When my brother beat me in the eleven-and-unders, I gave up sports (he went on to be a nationally ranked tennis player). I went toward photography, and I became an accomplished sports photographer at a *very* young age.

I was self-taught. By the age of fourteen I had won second, third, fourth, and fifth in the national Graflex Awards, which allowed me to work in summer of eleventh grade with Andy Lopez of the Acme News Service.

I took some pictures at the death march of Julius and Ethel Rosenberg from Union Square to Knickerbocker Village and I

started to publish at a young age through high school and college…
I started to get a big head and a very big ego. I hid my age from all
the big magazines around the world. Jacob Deschin, a writer for the
New York Times, called me a "pro at sixteen," when I was still in high
school. By the time I graduated from college I won the National
Press Photographers Picture of the Year award.

SS: What was the photograph?

LS: It was Nixon losing to Kennedy with a teardrop in his wife's
eye. I never considered myself a good photographer. I still don't.
I thought of myself as a hard worker. My camera was a sponge and I
had an instinct that athletes have—anticipation. Photography really
represents an enormous amount of anticipation—understanding
what might be there the next moment and being prepared for it. At
twenty-two years old, I was driving a Mercedes. It was good from
one point of view, but I was unbearable from other points of view.

SS: According to whom?

LS: According to my own reality and according to people who
wrote about me those days. I was being written up in *Newsweek*
and magazines all over the world. I refused to work on staff at magazines because I wanted to keep the copyright to my photographs,
so I didn't get the best assignments. Sometimes I would get back
at them emotionally, like photographing Marilyn Monroe in the
swimming pool, and charge them five times what they would normally pay just because they wouldn't give me some other assign-
ment I wanted to have.

I saw the end of the general magazine business at the end of the
'70s, and I knew I had to move into another profession when the
advertising dollar moved from magazines to television. The magazine business as we knew it was over. We were no longer the edu-
cators of the world. By 1972, I'm conceiving major projects…

beginning with an exhibit of twenty-four photographers' works of Marilyn Monroe. I said to a publisher, "Get me Gloria Steinem or Norman Mailer to write the text and you'll have the cover of *Life* and *Time* magazines the same week." Of course, they got me Norman Mailer.

SS: Was that the first collaboration?

LS: Right. But remember, ten years earlier I did not read and I didn't go to school. I was shooting Playmates for *Playboy* in my college president's home. I had a D+ average in high school, and Pepperdine was the only school that didn't look at my grades. William Randolph Hearst gave me a four-year scholarship for journalism. In 1962, I started to educate myself. Everything I did, I would do extensive interviews. I would go back to the people, time and time again, or move people into my home for six months and interview them every day—put microphones and recorders in their pockets, and I listened very attentively. This developed a unique style. In 1968, after I had done this big essay on LSD for *Life* magazine, a journalist interviewed me on the phone. When the book is published by the journalist—

SS: —this was Tom Wolfe?

LS: Yes. *The Electric Kool-Aid Acid Test.* I realized then that a good writer doesn't have to be where the story takes place to write about it. So the very next week, I hire Albert Goldman to write *Ladies and Gentlemen—Lenny Bruce!!,* which was the first major book that I published. It was not unusual for me after 1969 to seek out the most important writers I could to write books based on my ideas, my research, my interviews. Many people know of my relationship with Norman, because he decided to reveal it. I wasn't interested in revealing it. There are many, *many* other famous writers that I have worked with—

SS: —aside from those that are known…

LS: Yeah. There are *major* writers who have written books [based on my research]. If one looks carefully at the copyright page, you'll see my name. Writers of the stature of Mailer and even bigger. All over the world. I've had failures, don't get me wrong, but it wasn't beneath me to pick up the phone and introduce myself to Bernard Malamud and say, "I'd like to introduce myself to you and to come meet you. I think I might have something that's worthy of your skills as a writer."

SS: You talked about moving away as the business of photography changed. Of course, the fine-art photography market has taken off since the '70s. Is photography something you'll return to? I know there have been exhibitions…

LS: Those exhibitions have been part ego and part to produce some financial stability for my grandchildren's education. I'll give you an example: A very wealthy man calls me from a foreign country who's got a price on his head by two governments and the head of the Mafia in one country. He says, "I want you to photograph me," and I said, "Why do you want me to photograph you?" "Because you photographed Marilyn Monroe." You know that's, like, bullshit. I said, "Well, I charge a lot of money, and all the money has to go to charity." (That usually stops people dead.) He said he's prepared to pay. I said, "It's going to go to a charity for the misuse of donkeys in Israel."

SS: [*Laugh*] Is that your line?

LS: No, it's true. True!

SS: Why donkeys?

LS: Because my wife's an animal activist, and we were in Egypt for long periods. We saw how donkeys were mistreated. Therefore, we're involved in a sanctuary in Israel. So the guy pays me this exorbitant amount of money. I fly there—he sends a jet for me in London and I take the portrait. It was extraordinary! He had this face like an El Greco! Truly! He had been run over by a hundred trucks. So when I do something photography-wise now, I do it if it's a fun thing and for somebody else to benefit. I don't want to make my money off photography right now, because I don't consider myself as good as a thousand photographers out there right now. There are a lot of good guys out there—a lot of women, too—I mean, photography has become a women's profession, and, boy, I admire them. Annie Leibovitz, Mary Ellen Mark—whose books were the first books I published. I don't hold a candle to these photographers.

III. "WHEN YOU'RE BEING INTERVIEWED OR YOU'RE INTERVIEWING SOMEBODY ELSE, YOU ALWAYS HAVE YOUR VOICE TWO OR THREE OCTAVES LOWER THAN THE OTHER PERSON'S VOICE."

It wasn't the death-penalty issue that first drew Schiller to the story of Gary Gilmore. It was a newspaper article that mentioned the romance between Gilmore and Nicole Barrett and their double (failed) suicide pact that caught his attention. Over the years, Schiller maintained a taste for the sordid and the tabloid, drawn to those forced to air their business in courts. His oeuvre includes a book about JonBenét Ramsey (Perfect Murder, Perfect Town) and another about O. J. Simpson (American Tragedy: The Uncensored Story of the Simpson Defense).

SS: Have you ever changed your mind—I'm thinking about the JonBenét Ramsey trial—about the innocence or guilt of someone in your book?

LS: In that book, I refused to say who I thought committed the crime. Joyce Carol Oates in her review chastises me for that. I was flattered that Joyce Carol Oates was reviewing one of my books. But have I ever changed my point of view? No. I mean, O. J. Simpson is a cold-blooded, vicious killer. My daughter was his babysitter. And we lived across the street from him. I know about all the spousal abuse. I've had fights with him about it. In jail, I screamed at him and said, "Look at the good Rock Hudson did before he died, by acknowledging his sexuality and his illness!" I said, "If you get out of this fucking mess"—I didn't say "fucking mess," but—"If you get out of this, if you're judged to be innocent, you should go out and talk about spousal abuse. Do you realize how many women and men you could help?" "*I never did anyth*—" I said, "Fuck you, O. J." Of course, he continued to deal with me… but he's a cold-blooded killer.

SS: Didn't he try to bar publication in the end?

LS: He threatened at the beginning, and when the movie was made, he sued me, and the judge threw it out.

SS: I read some descriptions of the courtroom scene in a book called *Anatomy of a Trial*. The author describes you, Joe McGinniss, Dominick Dunne—it sounded like every writer who writes about the legal system and crime was in that courtroom. Where do you think you fit into that landscape?

LS: Hmm… the least professional writer of all of them, the least original writer of all of them. Uh. But the one that truly is the best Avon salesgirl or Fuller Brush salesman…

SS: You can't be this humble and get all this done.

LS: Look, you're interviewing me, so I'm obviously using some of my skills in the interview. One of the skills you may or may not have recognized yet. And that is when you're being interviewed or you're interviewing somebody else, you always have your voice two or three octaves lower than the other person's voice. That produces a certain ambience, OK? Which is very powerful, OK? And that was taught to me by a great, great lawyer called Edward Bennett Williams in Washington, D.C., when I was very young.

Otto Preminger also taught me some good things. And Bette Davis was my best teacher when I photographed her. She'd sit on the steps of her house and tell me what was going to happen in my first divorce, because she knew... Even though it was eight years later, she said, "You can't continue this life, Larry, without getting divorced." But I haven't always been this way. I've certainly mellowed as time has gone on—just as Norman mellowed. He was the boxer in the '60s and became the rabbi in the '80s and '90s. We both gained weight, we both have heart conditions, and we both lived on pills. I have five stints in me. There's a defibrillator in that room and one in the apartment. Since I had my heart attack, in 2002, we haven't had to use it. I want to be alive when I die. Honestly, I'd rather drop dead during this interview than die in a hospital bed the way Norman Mailer did...

SS: Not in *this* interview [*knocks on wood*].

LS: No, I'm very serious about what I said. I've been many things in my life, and that's what's very confusing even to me. Now I sit and I look at a dog and I try to figure out why a dog doesn't know the difference between right and wrong. My mind is occupied by things like that. Why do certain animals not know the difference between right and wrong? I guess those are things theologists think about. I don't know if that's a sign of where I am.

SS: I want to talk to you about reciprocity with all the people you've interviewed over the years. I know you do pay people for their time, in accordance with what they normally make sometimes... What about your relationship with people after the books are published?

LS: Well, Nicole Barrett drove up here in a truck. She arrived five days ago, and I had dinner with her, and I knew she was driving across the country to see me. She's still in my life. [Lee Harvey Oswald's widow] Marina Oswald is still in my life. There are a lot of men who are still in my life. I think some of them, like [Gilmore's uncle] Vern Damico, don't understand the business aspect of it, so they get a bit confused. But when you irrevocably alter someone's life by something you do, you have an obligation not to disappear, unless they want you to disappear. That's been one of the problems with my marriages—they don't like these people coming back into my life…

SS: Well, you have a lot of people, because there have been a lot of projects!

LS: That living room—[former FBI agent and Soviet spy] Robert Hanssen's children sat with other members of his family and his closest friend—he's still in my life and one of his kids is. Sometimes I don't speak to them for a long time. I've got as many enemies as those that have stayed in my life… I guess you have to make some enemies… and if you're as immature as I was in some of my ways for many years, you make stronger enemies.

IV. "I DON'T WANT [MY BIOGRAPHY] PUBLISHED WHILE I'M ALIVE, BECAUSE I WANT THE WRITER TO BE TOTALLY, TOTALLY FREE TO WRITE WHATEVER HE WANTS TO WRITE."

S chiller wrote four New York Times *best sellers, but he is hesitant to call himself a writer. Now he's heading a decidedly literary pursuit. Even at the writers colony he directs, Schiller has an air of someone who doesn't quite belong. Provincetown is certainly different than Hollywood, where he lives the other ten months of the year. He uses his status to his benefit; it defines his drive as an overachieving outsider with creative problem-solving skills. When he was squeezed out of the O. J. trial, for example, he squeezed himself back in by making himself part of O. J.'s defense team.*

Lawrence showed me Norman Mailer's study upstairs, promising that Norman's study "hasn't been touched, or even dusted, since the day he died." The room had a large Nautilus machine over to one side, and two desks. One of those desks was covered with his last project.

Mailer wrote longhand. His typical process involved faxing handwritten pages to his secretary in New York, who typed it up and sent it back to Norris, who printed out copies to give back to Mailer. Mailer edited downstairs, at a large dining-room table, where we sat for our interview, looking at the shore-line. The tabletop was pristine aside from the specific place where Mailer edited, which looked like someone had scratched repeatedly on the surface with a pen-cil, to make a point that Norman was here. I sat at the head of the table, with Mailer's scratches on my right and Schiller on my left. On the porch, a group of poets-in-residence were working with a visiting critic from Oxford.

Schiller feels a tension that has dogged and will continue to dog him: how to keep his own legacy separate from Mailer's.

LS: Norman was very special. He was one of the few writers in the world who was truly accessible to almost anybody. He would talk and relate to anybody whether they thanked him or not. He wrote about fifty thousand letters in his life. Eight thousand came from writers; sixty-five hundred were answered. Norman Mailer was interested in nurturing young writers.

He never wrote two books the same way. You have to constantly work on your craft. The word *intellectual* doesn't exist in my mind. If I were to appraise my capacity to have an intellectual conversa-tion, it would be very low on the totem pole.

SS: Well, what's your relationship to reading and writing now?

LS: I have to get on an airplane and fly around the world to read a book. I have to be totally isolated. The first book I wrote [*Ladies and Gentlemen—Lenny Bruce!!* "by Albert Goldman, from the journalism of Lawrence Schiller"] was a *New York Times* best seller. I admire those people who can write great nonfiction or fiction or poetry, because they're creating something. I absorb. Norman and I built a relationship because he saw a uniqueness in my interview process. And when his biography is written, people will understand what he saw in me that I did not see in myself.

SS: Why were you doing this, hiring these writers?

LS: These stories interested me, but having a book written was part of a larger plan. First, find a story that has depth and general appeal. Pray you can find a writer who has the same interests as you do. Second, once you have a finished manuscript and, if you're lucky, a best seller, you go looking for the right screenwriter. Third, with a good screenplay you have a movie.

SS: Are you still chasing stories?

LS: Well, the word *chasing* is a good word. I did chase stories in my life. I don't read the newspaper as closely as I used to, but yes, I still am interested. I think I care less about financial security now—it doesn't matter to me. One person has already accused me of hooking on to Norman's legacy, but Norris knows that's not true. I mean, the public doesn't know my real involvement, and maybe they never will, and that's fine. The colony is something that everybody said could never happen. I got it off the ground in nine months.

SS: I heard Don DeLillo was here...

LS: Sure. A lot of people who wouldn't normally venture out,

I call them up and tell them, "I need your help." That's my first line: "I need your help."

A lot of people don't like my personality. They don't like me. But they see there's value in what I could achieve.

SS: What's it like to work alone, since so much of your work is interpersonal?

LS: I don't work alone. I surround myself with talented people.

SS: Do you ever work alone?

LS: What's the definition of working alone?

SS: Sitting in a room. Writing by yourself.

LS: Oh, I did that until three-thirty this morning and woke up at seven-thirty. I forgot about your interview, but it beeped me on my cell thing. But quite honestly, yes, I work alone, but I called someone halfway around the world in the middle of the night to ask how to spell a word—all the way in Australia, because of the time difference.

SS: What was the word?

LS: That's immaterial! I'm not afraid! I stopped Christopher Ricks in the middle of a sentence over dinner and said, "What does that word mean, Chris?" Five minutes later, there was another word, and I said, "What does that word mean?" I mean, I've done that my whole life.

SS: How will you measure the success of this colony?

LS: If writers talk about the colony and writers are able to see something that benefits them, then it's successful. I've had failures—I've been in bankruptcy. I overextended myself on a movie in Chernobyl, and I pulled myself out of that in two years. I've made my mistakes.

SS: What kind of plans did Norman leave, in terms of the colony?

LS: Zero. He had no money. No life insurance. He left virtually no funds for his family. The family doesn't support this financially. I rent this from the family. This is an independent 501(c)(3). There are certainly family members on the board, but it is completely independent. That's the biggest battle I have. People don't understand that Norman has no money.

SS: How did you decide this needed to be done?

LS: About six months before he died, we were sitting here, and he said, "Random House likes this book, so I'm rushing to publish it." He says, "You know I'm not gonna be here by the end of the year, Larry." I didn't know what to say. A few minutes later he says, "You better figure out what's going to happen to this house and my legacy." Norris was talking to my wife in the other room. Four weeks later, he was in the hospital. He said, "I can hardly breathe." He said, "The scar tissue is strangling my lungs."

When I first saw him in the hospital, there was a nurse that just walked in and said, "I know who you are, Mr. Mailer, and I was wondering if you could give me some tips on writing." He looked at her and said, "What are you doing this weekend?" She said, "I'm going sailing with my boyfriend." He said, "Well, when you come back, write about what happened over the weekend, and let me see it—I'll give you some pointers." So, ten days later, she walks in with the papers. He's got more IVs coming out. Here he is editing her manuscript. He finally hands it to her and goes back to reading the *New York Times*. She starts reading it over and over, and she started crying. There the foundation [for the colony] was being laid.

Later, he was buried here in Provincetown, and I'm standing over there by that clock with a couple writers. One of them says, "What do you think is going to happen to the house, Larry?" I said, "I know Norman doesn't want it to be lost to history." A few minutes later somebody said, "Maybe it'd be nice to have a writers colony." I walked upstairs and stood in the room late that night where Norman wrote, and the next morning I said to Norris, "What do you think of turning the house into a writers colony?" She said, "That would be a nice idea." I said, "Would I have your support?" She said, "You'd have my support in anything you do."

I put some of my money in, called Günter Grass, Joan Didion, asked for their help—advising me and lending their prestige and their names. And then I was on the phone for three days. In three days, I had everybody. I don't think everybody thought it would happen. I called Tina Brown and said, "I need to have breakfast with you. I need you to teach me what fund-raising is about." Of course, that's my biggest problem—my personality doesn't raise money. It goes against raising money.

Twenty-five years ago, my personality would have chased everyone away. I couldn't have run this colony. But my personality was doing other things—it was getting into prisons. Or the attorney general's…

Norman and I had a big fight in Belarus where we hit each other and pushed each other down a flight of stairs. It was all about whom I was going to bribe and whether we were being set up, and why I had to bribe someone… We had our differences. Everybody changes.

SS: Is there anything I haven't asked you?

LS: You didn't ask me who I slept with last night…

SS: Who did you sleep with last night?

LS: Nobody.

SS: Do you know what's next?

LS: Everything just happens with me—nothing's thought out. I mean, there are lots of projects that aren't finished… but I think this project is worthy of the time that's put in. If we get one person out of the sixty scholarships, then it's worth it. My grammar has improved. I know the difference between *there* and *their* now.

SS: What about your biography?

LS: It's being written. I've given two years of interviews, twice a week, two hours at a time, eight months out of every year. The interviews are almost done. It will be published after my death. I don't want it published while I'm alive, because I want the writer to be totally, *totally* free to write whatever he wants to write.

SS: Did you choose the author?

LS: No. Several authors asked, and I'm giving complete access to one.

SS: Is that a secret?

LS: Yes. There's a working title, which is *I Survived My Mistakes.* Some people see a story in it. I just hope it's not episodic. If someone can find a through-line, that's fine. I can't. I'm very eclectic. I can't find a through-line.

SS: I wonder if you think writers need to be *more* eclectic. You have the longest hyphenated career…

LS: Well, it certainly happened by accident. I've been married three and a half times, so I changed my life four times. I reinvented myself four times. So each morning brings a little wisdom, and then you find out how stupid you were for most of your life.

SS: I want you to sign my copy of *The Executioner's Song*.

LS: Norman should sign it.

SS: [*I look at the empty seat to my right*] I want you to sign it.

LS: OK. Not on the title page—that's Norman's page. ✶

PANKAJ MISHRA

TALKS WITH

SARAH FAY

"YOU AREN'T JUST TALKING DOWN TO THE READER
FROM A POSITION OF PRIVILEGE AND AUTHORITY,
RATHER FROM A PLACE OF UNCERTAINTY—
NOT KNOWING EVERYTHING, KNOWING THINGS
PARTIALLY, WHICH MANY WRITERS CONCEAL
WITH AN ALL-KNOWING TONE."

People who have sublimated passion and turned it into insight:
Nietzsche's superman
Good writers
The Buddha

Though *we typically reserve the term scholar for erudite intellectuals sequestered in academia's ivory towers, Pankaj Mishra qualifies as a sort of maverick-scholar. He is a novelist, essayist, literary critic, lecturer, and reporter who travels the world writing on a wide range of topics, including globalization, the Dalai Lama, Bollywood, and the "Talibanization" of South Asia. His views on these subjects are both learned and unsullied. He regularly contributes to the* New York Review of Books, *the* New York Times, *the* Guardian, *and the* New Statesman, *and has written for too many international magazines and newspapers to list.*

Given his estimable résumé, it is striking to learn that Mishra was—for the most part—self-educated. Born in 1969, he was raised in Jhansi, a small town in the province of Uttar Pradesh in northern India. As a child, he developed a distaste for formal schooling because he said it kept him from what he loved most: reading. He later attended universities in Allahabad and New Delhi but describes his college days as "idle" as he spent most of his waking moments in the library immersed in books. When it came time for Mishra to enter the professional world and join the civil service as his parents had thought he would, he instead moved to Mashobra, a small village in the Himalayas. For five years, he read and wrote literary reviews for Indian newspapers and magazines. He also published his first book, a travelogue, Butter Chicken in Ludhiana: Travels in Small Town India. *After submitting an article on Edmund Wilson to the* New York Review of Books, *Mishra was "discovered" by the renowned edi tor Barbara Epstein. He went on to publish a novel,* The Romantics, *and two books of nonfiction,* An End to Suffering: The Buddha in the World, *and his latest,* Temptations of the West: How to be Modern in India, Pakistan, Tibet, and Beyond. *He also edited an anthology of writing on India,* India in Mind, *and wrote the introductions to new editions of books by Rudyard Kipling, R. K. Narayan, E. M. Forster, J. G. Farrell, and V. S. Naipaul.*

Our conversation took place over the course of two mornings at Wellesley College, where Mishra was the Robert Garis Visiting Fellow in Writing last fall. During the interview, Mishra—who has very dark hair and adumbrative eyes yet seems to emit brightness—described India as a phantasmagorical place, one where the linearity and fixed identities of the West still do not exist. In his books and articles, he often cautions against the notion of an unchanging self or ideal society. When I asked him what those of us living in "modern" countries in the West can learn from such sagacious skepticism, he referenced a quote from Friedrich Nietzsche: "If you gaze for long into an abyss, the abyss gazes also into you."

—Sarah Fay (March 2007)

I. THE LIFE OF THE WRITER
AS A LIFE OF READING

SARAH FAY: When you were twenty-three, you went to live in
the Himalayan mountains to read and write in the hope of someday becoming a writer. Did you have a clear idea about what you
were doing?

PANKAJ MISHRA: Well, I had a basic idea that I would go to the
mountains, where it would be cheap to live and there would be
lots of silence, lots of solitude. In retrospect, this was a completely
romantic idea. I wasn't making a living at that point—only a few
hundred rupees from writing reviews and articles for different magazines and newspapers in India—but this was in 1992 and the economy in rural India was on a different scale altogether. It only cost
me two thousand rupees a month to live, with my rent included—
that's forty-five or fifty dollars. I could live very comfortably on
that. The day began at five o'clock when the sun hit my windows.
The whole day was there ahead of me with nothing to do except
read and write. I wrote reviews—I loved reading books anyway, and
I was happy to write a few words about them and get paid. There
was no television, no telephone. I started on various drafts of a
novel, which eventually became *The Romantics,* but I mostly read,
about a book a day. I was able to finish a medium-size, 350-page
book in five or six hours.

SF: What did your family think?

PM: I'm sure they thought that I was doing something extremely
risky, but to their everlasting credit, they supported me. At least,
they never raised any objections, which in the Indian context is
especially unusual. It would be unusual here too, but in India people like my parents are anxious, generally, about what their children are going to do. My relatives often told my parents that I was

not doing the right thing and that I was going to end up badly. The fear is that if you don't do certain things at a certain point in your life—if you don't sit for certain exams, if you don't apply to certain colleges—you'll be left with nothing. In my case, there were no safety nets, no family money. But if my parents felt those anxieties, they never expressed them to me directly. I think my father may have had some literary ambitions of his own, which were reflected in the books he had around the house, and may have had sympathy for me. Otherwise I can't explain why they were so tolerant.

SF: Did you tell them that you were going to become a writer?

PM: At that stage, making a career as a writer in English wasn't the most absurd, unimaginable thing in the world. By the mid '80s, Vikram Seth's *The Golden Gate* had come out and soon after, Amitav Ghosh's first novel came out. I had no idea what I would write about, but I really didn't think too long about that. Initially, I saw the life of the writer as a life of reading, which for me was really an extension of the life of idleness that I'd been living as an undergraduate at university. Reading gave me so much pleasure that I felt that maybe I could continue that life indefinitely. I basically went from day to day, reading a lot, loving most books I read and making notes about them. I was just hoping that nothing would happen—like having to apply for a job or think seriously about a career—that would put a stop to the wonderful life I was leading. And, miraculously, nothing stopped me.

SF: What kinds of notes did you take when you read? Do you remember?

PM: I would record my personal responses to a book—notes that would be almost worthless to anyone else reading them. I remember reading a long story by Chekhov called "My Life" about the son of a small-town dignitary who tries to rebel against his father and nothing works out for him. One of the things that affected me most when I read that story—it's a beautiful, heartbreaking story—was that I could be one of those figures who had turned away from a professional career and could end up being a pathetic failure like that. But I also remember noting that there is not a single superfluous image in that story. Everything contributes to the overall mood.

Most of what I read now is for reviewing purposes or related to something I want to write about. It's slightly utilitarian. I definitely miss that sense of being a disinterested reader who's reading purely for the pleasure of imagining his way into emotional situations and vividly realized scenes in nineteenth-century France or late nineteenth-century Russia. Often I find that when I go back to those books by Flaubert or Chekhov—which I loved—I'm unable to summon up that same imaginative richness. That seems to me a huge loss. Now I'm thinking more about the craftsmanship of it—why did this paragraph end here—narrowly technical things.

SF: You were almost entirely self-taught, you had never left India, and you were reading in English, which is not your first language. How did you end up reading books by Flaubert and Proust?

PM: Actually, I had read a great deal of literary criticism by then—Edmund Wilson, V. S. Pritchett. This may sound strange, but I think that contributed to my understanding. I read and re-read Pritchett's massive volume of collected essays. It was not available in India, but a friend sent it to me. It was a treasure trove of writings on the writers I was reading at the time. Reading Pritchett's essays was like looking through an extremely alert, psychologically acute mind.

SF: That seems like the role literary criticism should play, but now it's so arcane.

PM: I know. It doesn't educate people in the art of reading in the way it used to. Pritchett was trying very consciously to get people to re-read "the classics"—Balzac, Zola, Maupassant—and to think about them again, to think about what made them so interesting and engaging. I don't know how many critics today are trying to make the act of reading a more enriching experience as distinct from establishing their own superior intelligence vis-à-vis authors.

SF: You mention that you often read travelogues and diaries by Western writers and explorers who journeyed through India. That must have given you a strange perspective on your own country.

PM: Those nineteenth- and early twentieth-century European and French writers were writing about India as the "other" of modernizing Europe. It's an Orientalist vision—although I use the word without its pejorative associations—in the sense that it portrays India as an extraordinarily exotic culture. To look at India through the eyes of these Western travelers wasn't strange, because the school and education system was almost entirely shaped by the long British colonial presence. I remember reading *Nicholas Nickleby* as a child. Perhaps that's why the West has never been separate from my conception of myself as a writer.

SF: You received a $125 advance for your first book, *Butter Chicken in Ludhiana: Travels in Small Town India*. Did that seem like a lot of money at the time?

PM: No. Given my salary at the time it was a fairly large amount, but once I actually started looking at the places I was going to be traveling to and how much the hotels were going to cost it seemed like a very inadequate figure.

SF: Is that how you got into reporting?

PM: It was a great stroke of luck: I wrote a piece for the *New York Review of Books* on the elections in Allahabad, and they became my main commissioner. That was in 1999. Soon I was traveling to Pakistan and Afghanistan. In the beginning I couldn't figure out anything, but I loved suddenly being challenged by everything around me. Often I would know the language, but the chords in which people spoke—the specific vocabularies—would be different. Slowly, I started to understand and every encounter became a marvelous store of perceptions and insights. I'd meet someone and then when I ran the whole film in my head of my meeting with them, I'd discover new things. It was wonderfully stimulating. I still love arriving in a new city and finding everything around me a sign that has to be deciphered and understood.

SF: In *Temptations of the West,* you describe the aftermath of a massacre in Chitisinghpura in Kashmir. You focus on a young girl whose father has been killed the night before and the people around her talking loudly and shaking her but then zero in on how the girl's "stony expression... did not break, the eyes remained glassy." How did you learn to write about such extreme situations without any formal training as a reporter?

PM: My initial training, or self-education, certainly helped me. I read and re-read books of literary reportage like Norman Mailer's *Armies of the Night* and some of Mary McCarthy's writing. Joan Didion too—primarily her early work. Tom Wolfe is an odd figure and though there's no trace of his style in my writing I did love his sharp sense of social class in those early pieces of reportage that he wrote for *Rolling Stone.* The 1960s and '70s were really golden years of world journalism, especially the writing that was coming out of Vietnam and out of the antiwar protests here. I learned a great deal from them, how they relied on particular details or vivid images that said more about the situation than any amount of abstract analysis. Of course, Mailer and McCarthy were primarily novelists.

SF: What is the difference between writing fiction versus nonfiction?

PM: When I was writing *The Romantics* there were many things I just left out because they didn't fit in with my idea of fiction—too political, too full of detail. I thought they threatened to overwhelm the delicate structures of fiction. Yet, for the past six years I've only written nonfiction, and I've felt confined by having to construct a narrative based on facts and not having the freedom to provide a different perspective. As a novelist, your impulse is toward multiplicity: multiple voices, multiple perceptions, multiple nuances—the ambiguity in human communication. Fiction really is the ultimate home for that sense of ambiguity.

SF: What do you think are the different responsibilities of the reporter, novelist, and essayist?

PM: Well, I feel the responsibility of the novelist is to create a very complex world populated by very complex individuals and to deepen that as much as possible. I don't think the responsibility of the reporter or journalist is fundamentally different, but I think the reporter or journalist is well served by having a responsibility to the powerless, to use a much-abused cliché. The voice of the powerless is in some danger of not being heard in the elite discourses we now have in the mainstream media. This is something that I've learned late. Obviously, I write for a very elite audience, but is there something else that I'm also responsible to? People who write about issues like poverty or terrorism are a part of the elite, and the distance between the elite and non-elite is growing very fast. You can move around the world but meet only people who speak your language, who share the same ideas, the same beliefs, and in doing so you can lose sight of the fact that the vast majority of the world does not think or believe in or speak the everyday discourse of the elite. Yet their lives are being shaped by these elites, by people like us. I don't mean this in a pompous way, but we have a responsibility to articulate *their* sense of suffering.

II. A NARRATIVE BASED ON FACTS

SF: In 2005, you were on a panel on the war in Iraq at the PEN conference in New York. What was your opinion of the war then and what do you think of it now?

PM: What I said at that time was not to underestimate the power of nationalism in a country like Iraq. In the modern world, nationalism remains a very important force. We delude ourselves into thinking that globalization has made all of that redundant and that everyone just wants to be like America. A lot of Iraqis would love to have the comforts and freedoms that most Americans experience, but they don't want a foreign army at their doorstep propping up a puppet government.

Now I think we are all aware that the war really is a disaster, although I don't know to what extent the lessons of that disaster have been learned. American credibility has really suffered such a blow. I've seen it as someone who often writes for American magazines and is identified with America in various parts of the world. Before there was contempt for American power, but there was also fear and now the fear is gone and the contempt is growing.

SF: In your new book, *Temptations of the West,* you describe the jihad as a kind of mob that recruits idle young men with no prospects and no hope. Is it more secularly motivated than it's made out to be in the mainstream press?

PM: Radical Islam became a kind of fashion much the way gangs became a fashion in America. Until Osama bin Laden emerged as a kind of gang leader, an inspirational figure, and franchises started to go up all over the place, delinquent British Muslims were turning to drugs and crime in towns in northern and central England. Then suddenly those idlers and drifters had a cause and a sense of victimization that made their lives seem meaningful. So the false sense of solidarity that you get from joining a group gets mixed with quasi-religious elements. But what tends to be written about and what we tend to be interested in is someone coming from Egypt to America who says, "This is a horribly decadent society and it should be destroyed," because this fits our prejudices about these countries and these societies. Instead of looking at the bland, xenophobic pronouncements of people like Sayyid Qutb or the struggle among modern Islam and mystical Islam and conservative Islam, I wish more attention was paid to the struggle within the souls of the people in these traditional societies. They are the ones growing into the modern world with very severe conflicts and contradictory pulls in their lives.

SF: Do you think that writers—or writing—can really bring about change?

PM: At this point there's no pressure for writers to respond in this way, but it seems important to change public opinion here—by here I mean in America and in the West—by talking about non-American and non-Western societies in intelligent and sophisticated ways. Martin Amis wrote a twelve-thousand-word piece for the *Observer* that basically said—I'm paraphrasing—that London is a multicultural society and Islam is the only thing that doesn't fit. His whole experience of Islam in that article is Christopher Hitchens buying an Osama T-shirt in Peshawar and he and his wife being refused entry to a mosque in Jerusalem after closing time. Amis spins out a whole paranoid fantasy about the man at the Jerusalem mosque and how the man could have killed him or his wife. I found it really disturbing to see a novelist writing a diatribe about Islam and Muslim radical extremists, blurring the distinction between the two. When the most sophisticated and well-read people in our culture start thinking along those lines, then we really are in trouble. I find it irresponsible because ordinary people in their everyday encounters with Muslims have an intuitive sense that "these are not terrorists.

These are not extremists with whom I've been interacting for the past ten years," whereas writers like Martin Amis are living at a vast remove from everyday experience. Many writers today live an extremely isolated and sheltered existence. They go from one literary festival to another, and they don't have those interactions with ordinary people anymore. If a writer doesn't have sufficient experience or knowledge to write about these subjects then fine, but then he shouldn't write about them in a prestigious forum, because what he writes has consequences.

SF: In *An End to Suffering: The Buddha in the World,* you write about your life, but in doing so you put your personal story in the background and the history, theology, and philosophy of the Buddha in the foreground. Most people would put themselves first. Is that how you set out to do it?

PM: I don't remember having any clear-cut ideas in the beginning as to how I was going to write the book, but I did have a sense that my story wasn't important enough to occupy the foreground. I could tease out certain ideas that were relevant to my account of the Buddha's life and his relevance to the modern world, but I never thought I was going to write a memoir. I had a sense that the form was going to be unusual. It was not going to be a historical re-creation of the Buddha's time, which was my original idea and was—thankfully—abandoned early on. It was not going to be a straightforward account of my discovery of the Buddha. I couldn't just say, "My life was shit and then I discovered Buddhism," because my experience was a bit more complicated. It couldn't be a straightforward biography of the Buddha because that's been done a million times and what could I really add to the existing genre?

Three books inspired me. One was Claude Lévi-Strauss's *Tristes Tropiques.* It's an extraordinarily radical book in that it's the mid-twentieth century and he's doing straightforward ethnography in Brazil while at the same time he's looking at his own experience as a Frenchman and the larger encounter that's happening between Western modernity and older cultures. The other book I had in mind was *Native Realm* by Czeslaw Milosz. It's another hugely fascinating example of someone mixing personal history with a larger historical account. My experience was quite different from theirs, I was neither an academic like Lévi-Strauss nor someone coping with very fraught political situations the way Milosz was, but these books were inspirations if not models. Also [V. S. Naipaul's] *An Area of Darkness,* which I think is one of the more interesting examples of experimental nonfiction: it's an essay, a travelogue, it's an instance of what today might be called cultural studies, it's certainly a memoir—a very angry one at times—there is a range of moods and a range of tones.

SF: You write about coming upon a statue of the Buddha on one of your first trips to the Sangla valley. You describe the statue's expression as lacking "passion." It's a cliché, but aren't writers supposed to have "passion" and suffer?

PM: That image that I describe doesn't reflect an absence of passion so much as passion sublimated and tamed and turned into insight. Nietzsche's vision of the superman is also of someone who's able to control and tame his passions and turn them into something richer than raw emotion and raw feeling. I think the best writing does that too. Untamed passion basically results in bad writing or bad polemics, which so many writers and public intellectuals are vulnerable to, especially in recent years. I think the Buddha presents an image of someone who believes in self-control. I think he's offering, perhaps, a critique of the romantic idea of the passions being this wonderful source of life or vitality that define you or your writing.

But so much of writing is fed by vanity and the feeling that what you are doing is the most important thing in the world and it has not been done before and only you can do it. Without these feelings, many writers would not be able to write anything at all.

If you think that what you're doing is not all that important in the larger scheme of things and that you're just an insignificant creature in the whole wide world, which is full of six billion people, and that people are born and die every day and it makes no difference to future generations what you write, and that writing and reading are increasingly irrelevant activities, you'd probably never get out of bed. You need to work yourself up into some kind of a state every morning and believe that you are doing something terribly important upon which the future of literature, if not the world, depends. Buddhism tells you that this is just a foolish fantasy. So, I try not to think too much about Buddhism early in the morning. From noon on, I think about it.

SF: In the book, you write about the many ways the Buddha tried to divest himself of his egocentric energies, and yet soon after you finished writing it you had to set off on a publicity tour. Did you ever feel that promoting the book was inconsistent with what the Buddha professed? I mean, he probably wouldn't have gone on a book tour, right?

PM: I wasn't making any high claims for the Buddha or Buddhism. The book was an attempt to think about the world we live in and to think it through Buddhist ideas, not an attempt to persuade or convert anyone to Buddhism, not an attempt to persuade anyone that my life is interesting and dramatic enough to read about.

I don't feel any great need to subscribe to a certain notion of Buddhism that says "You have to do this" or "You have to do that." Buddhism does not prescribe rituals or prohibitions in the way many religions do. The Buddha would not have liked people to call themselves Buddhist. To him that would have been a fundamental error because there are no fixed identities. He would have thought that someone calling himself a Buddhist has too much invested in calling himself a Buddhist. The Buddha saw life as a continuously dynamic process where every day begins anew and you have to start again.

Buddhism does have certain rules for monks and nuns. If you enter the order of the sangha as a monk or nun then you have to obey certain regulations within the community, but the message is of mindfulness and awareness. It asks you to consider speech and action very carefully and to keep monitoring your mind and ensuring that the mind is not weak before emotions like anger, envy, or malice, and to consider every situation calmly and soberly.

SF: Do you meditate?

PM: I meditate at airports because those are the places where I'm extremely tense, and I often meditate while I'm walking down the street. I have a thought and become aware of that thought and thereby create another level of awareness. That's really what the whole idea of mindfulness—which sounds like such a New Agey concept—is all about: having a second-level monitoring of your thoughts and being able to recognize them as being negative or harmful before they become a part of your being, before they become some kind of action like writing an angry letter to someone or speaking too strongly to someone.

SF: When you're written about in the press, people often comment on your earnestness. Do you think they're just surprised to find earnestness in a human being these days or do they have a preconceived idea that you are "the Buddha guy"?

PM: I don't think of myself as particularly earnest. I have long bouts of cynicism and skepticism. So much of my early life was full of uncertainties—it still is—the "Buddha book" expresses that. Perhaps that's what created this impression of earnestness.

SF: Years ago, you coined the term *modern spiritual tourists* to describe Americans and Europeans who jet off to India, as you say, to raise their kundalini while checking their Hotmail accounts. In the articles you've written recently, you seem to have grown more tolerant.

PM: In India, such people are too easily mocked because they are so highly visible, especially if they start wearing dreadlocks and tie-dyed clothes and start hanging out with the seedier elements of society. I think I was most hard on them before I visited the West. Coming to America and Western Europe, I began to see what they were trying to escape: the hyperorganized, hypermodern society where the pressure to have a professional career and dress in a certain way is intense. The '60s was the last time when large groups of people in the West searched for alternative modes of being. In a society like India's, which is still not fully modern or totally organized, and has a great deal of tolerance for otherness in general, they find the cultural license to try other things, to be whatever they want to be. I see this most recently with the large number of Israelis flocking to India, which is an extraordinary phenomenon. In India, Buddhism, Hinduism, drugs, sex is for them a way of escaping what is essentially an extremely harsh life as a conscripted young man or woman in Israel. I find it's hard not to be sympathetic to them, however outlandish their behavior might be—they can be very aggressive with the locals.

I suppose I've become less judgmental about individuals leading lives according to false ideas and false consciousness, because sometimes entire societies are prey to false ideologies and national delusions. While I've been in the States I've been reading that the top of the income bracket has enjoyed a 600 to 700 percent increases in their salaries since 1976 while the middle and low brackets have stagnated. In a poll in the *Economist* an extraordinary number of Americans denied that there was any inequality in America. A lot of us live with these national illusions.

III. REASONABLENESS OF TONE

SF:You live in London part of the year and in India part of the year. Are you associated with the writing community in either place?

PM: Writing in English in India really does not have a territorialized community, by which I mean a community that is based in one city or even in one region. You have extremely scattered communities. There is now a community in Brooklyn of Indian writers in English: Jhumpa Lahiri, Kiran Desai, Suketu Mehta, Amitav Ghosh. There's a group of Indian and Pakistani writers in London, but I still wouldn't call it a community, even though these are people who see each other on a regular basis.

But I've never really felt that being part of a literary community is all that important. It can be extremely detrimental to a writer. It can damage successful writers by giving them an exalted sense of what they've done, and it can crush less successful writers by infecting them with envy and malice at an early stage in their careers.

SF: What's a typical day like for you in India?

PM: I wake up at five or five-thirty, have a cup of coffee on the balcony overlooking the mountains, which is absolutely wonderful, look at the newspapers, start work. Lunch arrives—lunch is made by a family in the village, they deliver it.

SF: Really?

PM: They knock on the door and lunch is there.

SF: Wow.

PM: And then I have a nap after that. And then a cup of tea. And then I go back to work. I "leave" work around five-thirty or so and have a drink on the balcony and watch the sunset. Very soon dinner arrives from the family in the village.

SF: Of course.

PM: Evenings are usually polished off with a movie. For the past two years or so I've been in China a lot, so I load up my suitcase there with DVDs. You can get a whole box set of Truffaut for five dollars. I'm very interested in Jia Zhang Ke. He made a movie called *The World*. Then I go to sleep early, around nine or nine-thirty.

SF: What's a typical day like for you in London?

PM: More or less the same.

SF: A family brings lunch and dinner from the village?

PM: No. No food from the village. For lunch, I make myself ready-made Indian soup from Marks & Spencer. And no drinks on the balcony, alas. My wife and I usually make dinner or go out.

SF: Who encouraged you to become a writer?

PM: I wrote for many years without showing my writing to anyone, because I was constantly comparing it to what I was reading. You have to compare yourself to the best and feel totally inadequate. The people who encouraged me weren't necessarily writers or readers themselves. They were people who were just pleased to see me devote my life to reading and writing, such as my landlord in Mashobra [in the Himalayas]. He was a Sanskrit scholar. He did not read in English and didn't really have a sense of the books I was reading or what I was writing, but he liked the idea that I was a scholar. In India, there is a great tradition of revering learning for its own sake. He encouraged me in all kinds of material—for instance, he sent me breakfast every morning—and nonmaterial ways.

But, as I said, Barbara Epstein at the *New York Review of Books* was a huge influence on me. Civility of tone, reasonableness of tone, was her preoccupation. They make possible a kind of dialogue with the reader. You aren't just talking down to the reader from a position of privilege and authority, rather from a place of uncertainty—not knowing everything, knowing things partially, which many writers conceal with an all-knowing tone. She was the first person to look at my writing and mark certain passages and say, "You're lapsing into a more aggressive tone here." It was a revelation. By that stage—it was 1997—I had published a book, many articles and reviews, but I'd never had the benefit of having someone comment on a piece of my writing in that way. It made me realize that I had to learn a lot more and do a lot more than what I'd done before. It's shaped everything I've written since.

SF: Do you write with a specific audience in mind?

PM: There is a lot of anxiety in India about writers selling out to foreign audiences, but I'm neither flattering the Indian audience nor the American audience. I'm uneasily somewhere in the middle. I think there may be a new audience coming into being. The internet has created a transnational audience. If you publish something in the *New York Times,* it's read all over the world. Who knows how big this audience is or how long it will last?

Ideally, the act of writing should not be accompanied by the sense of an audience, someone peering over your shoulder, but in nonfiction I think it's almost imperative that you identify an audience so you can confirm or challenge or undermine whatever ideas or prejudices they might have about your subject. You have to have a sense of what they might be thinking about the Indian economy or terrorism or Islam based on what they may have read. I find myself writing more and more of these kinds of pieces with this in mind and having to reckon with prejudices which are multiplying very fast.

SF: When you first moved to London to start your writing career, did you encounter a lot of racism?

PM: When I moved there in the 1990s, London had changed a great deal. Racism had become deeply uncool. But there has been a return of racism in the guise of "antiterrorism." People who look like myself are immediately suspect. I've become extremely self-conscious about going into crowded public places. I'm constantly being stopped and asked to produce my identity. At airports, it's gotten to the point that you start to have the sense that everyone at the airport is looking at you wondering if you are the guy who's going to blow up the plane. It's deeply unpleasant, and it's now a disturbingly commonplace experience.

IV. POLITICAL
AND LITERARY POSSIBILITIES

SF: In *Temptations of the West,* you write about the corruption of the Tibetan monks who were in power before the Chinese invasion. In America, we have a rather Hollywood conception of Tibet.

PM: The whole Hollywood conception of Tibet as this peace-loving country denies the complex humanity of the Tibetan people. Their ideas exist in a high degree of tension with impulses toward corruption, toward violence, toward all sorts of things. The Dalai Lama himself would say that he has to fight these impulses himself on a daily basis. There's no fixed state that he's arrived at where holiness is guaranteed no matter what you do. Like any other ruling class set up, the monks in the early twentieth century in Tibet were corrupted by power. Any kind of power unchallenged will enfeeble rulers morally, and that's what happened there. But the innocent

Tibetan Buddhist is a counterimage of the West, and therefore China is horribly cruel because they sent the Tibetans into exile. But the story is much more complex than that.

SF: You also talk about how the human rights abuses in Nepal—which are horrifying—are completely off the radar of the mainstream press. What does that mean to a country like that?

PM: Well, obviously Condoleezza Rice is not taking meetings about Nepal—she doesn't have time to do that—so there are people at very low levels of the government making important decisions about it. And these people are sometimes making horribly wrong decisions. If you belong to a small country that is geopolitically not that important, or strategically not that important, you have no place among nations. Those countries are neglected and left to fend for themselves. Nepal only appears on the radar when there's a fantastic incident of regicide where the entire royal family is murdered, or if it embraces democracy in a very public fashion.

SF: You've been criticized for speaking out about the Indian government's involvement in Kashmir.

PM: Seventy thousand people have died in Kashmir—many, many times the number of people who've died in the violence in Palestine, but it simply does not occupy the kind of mainstream space that so many of these other conflicts occupy. I published a series of articles that came out at a moment when India was trying very hard to ally with the United States and make the Americans more suspicious of Pakistan. The government at that time was the BJP Hindu nationalist government, so I became a kind of hostile figure in their eyes. My parents were visited by a couple of officers from the intelligence bureau in India asking them why I had visited Pakistan. My phone was tapped in Delhi, but that's a very commonplace occurrence.

I think all of that is in the past, partly because Kashmir has become a slightly marginal issue to the main story, which is the rise of India as an economic superpower. There's this idea that India is a democracy, Pakistan is a dictatorship, there are fundamentalists out there—as for Kashmir, it's complicated, and few people can be bothered to come to grips with it.

SF: If you could have every American read one book, what would it be?

PM: *A House for Mr. Biswas.* It's quite removed from the glamorous notions of what a great novel should be. It's about a man in the middle of nowhere working his way out of a background of deprivation and wanting a house of his own for his growing family. The frustration and partial fulfillment of that desire is described with great insight and humor, and, most extraordinarily, with no sentimentality. Apart from other things, reading that book makes you understand—intuitively—the violence in the world today.

SF: In America, memoirs of suffering are written and published and read ad nauseam—and yet we're so incredibly privileged. Why do you think that is?

PM: Paradoxically, I think it is because suffering is largely invisible in this country. In a place like India it is in your face all of the time. That is why so much is made of it when it is highlighted in a book or memoir about this bereavement or that medical condition. In some cases, these books are extremely well written, powerful pieces of writing, but the memoir does have a special place here in America that it doesn't have elsewhere. European and English literatures don't exalt the genre as much as you do in America.

SF: Occasionally, you teach creative writing at colleges in the United States. The idea of teaching "creative writing" is almost unheard of in Europe and India. Do you enjoy it?

PM: It's a very different way of learning. Some of my students seem to want to be able to write without actually reading, which seems utterly bizarre. When I assign certain readings, they often say, "I can't *relate* to this," which means whatever story we're reading is so far outside of their experience—which tends to be limited—that they will not make the effort to understand what it is about. I find this a crippling attitude to have toward literature, toward history, toward all sorts of things.

Some of my students don't have a sense of whether their writing is any good or not. They think it's good just because it comes out of them and it's a part of their being. To criticize their writing is to criticize them in some profound way. It's as if they've been taught far too much self-confidence—and maybe not much else.

SF: Has the internet made this worse?

PM: The internet has spawned people for whom knowingness is more important than knowledge. It equips you with the illusion of offering knowledge instantly—and quite easily—so you can read a few articles on a few subjects and feel well informed but not actually know any of those subjects in any depth.

SF: Do you see the same trend in young professional writers in America?

PM: This may be a huge generalization, and there are many exceptions of course, but if you look at the average trajectory of the American writer today—he or she goes to high school, college, does an MFA after that, gets a writing contract and advance soon afterward, publishes a few short stories in *Ploughshares* or the *New Yorker,* and then creates a career for him- or herself—life experience is almost absent. This is a relatively new development. If you look at the life of someone like Philip Roth, who was very actively involved in the antiwar movement in the 1960s, his later career would have been impossible if he had not immersed himself in the politics and the world around him when he was a young man. In a *Paris Review* interview he says that the '60s were a "stunning" education for him in political and literary possibilities. In the books he wrote in the '90s, *American Pastoral* and elsewhere, he went back to those experiences, and they help give his later fiction its particular social and political density. Are there young American writers right now undergoing that kind of education? I often wonder about this because the American writer right now is a very pampered figure—by foundations, by fellowships, by publishing advances. Even though I am not American, I have been pampered enough myself to know how it can make your life too frictionless.

SF: Are you ambitious?

PM: Well, I feel very privileged to get to read and write and not to have to do things that I don't like, and I don't want to give that up. Everything else is just a bonus and often a distraction from the writing, reading, and traveling that gives me the most pleasure. I feel that I already have the life I love and I don't see how it could be improved radically by any greater material success I might have—bigger advances, more prizes. It's a kind of madness. And the culture of prize-giving is so corrupt. To think of what someone like Flaubert would have made of it, what kind of utter disgust and scorn it would have aroused in figures like Tolstoy or Dostoyevsky. What would they say if they were told they all had to compete for these little trinkets that were given out? Yet the longing for a very garish kind of success seems as widespread among writers as among investment bankers.

SF: In a piece you wrote on the Indian writer R. K. Narayan, you talk about how he wrote about marriage as a deeply fulfilling engagement for a man. That seems so far from the view we have of it in America.

PM: In the context of those men in India who are faced with all sorts of professional burdens and are asked to create an identity for themselves in the modern world of careers and jobs, women often play a great role in rescuing men from this very drab world of adult responsibility and bring them back to a world of carefree freedom and happiness. In Narayan's case, in his scenes of marriages, there is that sense, which I find very attractive. In India, love often follows marriage. I know many people who are still very deeply in love with their wives, who they barely knew before they were married. In America there's this idea that "how could someone get married without being deeply in love with each other?" but in a lot of these cases feelings of love and affection actually grow after they've been legally and formally brought together. I don't think the experience of romantic love between two well-adjusted people has been satisfactorily described in fiction, but maybe I'll write about it in my next novel. ✶

JULIE HECHT

TALKS WITH

DREW NELLINS

"NOT THAT ANYONE'S GOING TO READ
THE BOOK, OR THE BIO, BUT JUST IN CASE.
YOU DON'T WANT TOO MUCH IN PRINT
ABOUT YOUR OWN LIFE."

Discussed in this interview:

Shadow of a Doubt
The way things are now
Andy Kaufman
David Letterman
Swedish people

Julie Hecht's work has been described as "subversive," "devastating," and "neurotic." While those words are certainly accurate, they don't begin to suggest the singularity of the writer or her career. After publishing two stories in Harper's in the late 1970s (winning the O. Henry Prize for the second), she didn't publish any work for a full decade. Then, in 1989, her unusual story "Perfect Vision" was accepted by the New Yorker. Over the course of the next nine years, the New Yorker published ten of her stories.

After her editor at the New Yorker, Daniel Menaker, moved to Random House, he collected her stories in the acclaimed 1997 book Do the Windows Open? The next year, she was awarded a Guggenheim Fellowship.

In 2001, Random House released Was This Man a Genius?: Talks with Andy Kaufman, *taken from a book-length profile Ms. Hecht had written in 1979. Originally intended for* Harper's, *the manuscript sat in a drawer for years before being excerpted in the* New Yorker *and later printed as a book.*

Julie Hecht's first published novel, The Unprofessionals, *was sort of released in 2003. Midway through the publishing process, she followed her longtime editor as he left a stint at HarperCollins and returned to Random House, where he took over as editor in chief. Though it was slated to be its lead literary fiction title for the fall,* The Unprofessionals *was lost in a corporate shuffle and fell victim to major distribution problems. It could only be found in a few bookstores across the country. As a result of the error and the immediate fallout, Ms. Hecht split with both her agent and her editor, and* The Unprofessionals *received almost no exposure. It disappeared in spite of overwhelmingly positive reviews and being named a notable book by* Publishers Weekly *and the* New York Times.

Her fourth book, Happy Trails to You, *is a collection of short stories set to be released by Simon & Schuster in May of 2008. Simon & Schuster will also release a paperback edition of* The Unprofessionals *in late summer of this year.*

Ms. Hecht and I began communicating at the beginning of 2007. Because she rarely uses email, we communicated mainly by telephone. She has given fewer than four interviews in her life.   —Drew Nellins (May 2008)

I. "I'M TALKING ABOUT A TIME WHEN WOMEN DIDN'T WALK AROUND INTENTIONALLY SHOWING THEIR ROLLS OF FAT AND TRYING TO LOOK LIKE PROSTITUTES."

DREW NELLINS: In past conversations, you've described publishing as "a pigsty." Why the bleak view of the industry?

JULIE HECHT: Oh, but that was a compliment!

DN: Is it really so bad?

JH: When I said that, in conversation with you, I was thinking about the movie *Shadow of a Doubt,* where Joseph Cotten says, "The world's a pigsty." People who've read my work know I'm always thinking about that movie.

It's not the people in publishing. It's the whole world situation. Publishing is now a corporate industry run by conglomerates. Everyone in publishing is affected by this.

DN: Well, you published a great deal at the *New Yorker,* especially in the 1990s. You seem to have had a fairly favorable view of publishing there.

JH: That's because there were copy editors, proofreaders, lawyers, literary editors, and more I can't even remember now. There's no time for that kind of editorial consultation in book publishing now.

An illustrious publisher once called me in the hopes of convincing me to take his offer instead of another, much larger, one. He said how much he liked the book, and I said that I knew it needed editing. And he said, "Oh no, I think it's fine the way it is." And then I realized, Oh, this is what publishing is like now! From the top to the bottom. There's no more editing.

DN: The earliest publication I could find of yours was the October 1977 issue of *Harper's.* Is that the first story you ever published?

JH: Yes, and the first I ever submitted there. I had an agent at the time who said, "You'll never get a story in *Harper's* because it's a monthly, and they publish only one story a month. The *New Yorker* publishes three or four a week." But then *Harper's* published the first one she sent.

DN: How did you have an agent before you ever published a story?

JH: I always had agents because they liked the stories and thought they were going to grow into a book.

DN: So before you ever had a story published, you had an agent? That's very unusual.

JH: Not at that time.

DN: You must have thought you were so cool.

JH: Not at all.

DN: I would have.

JH: Well, you're an idiot.

DN: Thank you. You won an O. Henry award in that period for the second story you published in *Harper's*.

JH: The O. Henry was a great thing for a writer starting out. I never thought about awards. I don't even know about awards. People always have to tell me. So when my editor called to tell me that I had won the O. Henry Prize, it was a complete shock. She said, "I thought it might be considered for the prize." And I said, "No one mentioned it to me."

Then someone had to tell me to apply for a Guggenheim. I never think that way about my own work.

DN: What was it like getting the Guggenheim?

JH: That was great. That was unbelievably great.

DN: Because it gave you freedom to write?

JH: No. It's not the MacArthur. It was a great form of recognition. I associated it with Raymond Carver because I remembered reading that he was so happy, that it was so important to him to get the Guggenheim.

DN: I notice you always thank the Guggenheim Foundation in your books.

JH: I'll never stop thanking them. It was so important. I remember when I told my mother about the O. Henry Prize. I called her on the phone. She had been an English teacher. She showed a combination of disbelief and excitement. At the time, my work wasn't taken seriously by my family. I was always just treated like a girl. And when I said I was a writer, people just didn't believe it. They'd snicker. Well, men would. They would say things like "You remind me of Goldie Hawn." Or "You remind me of Teri Garr in *Young Frankenstein.*"

When I was an apprentice at Summer Stock, I was given a very small part in the play *Death of a Salesman.* The part was a trampy girl in a bar. After the play was over, the set director—who had always been mean to the apprentices—smiled at me and said, "Very funny, very good. But you'll always play a dumb blond." So I needed to get some prize for anyone to take it seriously that I was a writer.

DN: Before you found real success, did you always think of yourself as a writer anyway?

JH: Did I find real success? I thought of myself as a writer, but I knew that nobody else did. They thought I did nothing—especially my mother and my husband's mother.

DN: And the O. Henry changed that?

JH: Maybe for a day. People didn't think of my work as a real career.

My family thought the stories I wrote in childhood or a story I told—they thought they were entertaining. They didn't think I would have a career as a writer.

DN: Do you think of writing as a career now?

JH: I think of it as a bad habit. In my childhood, stories were respected and revered. I understood from my teachers that there was nothing better you could do than write a story, paint a painting, play a musical instrument. And then I grew up into a world where none of that matters. A world of a million TV channels and terrible movies and music.

DN: You grew up in one world and ended up in another.

JH: The world changed. But I was still writing, unaware of what lay ahead.

DN: There's a real strain of nostalgia and regret in all of your work.

JH: I keep telling you, the world has changed for the worse. Everyone in my generation is nostalgic, and even unhappy about this.

DN: But don't you think every generation is doomed in this way? Thinking that everything is getting worse?

JH: No. My parents were interested in what was going on with the next generation. They liked the Beatles. They liked the things that were happening until the '70s. Then things started getting worse. I mean, I'm not wishing for the age before plumbing. I'm talking about a time when women didn't walk around intentionally showing their rolls of fat and trying to look like prostitutes.

DN: Your narrator talks a lot about being appalled by the public. There's a line in your new book, *Happy Trails to You,* in which she says, "I'm never prepared for people in our society." Do you have this in common with your narrator?

JH: Well, there's a lot of alcohol use now. And screaming in restaurants. I'm not prepared for that. Terrible loud music blasted in stores.

DN: Is it that you don't like coarseness?

JH: Like all these Republicans with whom I have nothing else in common—like Patrick Buchanan. I've heard him say things about the "coarsening of our society."

There are more people everywhere now. Coarseness and lack of civility might have to do with the larger population, but I'm sure there are other reasons as well. Maybe they're encouraged by corporations who want people to smoke and buy fast food. I'm not an expert. I'd have to think about it more.

Then there's the glorification of Hollywood. And the trashiness in movies and on TV. People want to copy that. I don't know why.

DN: I've certainly heard you complain that it's hard finding clothes now that aren't tight or trampy.

JH: The last time I saw normal clothing was on a night when I was flipping channels and I saw a woman showing some clothes to another woman—examples of proper clothes for teenagers. They were things like pleated skirts and little sweaters. They were like clothes I wore in the '60s and '70s. And then I saw that this was on CBN—the Christian Broadcasting Network. I couldn't believe I had anything in common with Christian conservatives. That's how far things have gone.

II. "I THINK BAD WRITERS WRITE WITH A PLAN AND THEIR WORK SEEMS CONTRIVED AND CONVENTIONAL."

DN: How do you explain your work to people?

JH: I don't explain my work to anyone. Writers write. They edit their work many times. They don't have to explain it.

DN: If you meet someone and they say, "What kind of books do you write?" what do you say?

JH: I say as little as possible. I say that I write stories. And if they say, "What are they about?" and if I'm forced to be polite, I say, "They're about the way things are now."

Some people say, "I know what you mean." Others don't know what I'm talking about. Of course, they would never read a book or a story, or even part of one. Most people don't think of reading anymore. When you say you're a writer they try to show interest, but you can see they have no interest. Not just in my writing. Any writing.

DN: You know, there's kind of a cult associated with your work.

JH: I know of no cult.

DN: I'm sure you know that there's very little information out there about you. One of the things that made me want to track you down even before I knew you had a book coming out was the bio that appears on all of your book jackets, completely unchanged. It says almost nothing about you.

JH: That's good. One likes to maintain one's privacy. Not that anyone's going to read the book, or the bio, but just in case. You don't want too much in print about your own life.

DN: One thing that's generally known about your work is that the narrator in your stories is always the same, like Proust. Or—one could argue—even Carver, whom you mentioned earlier. Is this a conscious plan?

JH: As for being in a group with Raymond Carver and Proust, that couldn't be better company, but, no, it's not a conscious choice. People write the way they write. Good writers write the way they write. I think bad writers write with a plan and their work seems contrived and conventional. Best sellers—usually those people have a plan. I couldn't even think of writing that way. I have no idea how to do it.

DN: Truman Capote was famous for plotting his career.

JH: When I read that about Truman Capote, I wished I were more like him in that way. I wish I were like a hustler. I wish I'd had a plan.

DN: I read an old review of one of your books in which the reviewer suggested that you were satirizing your narrator. That's not how I read your work. Is that what you mean to do?

JH: No. They don't get it. It's not a satire of anything. It's not a satire.

DN: How conscious are you of trying to "write funny"?

JH: I'm not trying to do anything. I just get an idea and then write it. My editor at the *New Yorker* once said to me, "It's hard to be funny," and I said, "What do you mean?" He read me a sentence from one of my stories and said, "Are you telling me you didn't try to make that funny?" And I said, "No. That's just how it occurred to me. I just write things the way I think of them."

DN: In terms of your personal reading tastes, I'm always asking you,

"Do you like this author?" or, "Do you like this book?" and you always say, "No, because it's not funny." Is it really true that you only like funny writing?

JH: It's almost true. Even the greatest books—I can't read them unless they seem funny. In Kafka, in *The Trial,* for instance, there's that phrase "the bandy-legged student." That might be an incorrect translation, but I remember in college I had a friend who loved the phrase "the bandy-legged student." She used to refer to another student that way. So, even in *The Trial,* the parts that aren't meant to be funny seem funny.

DN: Do you focus on absurdity in real life as well?

JH: I don't focus on anything. This is the way people are. What they notice or don't notice.

DN: So when other people are looking at your work—and surely you've read some reviews of your own work—is there anything you wish they'd notice that they don't pick up on?

JH: I don't expect anything from reviewers. I don't read most of them—about other writers' books either. I might skim one if someone tells me to. They usually give a plot summary the way children did in fourth grade. Who wants to read that? I don't expect them to get it.

There's one review that I really liked. It was in the *San Francisco Chronicle,* I think. They said my stories "seem to touch on everything and contain the whole world." That was my favorite quote in any review. I thought it was the best compliment, because some people find that annoying—that the stories contain too much. They don't have the attention span for stories that go everywhere.

Had my *New Yorker* editor been a book editor, each of the stories might have been a book. But I had to keep cutting. Cut, cut,

cut for the *New Yorker.* If I had kept going instead of kept cutting, I might have a lot of books instead of a lot of stories.

When my editor became the book editor for the Andy Kaufman book, it was "Expand, expand, expand." It had nothing to do with the work itself. It only had to do with what was to be published where.

DN: Between 1989 and 1998, the *New Yorker* printed ten of your stories, all with the same narrator. Sometimes a couple of stories a year. Did they take everything you wrote?

JH: They took every story I wrote during that time.

DN: In 1997, most of those stories were collected in your first book, *Do the Windows Open?* It got a lot of attention, particularly for a book of literary short stories. What was that success like?

JH: I didn't really take it in. I guess I was glad the way it turned out. It was better than a failure, but I wasn't jumping for joy the way writers do when they're in their twenties. If the book I wrote in my twenties had been published I would have been crazed with narcissism.

DN: Your next book, *Was This Man A Genius?,* was published in 2001. It was a profile of Andy Kaufman originally written for *Harper's* in 1979, and then not run because of its length. How did you begin that project?

JH: I called his agent. I called Andy. I talked to him for a long time. His agent suggested I go meet Andy after his performance at Great Neck North High School, where he had been a student. After that, my way to continue the project was to meet him when he came to New York to be a guest on *Saturday Night Live.*

He was the one who suggested using a tape recorder. Before that, I was just watching and listening. This conversation is in the book. I was very young. I knew nothing. I forgot to ask for expense money or an advance.

Andy was just starting out. I remember I met his manager's girl-friend after his Town Hall performance. She thought I was writing for *Harper's Bazaar*. They had never heard of *Harper's,* and they didn't care.

I would have to meet Andy at his dressing room at *Saturday Night Live* and hang out there in the hours before the show. That's when I taped all this really interesting—well, *I* thought it was really interesting—conversation.

DN: Why did you do that book? It's so different from your other work.

JH: I wanted to know. Andy was unique. His act was fascinating and funny and bizarre. I had never seen anything like it. I wondered, How did he ever come up with this? It was unbelievable to me.

DN: Were you distressed when *Was This Man a Genius?* didn't get published immediately?

JH: It didn't get published for twenty years—and then just because some movie had been made, supposedly about his life.

DN: Were you upset at the time that you wrote it and it didn't go anywhere?

JH: You see, being a writer, I was used to all things being discouraging. I was upset by people publishing ordinary, junky stuff and not wanting to publish much unusual writing. So, yes, I was unhappy, but I was used to rejection. The early life of a writer is to be rejected. Like the life of the actor. It was a way of life, and I got used to it. That's why having that first story published in the *New Yorker* was probably the most exciting thing that ever happened to me.

DN: Speaking of discouragement, what can you say about your novel *The Unprofessionals*? I know it was well reviewed, but it ran into some kind of distribution snag. I did some research—it sounds like a giant clusterfuck.

JH: What's that?

DN: It's when a bunch of morons get together and fuck something up.

JH: That's so funny. I never heard that expression. But my agent and editor weren't morons. They were smart. If there were any morons, they must have been behind the scenes.

DN: Dealing with that book must have been a nightmare.

JH: Yes, and it still is. I don't think I should get into it. My husband went to Barnes & Noble in New York and the book wasn't there. They looked in the computer, and saw that it wasn't anywhere. That day began a series of emails between my agent, editor, lawyer, and publisher—many, many emails that never resolved anything. Very few bookstores received copies of the book, and the publisher was disinclined to do anything about it.

DN: I understand you stopped working with both your agent and your longtime editor, Dan Menaker, after that.

JH: Yes. I regret that we don't speak anymore. He helped me with my stories since my first story was published at the *New Yorker*. He worked really hard with me on those stories and on the story collection. I'm indebted to him—for whatever career I have.

DN: Like a lot of readers and reviewers, I really love that book. Aside from the obvious negative associations with *The Unprofessionals*, what did you feel about it? How did it feel writing a longer piece?

JH: I didn't think of it that way. The problem was: no editorial guidance. I don't know if the editor even had time to read the second half of the book because of his new position. I was on my own. When in doubt, I kept cutting.

III. "I USE MUSIC THE WAY OTHER WRITERS USE DRUGS OR ALCOHOL."

DN: Do you look back on your earlier work very often?

JH: No. When I look at a work from before, I don't like it and wish I could change it. For example, my new book—two of the stories were published a few years ago. I had to improve them.

DN: A friend of mine worked at the Harry Ransom Center at the University of Texas, which purchases a lot of author archives: Don DeLillo, Norman Mailer. Knowing him sort of trained my mind to think about their legacy—the big pile of paper they leave behind. It seems normal to me to look back at all that stuff, for better or worse.

JH: I think male writers are more egomaniacal and they often have devoted wives who manage everything for them. Men get to take themselves very seriously, but women don't have the time. They're mothers and they're running houses. Millions of distracting details. Of course, some women writers don't have children. Louise Nevelson said a woman should think a million times before giving birth.

DN: I've always wanted to ask about your fascination with David Letterman. You've mentioned him in several stories.

JH: I'm not fascinated. I love to watch the first half of his show, when he talks to Paul and you can see what he's like. When I see a Hollywood actress begin to walk out onstage in a black slip, I know it's time to change the channel. I like him because he decries the lack of civility in society. He's also very quick witted and funny.

DN: I received a special request to discuss the story "That's No Fun" in *Do the Windows Open?* from someone who was fascinated by your fixation on Swedish people.

JH: That story is the favorite for many people. I received a lot of mail about that story.

DN: So do you have a particular interest in Swedish people?

JH: I knew a Swedish woman. She was always talking about how great Sweden was, and I believed her. The thing I liked the best was that they took their shoes off before they came into their houses.

She was nostalgic for Sweden. She loves the outdoors, the cold air. I do, too. In the winter, she used to put her baby outside on the screen porch to have a nap. And when she brought him in, she said he looked so healthy. She'd bundled him all up in his carriage. She said that's what they do in Sweden.

She was always doing these kinds of things and saying, "That's what we do in Sweden." And they were good ideas. It sounded so interesting to me. But mainly I love the shoe part. I couldn't understand why all these Swedish people live here if everything's so much better in Sweden.

That was before things were so crazy here. Back then, they were just crazy enough. The whole country is like the Wild West now. No, worse.

I'm looking at the TV now with the sound turned off, and it's all these children in a band. And they're all overweight. Some are obese, but all are overweight.

DN: What writers would you want others to read?

JH: Which other people?

DN: The reading public, I guess.

JH: What's that? Anyway, it's not my job to tell people what to read. I'm just a writer. I haven't read enough.

DN: You've mentioned a few other writers whom I've never read. Thomas Bernhard and Robert Walser. Would you recommend them?

JH: I recommend those books only to people who I know have a great sense of the absurd and are interested in literature.

DN: Speaking of the absurd, I thought of you today when I read about a professor who hates typing on computer keyboards, so he types letters on a typewriter and then scans and emails them. You've talked a great deal about your hatred of technology.

JH: Well, I really can't type. I don't know how to type, because in my high school that was for the secretarial department.

DN: Not learning was a feminist thing?

JH: Yes. A goal was to become some man's assistant. People have said to me, "You've made your point, now you can learn how to type. All the men are typing now, too."

DN: You write in longhand?

JH: Yes, and I then have it typed. I had to get a Mac PowerBook so I could have my work emailed to me. Then I make corrections and fax them back to the typist. It's not very efficient. Fax machines rarely work. They're a kind of hell.

DN: What is your work area like?

JH: I live in a small house, and I don't have a desk. I don't even have a room I could fit a desk into, unless I gave up this little tiny dining room, which is filled with books because it's impossible to get anyone to build bookshelves. All the carpenters and builders just want to build big houses around here. So my books are on the floor, piled up everywhere. I write in the living room on the sofa.

DN: Do you write on legal pads?

JH: No, fax paper.

DN: Unruled paper?

JH: Yes.

DN: I can't imagine writing on unruled paper.

JH: Maybe I should get ruled paper. I never thought of it. My typist is too polite to tell me. And my writing is all at an angle, I just realized!

DN: You talk a lot about music in your books. Do you listen to music when you write?

JH: Yes. I use music the way other writers use drugs or alcohol. Mozart works best. But I listened to Leadbelly singing "Goodnight, Irene" over and over while I was working on something. I did the same thing listening to Elvis Presley singing "Blue Christmas"— and to the Paul McCartney song "I'm Looking Through You," after I used up everything by Mozart.

DN: We should talk about your new book, *Happy Trails to You*. What can we say about it? How are you feeling after spending so much time with the manuscript?

JH: Indescribably bad. It's not the book. It's the book production stage. It wears you down. You have no other life during this stage.

DN: I'm sorry to hear that, because it's such a great book. It's so funny and sad.

JH: Oh, I forgot about what's in the book. The fun part was writing the stories.

DN: What was hardest part of writing for you?

JH: Sitting.

DN: Are you happy with your body of work?

JH: No. What body?

DN: Do you wish you had written more?

JH: I *have* written more. I gave up publishing my early work after just a few turndowns from the *New Yorker*. For me, submitting the stories is more difficult than writing them.

I wish I had more time and energy for it. I wasted so much time looking for curtain material when I lived in New York. I didn't have much money, so I was always looking for beautiful things that weren't expensive.

DN: Do you have any idea what you'll write next?

JH: Yes, but I wouldn't want to talk about it. I have an idea, but I think it will probably take several volumes, like *Remembrance of Things Past* or Carl Sandburg's four-volume biography of Abraham Lincoln.

DN: You started having second thoughts about going through with this interview when I used the word *departure* to describe the content of your new book.

JH: *Departure* is a word from a transportation schedule.

DN: And the word *process* made you even angrier. How did you feel that the rest of it went?

JH: Well, I tried to train you in advance. So, I think it went better than when it started out.

DN: You never do interviews. Why did you agree to this one?

JH: I don't know. I wish I hadn't. It's really wearing me out, thinking about all these things from the past.

DN: Well, we can stop here.

JH: It's too late. The damage is done. ✶

VICTOR LaVALLE

TALKS WITH

KAITLYN GREENIDGE

"I'M A BLACK WRITER IN THE SAME WAY JAMES JOYCE
IS AN IRISH WRITER, TOLSTOY A RUSSIAN,
FLANNERY O'CONNOR A WHITE SOUTHERNER...
BUT THOSE IDENTITIES, THOSE CULTURES,
ARE JUST THE DOORWAY
TO SOMETHING MORE UNIVERSAL."

Incomplete list of conclusions drawn in this interview:

Fear is a powerful motivator
Readers are masochists
Specificity is the route to the universal
Making yourself out to be a monster is a form of self-flattery
High drama and deep philosophy are not mutually exclusive

Victor LaValle's debut book of short stories, Slapboxing with Jesus, won the PEN Open Book Award. His first novel, The Ecstatic, was a finalist for the PEN/ Faulkner Award. His writing draws comparisons to Gabriel García Márquez and William Faulkner. Mos Def named his 2009 album after LaValle's novel. In addition to this honor, LaValle has been awarded a Whiting Writers' Award, a Guggenheim fellowship, and the key to Southeast Queens. His latest novel, Big Machine, was named one of the ten best books of the year by Publishers Weekly. It was also awarded the 2010 Ernest J. Gaines Award for Literary Excellence.

LaValle was recently a writer in residence at the Dutch Foundation for Literature in Amsterdam, working on a film adaptation of Big Machine *in cooperation with Amsterdam's Binger Filmlab.*

Big Machine *details the complicated history of the Washburn Library, a research institute based in Vermont that takes in former addicts and ex-criminals, all black, and trains them to investigate supernatural occurrences. The book's main character, Ricky Rice, a recovering junkie and former childhood member of a dangerous Afrocentric religious cult, is pulled into solving the mystery of the Washburn Library's purpose and its early history as the legacy of Judah Washburn.*

LaValle's novels complicate traditional narratives of American history and African American history in unexpected and imaginative ways. His work focuses on characters who are outside the mainstream, the type of people less-imaginative observers might deem "outcasts."

—*Kaitlyn Greenidge (May 2011)*

I. "I MADE MORE OF AN EFFORT TO BE A STORYTELLER… WHICH IS DIFFERENT FROM BEING A WRITER."

KAITLYN GREENIDGE: How old were you when you first started writing?

VICTOR LAVALLE: Ten or eleven. Twelve years old. I would copy Stephen King and H. P. Lovecraft stories. What I mean is, I would read a story by one of them and try to write exactly the same story. But I don't know anything about small-town life in Maine, King's specialty. And I don't know what it's like to be a misanthrope in Rhode Island, which was Lovecraft's. So my stories were always sort of vague and fake. But I kept trying.

KG: When did you feel you could call yourself a writer?

VL: I never had any qualms about saying I was a writer. I didn't come from the kind of people who talked about writers as some rare and cherished beings. This is because we didn't actually talk about "writers" at all. There were a few books in the home: the Bible and the *Encyclopedia Britannica,* that kind of thing. My uncle was always a voracious reader, and sometimes he'd leave books at our apartment when he visited. But the role of "author" wasn't deified, so I didn't overthink the title. I didn't imagine it was a privilege. When I found I liked to scribble little stories, I became a writer. As long as I was producing pages, I was a writer, no matter what actually happened to those pages later. Publication wasn't proof. That wasn't the test.

KG: The first story you wrote was a horror story. And you've listed some of your influences as Shirley Jackson and Stephen King. How does horror influence your writing? What elements of horror do you see in your work?

VL: This most recent novel is the most obvious because there are monsters in the book. But also I made more of an effort to be a storyteller this time. Which is different from being a writer.

I love tales. In the campfire sense. In the scriptural sense. Folklore. The kind of stories that get passed down like wealth because they are riches. Those kinds of tales usually have some pretty basic lessons to impart: about bravery or cowardice or greed. But they also tend to play on certain primal emotions, fear being one of the surest. And they do this because it *works.* Fear is a powerful motivator in human behavior, for bad and for good.

But then how do you tell a tale that gains access to that place? Sometimes you have to indulge a little of the fantastic, the impossible, to access that deeper wisdom. And to relay that wisdom to a reader. Whether it's a wolf that can actually dress and talk like Grandma long enough to lure a child into its bed, or the idea that a column of smoke, a column of fire, actually moved with the Israelites, smiting enemies and taking over towns. Talk about eminent domain! It's not actually important that you believe either story happened, but when you hear each, you know exactly what they're trying to convey.

KG: How did this approach—thinking like a "storyteller," as you say—work while you were writing *Big Machine*?

VL: So for this book I tried to access that power. Mixing the mundane and the mythic. For me, few "genres" do that as exceptionally as horror. That's certainly why I was drawn to it as a young reader. One of the things I'm always telling my writing students is that they should find ways to externalize the internal dilemmas of their characters, of their books. If they externalize the dilemmas, there's a chance that something might actually *happen* in their work, and I have a selfish desire for that, as a reader. But I also push them in the hopes that they'll create a *beast* of some kind, whatever that actually ends up meaning to them, one that any reader might understand on the deepest level, instinctively. In this book there are a number of beasts: some are humans who act like devils, but others are something else, literally.

I think in order to like horror and supernatural stuff, in order to believe it, you have to have been a person who's lived a life where terrible things happened and there is no easy explanation for why they did. With [*Big Machine*], it's been interesting. Some of the people who have the hardest time going with the final section of the book, where things get particularly strange and insane, when I talk with them, not to be dismissive, they are often people who feel life follows a certain logical order. People who feel, even if cancer kills your parents, you can say, well, they lived next door to the such-and-such plant and that caused the cancer, so they died. As opposed to saying, I live in such-and-such a place, and without my even knowing, a civil war popped off, and a plane dropped a bomb on my house and killed members of my family. And that is a truth that is really hard to explain away.

Or, more particular to me: people in your family are born with illnesses that are never healed. They are only managed. And science can't particularly explain why these illnesses exist. And for me, it's an easy leap from that scenario to "OK, there're monsters. There's evil in the world that just can't be fixed." That's the influence I get from horror.

KG: In this book especially, and also in *The Ecstatic,* it seems like there is a real sense of faith in each of the characters. It is very up-front that that is what they are struggling with: a sense of belief or a belief system. I'm wondering what advantages you get when you have a character's belief system so plainly delineated?

VL: Well, first I'll admit I didn't know they would have that strong sense of faith, or that they would be wrestling with faith, until about twenty drafts into the process, about two or three years into the book. But one of the advantages of having a character with a specific belief system, with stated ideals or goals, is I get to avoid the excessive ambiguity that I find a little aggravating in some strains of contemporary literary fiction. The idea that ambiguity is all. That a character's motivations, their beliefs, are supposed to slowly spool out, until you have a mess of yarn in your two hands. But the danger of that approach is that the human beings don't actually move forward in time; their lives are all stasis. Now this might be how people *feel* at certain times, but it's rarely actually true. You still have to get up, go to work, encounter the world, no matter how much you'd like to stay home and ruminate. Rumination doesn't pay what it used to! I wanted to write characters that had some forward momentum. As a result, they couldn't sit around for sixty pages, thinking about the delicacy of faith, and describing that condition through the details of a lamppost or something. I wasn't interested in that.

II. "IF YOU'RE GOOD, YOUR IDENTITY IS A PORTAL. IF YOU'RE BAD, YOUR IDENTITY IS A WALL."

KG: When you were editing *Big Machine,* what did you fight to keep in?

VL: My biggest fight was to keep the creatures, called the Devils of the Marsh. My editor, Chris Jackson, is incredibly smart, a wonderful editor. But he's also much more of a realist. He had a hard time cosigning on some damn monsters. So he'd ask, "Can't they be psychological monsters?" But then I'd ask, "Well, how's Ricky gonna get pregnant then?" Which led to Chris's next question, and our second-biggest argument, "Does Ricky have to get pregnant?" And I knew he did. Yes.

KG: How soon did you know you wanted the protagonist to become pregnant?

VL: That turn was in the earliest drafts of the book. And it made no sense then. I wrote the first draft while I was on winter break at Mills College in Oakland. It was a short novel. One hundred ninety pages, if that. A pure detective novel. There was stuff about the secret society, but nothing about the Voice, nothing about faith, and there definitely weren't any monsters. Ricky joins this group, there's this former member who flips out and rebels. Ricky is sent out west with Adele Henry, to kill him. In that version, Adele, the Gray Lady, as she's also called in the book, actually betrays Ricky at the end. As soon as the villain, Solomon Clay, is killed, she was meant to murder Ricky. He was Oswald and she was Jack Ruby. And yet, even in that one, Ricky Rice became pregnant. Even though there were no monsters, he was still pregnant; he had something growing inside him, even though it wasn't explicit, as it is in the final version.

KG: And why was it important to you that he become pregnant?

VL: I was dealing with a relationship that was falling apart at that time. Had fallen apart. And in that relationship, I got my girlfriend pregnant. And she and I battled about what to do next. Those aspects made it directly into the book, in some of Ricky's flashbacks. They are how I remember them, which of course doesn't mean they're accurate. But I was trying to tackle that, too. Why we remember our stories, our pasts, the way we do. Whether we damn ourselves in those stories, or praise ourselves, we're always doing it for a reason. The way people usually remember their pasts flatters something in themselves. And making yourself look horrible, like a monster, is a very traditional form of self-flattery. I wanted to engage with all these ideas, and, for me, the story of that pregnancy was the way to do it.

None of this was conscious, not for a while. The elements stubbornly refused to be erased, no matter how many times I deleted them from the page. After a while you've got to stop fighting. Those deeper concerns wore me out. So finally I let them in fully.

KG: Is it always easy for you to draw that connection between your actual life and what you write about?

VL: There are many different ways to approach having your real life in your work. I want to tell other people a good story, but if I'm going to spend years on a book, I better get something out of it that benefits my real life, too. I want the work to be worth more than an advance, because I'm going to spend that advance soon enough. My previous book, *The Ecstatic,* was about working out really conflicted feelings about my family: hating and loving them, wanting to escape them. Pretty normal concerns. But luckily I was able to acknowledge that pretty quick in the writing process, and I just decided that if I was going to really wrestle with this stuff, I might as well throw in as many true-to-life parallels as I could. Unfortunately, my family did find out that I'd thrown in so much, and we had a rough patch because of it. But that's the other side of being so willing to toss all your autobiographical bits onto the page: those damn human beings won't just act like characters in your book! They actually have different ideas about what happened and why. But they usually don't have the luxury of being able to write a book to refute you, though my sister did get a few really solid punches in after *The Ecstatic.*

KG: Both novels, *Big Machine* and *The Ecstatic,* contain extensive rewrites of American history. Why did you decide to include these fantastical historical sections?

VL: They weren't in most of the early drafts [of *Big Machine*]. But my editor would constantly say, "How is this aspect of the story possible?" Meaning, what explicable history led to this or that element? And I just didn't know. And so I created not just a complex present-day, but an equally complex past that made the present possible. Which is history. It was exciting.

But the other thing that I wanted to do was I also wanted to have… you have a black American runaway slave and you have these Native Americans from this tribe I made up. I took a lot of pleasure in making them all act really badly. They're terrible people, actually. At least, they have terrible moments. I knew both ideas were offensive to ideas of what you are supposed to do with certain historical types. They were both supposed to be noble or righteous and nothing else, that's the received wisdom. Which is, of course, horseshit.

KG: It's interesting that you see these stereotypes as strengths and try to use them.

VL: When a writer just supports a stereotype, that becomes cliché. But when a writer subverts the stereotypes in a surprising way, then the received wisdom can be enormously helpful. And instead you can introduce a type of person that readers expect they already know. And when you take a sharp turn away from the expectations, it can cause some very satisfying whiplash. Satisfying to the reader because his or her expectations have been challenged. It's almost like slapping the reader awake. And, to my great surprise, many readers tell me they appreciate the feeling. So the conclusion is obvious: readers are masochists! If you do it right.

KG: Would you define yourself as a black writer? Or does that term even mean anything to you?

VL: I would. I'm a black writer. I'm a black writer in the same way James Joyce is an Irish writer, Tolstoy a Russian, Flannery O'Connor a white Southerner, just to make three self-aggrandizing comparisons. But those identities, those cultures, are just the doorway to something more universal. That's the hope, anyway. If you're good, your identity is a portal. If you're bad, your identity is a wall.

Of course, there's the other side of the issue: the reader. You can't actually control how readers will embrace or flee from the identity before them. Some people love the Brits and others loathe them. Simply setting a piece of fiction in London can be enough to turn some readers away. But what's your alternative? Set your story in the city just because you don't want to turn any readers away? That's a recipe for blandness, most of the time. Specificity is the route to the universal. It's pretty hard to be specific if you run from all markers of identity. Imagine if Joyce, an Irish Catholic, never played with or referred to the rites and rituals of Catholicism! Can you imagine James Joyce the Unitarian?

III. "I USED TO WANT TO WRITE GREAT SENTENCES. NOW I WANT TO WRITE GREAT BOOKS."

KG: In *Big Machine* and *The Ecstatic*, I noticed a lot of physicality in your characters. They're very much defined by the way they move in their bodies. When creating a character, do you start from gesture, or is that something you work on?

VL: It's always worked on. My first impulse is to write dialogue. I have a good ear for it, and I can usually make it all sound quite real. But that means I also rely on it too much. Ask the dialogue to do a lot of work for me. But that becomes indulgent.

So on the second, third, fourth, however many drafts, I start thinking: OK, I have to start picturing them moving. They have to have bodies. And then I'll usually come someplace like a coffee shop, and then I'll have in mind: OK, it's two people breaking up, and I'll try to pick two people who seem to be having a rough day, an argument. Then I just watch them and take notes about how I know they're fighting, even if I can't hear a word. Their bodies are telling me everything.

The way people move is all the backstory you will ever need. Because they tell you their whole lives through their bodies. If you want to illustrate an aggressive personality, you don't need a whole scene from his childhood where you explain how his mother and grandfather had been aggressive, too. Just show him pushing ahead of five other people on a line, and even as others are grumbling, he never even turns around. He just pays and strolls out. The other people just crumple and accept it. And a reader will think, All right, now I know that person. They might not like him, but they sure know him.

KG: Do you start with an image, an idea, or a combination of the two?

VL: It's always the first sentence. I know I'm really ready to start a new project when the first sentence is an ass-kicker, when it excites me. Some images, some ideas, some characters have been percolating in my mind for a few years, but it's not until that first line appears that I know the coffee's ready.

KG: So language is the key for you?

VL: Early on I would've said that the sentence is all that matters. I used to think it was a compliment to say someone's book was full of incredible sentences. And it was a compliment, at the time. But these days I tend to take a few steps back from the page. I don't think it means that I care less about sentences, just that I care more about the book. When I used to coach people to focus only on the sentences, when I used to write that way myself, it was because I needed to focus that sharply on the issue. There's nothing wrong with lyricism. I'm not trying to degrade the art of a fine line. But when your book just becomes a pileup of fine lines, it makes it much harder for a reader to appreciate the book as a whole. In fact, sometimes the book as a whole is really beside the point. And these days that seems like bad news. I used to want to write great sentences. Now I want to write great books.

KG: How do you know you're done with a project?

VL: When I feel that I've gone as far as my powers can go. When I can't imagine what else I could do. A year, two years, two days after it's published, I know I'll come up with a dozen solutions to the problems, the limitations, of that book, but that's why I write the next one. With *The Ecstatic,* I wasn't trying to write a narrative-driven tale. I felt I hadn't ever read a book that actually captured how a bipolar mind, or a schizophrenic mind, truly works. The two aren't interchangeable, but I felt I had enough experience with both to pull it off. So that was my mission, and I'm pretty proud of the results. But, in part, that was also my mission because I couldn't do any more than that. I mean that I could capture the workings of an ill mind, and I could show that mind in a kind of episodic adventure, but I couldn't also create a traditional narrative for the book. That's my long way of saying I didn't know a damn thing about plot. But I didn't realize this limitation until

I was writing the new book, and suddenly it seemed like I had developed this brand-new power. Narrative! But in reality it wasn't sudden. I'd spent years teaching myself how to do it by not being able to do it.

KG: How did your newfound interest in narrative lead to your decisions on structure for *Big Machine*?

VL: That also was long into the editing process. In the earlier drafts, the chapters were actually about forty pages long. A few years into the writing process, that started to feel like one very long breath. A lot of little things that seemed essential were being lost. I wanted to be able to stop and let the reader think about this idea or that idea, to build my themes slowly over time. But I found that when I had a forty-page chunk, even my closest readers would miss a lot. Not that they were lazy, but that there were only so many details, clues, ideas that I could ask them to juggle at one time. So I was facing a real problem: how do I communicate a lot of big ideas and beliefs without overwhelming the reader?

Luckily, I was reading *Moby-Dick* and I saw that *Moby-Dick* has these incredibly tiny chapters. This made it read, at least in the beginning, like an adventure novel. An adventure novel interspersed with moments of philosophy or wisdom. You need to have the sermon at the church as a stand-alone, because if it was buried in another chapter, you might forget, or overlook, the ways that Melville is smacking you in the cheeks with all the themes and goals of the book. As its own thing, you can read it and then put the book down and sort of think about all the points he's hitting there. I really liked that structure.

Then as the book goes on, the chapters get more and more dense with theory and philosophy. Melville started the book as more of an adventure novel, but then when he discovered that no one wanted to buy it, he was just like, "Aw, fuck this, I'm just going to do whatever I want." It can seem like Melville is such a genius, and he is, but what's also true about this great book is just that it ran smack into reality, too. He tried to make money off of it, that didn't work out, so he switched gears. And to his credit he didn't go back and remove the more adventurous, propulsive chapters. He just mixed them all together and trusted, hoped, that this only made the book better. The high drama and the deeply philosophical. Melville knew that you can offer a reader both and remain highly serious. And I learned that from him.

IV. "AMERICANS DON'T BELIEVE IN MAGIC, BUT WE DO BELIEVE IN MYTHS."

KG: In both of your novels, most of the characters are outsiders. What's the advantage of writing outsiders, if you would even call them that?

VL: I would call them outsiders. I would, because enough people have brought it to my attention. Enough people have used that term. But I never think of them that way myself. These are just folks that are misjudged or maligned or underappreciated. That's who I find interesting.

I have a wonderful family, on both sides, but I would say a lot of them got a lot of bad breaks. And I didn't. I've been really lucky in so many ways. I never thought so when I was younger, but that's because self-pity comes pretty easy to the young. But I'm a grown man now, and it's become pretty difficult, if not impossible, to play that *poor me* card much anymore. So part of me feels like one way I can drag my family, these beautiful but often unappreciated folks, into the public consciousness is by writing about them. One way I can give their lives their due is to make them into stories. But I also realize it's because I want to save them.

KG: What do you mean by "save them"?

VL: Well, one of my beliefs is that people, in the sense of a group, a people, are real only when there are myths about them. Only if they join the legendary: *The Iliad* or Faulkner's Yoknapatawpha County, Toni Morrison's black Ohioans, or Murakami's Japanese. These are stories about real people, but they're all tinged with legends, with myths. And that's why I think they reach a different scale than a Dos Passos or, I don't know, Alex Haley. It's no surprise that Haley's most enduring book is *The Autobiography of Malcolm X*. Because it's a personal history, but it's also an epic in the oldest sense.

Since I'm a reader, my version of being real, and lasting forever, is that there are books that create your legend so that it lives on long after you do, long after the storyteller does. And the specific brand of outsiders, the weirdos that I love, that I feel an affinity for, haven't been represented in the way I think it should be done. The particular geography I want to map in the world of literature is defined more by the eccentricities of its inhabitants than by their races or their countries of origin. They tend to share the same class, though. Working-class oddballs. The mythic lower middle class! It sounds silly when you say it out loud, but that is actually what I mean.

KG: Do you see yourself using realism again?

VL: I think *Big Machine* is realism. Mythic realism. That's the term I want to use. I think I came up with it. If so, I'll file for the copyright. It's not magic realism. The distinction seems to be that magic realism is what you call it if the writer isn't an American. So Márquez qualifies, of course. Murakami. Ben Okri. Atwood maybe. Doris Lessing. But if you're an American writer, it seems like this is a harder fit. Americans don't believe in magic, but we do believe in myths. Which is just another kind of enchantment.

I remember years ago, when my first book came out, I did an interview with this guy from a magazine that no longer exists. We spent a good while talking, and the magazine ended up writing a very nice piece, with my picture and everything, so it was very gratifying to the ego. It was the thing I could show my family, and they could enjoy their kid getting the shine. But I remember at one point me and the reporter were talking, and he said this kind of cast-off line. He asked me what it felt like to write books for people who don't read. I had a good laugh at that and proceeded to chew his head off. We had a tense few moments as I defended black readers, or urban readers, or younger readers, all the various groups he meant to suggest I couldn't rely on. I wasn't actually hurt by his question, though, because I also realized that his question meant one thing to him and something else entirely to me. He meant it as this real-world issue of how many readers are there for a black book, a book of stories, that kind of thing. Business concerns. Valid questions to raise in a business context. But when he asked the question, my mind had gone in an entirely different direction. I thought of those artists who wrote with a knowledge, a hope, that seems to go beyond a specific moment in their own lives. I'm thinking of Herman Melville, or Henry Green, or Vincent van Gogh, or Zora Neale Hurston. I'm thinking of this great line from a Hunter S. Thompson book, "A Man on the Move, and just sick enough to be totally confident."

Even at that age, when me and this reporter sat across from each other at a Russian vodka bar in midtown Manhattan, even as I gave him hell about his prejudices, I still understood the difference between us as this: He saw reality in finite time. Questions of success or relevance or impact were answered that day, or that week. My sense of time was a bit grander. I was twenty-seven, but I believed I'd be sitting here, someday, talking with you about another book. I believed I'd write so many books. And I knew that every person who ever read one of my books and was touched by it, affected, was there with me in that bar. That reporter looked at me and saw one young man at a table. He didn't realize I had a fucking army with me.

Goddamn, was I an arrogant bastard! Still am. ✶

MARK LEYNER

TALKS WITH

BRIAN JOSEPH DAVIS

"I REALLY WANT THIS WORK TO FEEL EMANCIPATORY TO PEOPLE."

Great examples of American surrealism:
Chuck Jones
Spike Jonze
Andruw Jones of the Yankees

It has been almost fifteen years since Mark Leyner's last novel was published. Many authors have gone longer between books— Thomas Pynchon went seventeen years between Gravity's Rainbow and Vineland—yet most authors who have left public life did not have quite as public a persona as Mark Leyner once did. With pages thick in perverse, pop-artifact-studded automatic writing, his 1990 collection, My Cousin, My Gastroenterologist, still reads as it did then, as a midnight movie on fast-forward, told through non-sequitur skits and saturated with advertising jargon honed from the author's years spent as a copywriter. At his best, Leyner would go on to capture, and atomize, the Manic Panic–millennialism of the Clinton era.

313

After Leyner's breakout hit, he established a fictional Mark Leyner character in his novels, composed of signature riffs wedged into self-referential frameworks: Mark Leyner, world-famous author and corporate brand, in Et Tu, Babe; *and thirteen-year-old Mark Leyner, literal enfant terrible, in 1997's* The Tetherballs of Bougainville. *Then the onetime poet truly joined the mass media when he started writing scripts, including the divisive 2008 John Cusack film,* War, Inc. *Audiences expecting a sequel to Cusack's previous assassin rom-com,* Grosse Pointe Blank, *instead encountered a frenzied update of Dr. Strangelove for the age of Blackwater and indeterminate incarceration.*

In Leyner's most recent novel, The Sugar Frosted Nutsack, *he has created a pantheon of new gods ("The God of Dermatology," for example) who toy with everyone from Red Sox Ted Williams's frozen head to the novel's central character, a paranoid mortal in New Jersey named Ike Karton. Told in a poetic, recursive style,* The Sugar Frosted Nutsack *is Leyner's most complex work to date, and his most raw. For a novel about a fiction that contains all of existence, Leyner's cosmological reality show intriguingly lacks his most famous creation: Mark Leyner.*

When we met at Manhattan's Old Town Bar last April, I knew I wouldn't be interviewing the exact Mark Leyner from two-decades-old magazine profiles. The author I met was as much a middle-aged father—nervous and humble at the prospect of talking about his return to fiction—as he was a writer who could effortlessly weave Jersey Shore *and* The Iliad *into an improv thesis on storytelling.*   —Brian Joseph Davis

I. PAPA WAS AN INFINITELY
HOT AND INTENSE DOT

BRIAN JOSEPH DAVIS: Writing about gods and myth is very much in the tradition of classic poetics, which is what you originally worked in. Going back, even before *I Smell Esther Williams,* when did humor creep into your writing? Baudelaire and Rimbaud are not innately funny guys.

MARK LEYNER: No, I have a feeling they were not particularly fun to hang out with. I realized, at the age you realize these things, I had a capability of making people laugh. Once you realize that, you don't want to stop. It feels too good. "What did I just do? I want to do that again!" So there was a kind of crucial time—and it very much has to do with me trying to write prose—when I wanted to write something as linguistically eventful as poetry. That was my embarkation point toward, and I say this in all humility, what is unique about my work.

BJD: Coming of age in the 1970s, what comedy spoke to you? I ask because I've always wondered about the influence of something like the early *National Lampoon* and that window where the avant-garde and comedy crossed over.

ML: I don't think I was a devotee of comedy at that time, or any kind of contemporary, oddball, or transgressive comedy. I can tell you what things I loved as a kid. Those things tend to be much more meaningful, or enduringly meaningful, to me. If you asked me what I thought was a great example of American surrealism, I would say Chuck Jones.

BJD: And Spike Jonze? All the Joneses?

ML: Yes, Andruw Jones of the Yankees. He's very funny. I'd also say Charles Fleischer cartoons, and the sort of stand-up comedy on TV that anyone sitting in a living room in the late '60s or early '70s would see, comedians that you would watch on a talk show, like Rodney Dangerfield. Stand-up comedy had an interesting effect on me in terms of how I started to think about constructing things, because I really loved the interstices, the linkages, or lack thereof.

BJD: Poetry and comedy are very much related in their dependence on language.

ML: They are very much related. I'm reading this book from the 1940s, *The History of Surrealism* by Maurice Nadeau; it's wonderfully erudite, and throughout it makes the point that comedy is effortlessly surreal. Now, I wasn't thinking these things at the time, but I was very interested, when I started doing whatever you'd call what I do, in those elements that make cohesive a stand-up routine. Sometimes it's just a refrain, an arbitrary thing. And we know these things so well, like the phrases *What're you gonna do?* or *What's up with that?* That can link a list of fifteen or twenty things. It's only the later style of comedy where there's a naked lack of linkage, but in an old Rodney Dangerfield routine it's just bits linked by his animus toward his wife or mother-in-law— you know, hackneyed things that comedians hate now. But these links did get me thinking about how it might be possible to have explosive or incandescent imagery with some kind of narrative drive. I don't think I've written a book that was as pure and intransigent an example of how I wanted to write as *The Sugar Frosted Nutsack,* which is odd, as here I am, and I ain't a kid. But maybe that's why?

BJD: You killed the character of "Mark Leyner" at the end of *The Tetherballs of Bougainville,* and in the new novel there is no Leyner character. Despite a fourteen-year gap, it seems like you had a consistent plan for where your writing was going.

ML: I know it seems like I made some great religious repudiation of fiction writing. I wish! I should. But it's a very easy thing to explain. In terms of the work, I did feel like I should stop for a while. I thought at the time, looking at *I Smell Esther Williams* through *The Tetherballs of Bougainville:* Here's a full demonstration of these postulates; here it is, to the extent that I'm able to do this and show how this might be done; and OK, that's good for a while. I also remember trying to resist this as a career. It is my life. The most deeply felt, most profoundly felt thing that I do is this work, but I was trying to resist this idea of having a new book every couple of years so you could renew your membership.

BJD: It's easy to have that panic, though.

ML: It is. And when I had my daughter and started thinking about money in a certain way, some opportunities to write scripts came up, and I saw script writing as a tangential adventure, a more lucrative version of journalism or teaching. The idea of me doing that seemed much more outlandish than script writing—I'm not a good teacher.

This adventure isn't over; I'm still working on some projects, but something interesting happened to me, and it's a great deus ex machina. I got hit by a car in L.A. when we were doing postproduction on *War, Inc.,* which completely fucked my knee up. I flew back and I couldn't walk for a while and just started reading in a different way. It was an enormously galvanizing experience to me and I decided: it's time. Enough time had passed, and I had ideas on how to proceed without just redoing something I'd already done. I was making progress on the novel—it was due sometime—and I had at least a hundred pages of notes for what I was feeling was the last third of the book. Then I got an incredible case of the flu, or maybe I'm just being vain about it. But this is my version of the flu, and I'm lying in bed, and I can be very dramatic when I'm sick. I moan and thrash and ask people to bring me things. I'm hot, then cold. I couldn't eat anything. My wife brought me food from McDonald's and Dunkin' Donuts and I couldn't eat even that. I had a complete, universal revulsion about everything, including my book. Not what I had already but all my plans for it. It was an enormous problem, and I decided on a radical upheaval in the book, which turned out to be the perfect thing. I can't imagine what the book would have been like if I hadn't done that. It involved inventing two characters.

One of those that had been very peripheral but became very important is Meir Poznak. I needed a character to come and dramatize or express my revulsion at a long, well-crafted denouement.

It was sickening me that I would fall prey to that! The book is fated from the beginning, and I was very clear about this. I wanted the reader to feel as if everyone knows this story, as it's an epic based on a myth.

When you read *The Iliad* now, it's not like you say, "I can't wait to find out what happens to this Achilles guy." Everyone knows. It's in the introduction! So I wanted that to be part of the book. Everyone knows, and I repeat it a trillion times: Ike wants to be the martyred hero, not only waiting but eagerly awaiting his demise at the hands of—as in the mind of any great paranoid—the Mossad. The refrains and repetitions are there to give the idea of the story being folkloric. If people asked me what it was like when I was writing, which is a better question than what's it about, I would say: it's like a book you would get, an old book, with an introduction about the mythology that the epic is based on. And the book itself is not necessarily the epic. It's about the epic. I realized that if that's the given of the book, wouldn't that mean that once you allow for marginalia, or something like Talmudic commentary, it would begin to be this creature that's embracing and devouring everything?

II. THE TROJAN SHORE

BJD: You give your gods Greek-like involvement in the lives of mortals. Until I read *The Sugar Frosted Nutsack,* I never considered reality TV as a classical form, where common lives take on dramatic importance, but in a very staged and static way, and the crew members are like gods hovering in the background. What's funny, though, is cinema vérité got us to reality TV, but it's kind of the exact opposite of cinema vérité philosophy. And two centuries of the realist novel has only created a market for fake memoirs. I think this speaks to a continued need for fiction—as much as we want more real content, it all becomes part of the fiction.

ML: I hate to use the word *discourse…*

BJD: There are much worse words than *discourse*.

ML: I'll use them, I'm sure. I have a new interest in things that people were sick of even in the 1970s—I'm an enormous Gilles Deleuze fan. Anyway, when I was fifteen or sixteen I was into those long, twenty-page *Rolling Stone* interviews. They'd always be known as "The Pete Townshend Interview" or "The Keith Richards Interview." I devoured these things, being a big music fan, but I always thought it would be interesting to apply that kind of obeisant interest in someone to an anonymous person. I had this idea at the high-school newspaper that we should do these big long interviews with just us. I don't think I'm so terribly prescient, but it really was an embryonic impulse toward what we see everywhere now where it's almost, you know, *enough!* But then we're such voyeurs you can never get enough of watching someone. Just watching someone who needs to get into the bathroom and they're pounding on the door and the person in the bathroom won't let them in. I mean, you could just watch that for a good forty, forty-five minutes.

But I also didn't want the new book to be a parody, and I was careful not to strike that tone. One of the things about mythology is how childish and silly it can be. Sometimes if you read a Norse or Hindu myth it sounds like something a kid made up as they went along, and now it's stuck for time immemorial. You know, like: so a guy rises out of an ocean and brushes something off his erect penis and it's, like, a large, rough piece of sand; he flicks it off into the sky and it becomes the moon and then the moon winks.

As well, when you look into the story behind the Trojan War, the story behind the story.

BJD: The director's commentary.

ML: Or a reality-TV show. Of course Helen gets stolen, but, from the Olympian perspective, it started at a wedding where there were three goddesses who asked Paris to pick the hottest goddess. For some reason Paris took part in this. Every other mortal said, "Uh-uh. Not getting involved in this. This couldn't be good, as I'm going to piss two goddesses off." But Paris did piss two goddesses off, and hence this whole series of events happened. and I thought: That's it? That's how all this happened? Is that not out of reality TV? When two girls come into the kitchen on *Jersey Shore* and ask, "Who do you want to fuck most? Pick one." Then someone gets pissed off.

So that stuck in my head. Again it's one of these odd transpositions between most trivial and most important. Those distortions of scale, I think, are at the basis of both what's poetic and what's funny.

III. BIGGER THAN VICTOR HUGO

BJD: One standard criticism of work that uses the language of pop culture or technology is that it will be dated, but I think it's fiction's job to have an accidental, documentary quality. When I was re-reading *My Cousin, My Gastroenterologist,* I was struck by how much, without even trying, it sponged up our cultural and political obsessions of the late '80s and early '90s.

ML: Now, I think that's something that's consistent in my writing, but it's also something I was, again, very aware of in *The Sugar Frosted Nutsack,* because the creature of this book purports to subsume everything extrinsic to it… Somehow I had concocted this thing that couldn't be killed—and god knows I tried. I'm always trying to kill it and subvert any premise that was prevailing for a certain number of pages, and pleasurably so. Then I realized the book wouldn't die and I was just beating it and impaling it and eviscerating it and there it was, there it was.

BJD: The book that wouldn't die!

ML: I would force it to be a kind of *TV Guide* for a little while, and then coerce it to become, again, more literary, or suddenly the *TV Guide* looks like a poem. There are moments in the book where it feels to me like the technology of the book is in perfect accord with my boredom with something I was doing, or my impulsivity in maintaining this character. As we were saying before, there's a moment when another character basically takes over, when it appears that the god named XOXO will be happy to let the book go on forever, or, as he says, "give the epic a cosmic case of blueballs." When that accord happens, it feels good. It's... what's that word when astronomical bodies align?

BJD: I know the one, it sounds like a Czech village.

ML: *Syzygy.* Yes, it's thirty kilometers that way. But writing is like any human activity. You get bored with it, you feel guilty about not tending to it, and you feel disgusted with it. You can be wildly megalomaniacal with it. That's always a sign a big crash is coming, and it ends up becoming a kind of a high-stakes game. This book was a big deal for me. I did face it with some degree of trepidation, and I felt I had to stand up to it in my way. I have an awful physical and psychological combination of being small but thinking I'm tough. That usually creates a horrible, gnarled person who challenges much bigger people in bars.

BJD: You could say that's the state of the writer in general. We don't have much power over the universe, but we have to think that we do.

ML: I'm fascinated by Raymond Roussel. He had a system for using the French language in such a way with similar-sounding words. It was a schematic way of generating the most gorgeous, surrealist text. He did a number of intriguing things. He traveled around in one of the first mobile homes, at times with his deceased mother. He was a little divorced from the reality of how his work would be perceived. He thought of himself as kind of a popular writer.

BJD: He thought, I'm going to be bigger than Victor Hugo!

ML: He did! He very much admired Victor Hugo and Jules Verne, and thought he would have the same kind of acclaim. But even more interesting is that he believed his writing created a kind of refulgence, a kind of light. And when he would write he would shutter up the room he was writing in so that the light wouldn't disturb the people on the streets of Paris. Like they'd see this bizarre light flooding out and it would create a panic. So there are sometimes disproportionate feelings of importance, but, again, I had a kind of psychological truculence about doing *The Sugar Frosted Nutsack*. I'm glad I did.

BJD: What I really liked was how even though the story is falling out of these multiple frames, there's a heft to the character of Ike Karton, and there is a progression that wouldn't be there in, say, an antinovel.

ML: This novel isn't anti-anything. And that goes back to avoiding a parodic approach. There is a completely clear, predetermined plot. It's fated. Fate is the primordial plot device. And a number of times in the book I will go through the entire story again just to remind people: this is what happens; Ike is making a bread-crumb mandala; he's going to the Miss America Diner; his band is performing; he will be killed by the Mossad. It's a time-honored exposition device.

BJD: Again, very popular on reality TV.

ML: I do appreciate that, and while I was writing I was acutely aware of and playing with that. If you look at the percentage of the new footage on a show after a commercial break, it comes down to maybe 2 percent, and the rest is just a recapitulation of what you just saw a minute ago, which I think is kind of fantastic.

BJD: And they sometimes use different footage, or a B-roll, then you're left questioning what you just saw.

ML: And I really do like that. I think the forms of those shows are fascinating. And again, while I was aware of that, I didn't model the story on it. This is how we tell stories in any number of ways. It's how we tell stories in terms of intimate human communication. It's how we tell stories as teachers and students. How we constantly remind people of things. It's having patience with people that are not as fixated as you are or haven't fetishized something to the extent you have. So I love it very much. It's a narrative approach that is very generous. More importantly, with this book, it reiterates the fact that this story is known, that this is a kind of primordial tale, and it's not a matter of what may happen, necessarily, though something interesting does happen in the end.

BJD: Are you a classicist who's long been mislabeled a postmodernist?

ML: Yes. And it's not that I cringe at the word *postmodern*. I don't mean to sound aggressively disdainful about what anyone wants to think, but if you know anything about what any of these terms mean, and if they're useful in any way, I'm so much more of a modernist than a postmodernist. The people that I love are from an era long before there was any such a notion of postmodernism. And there's a moral component to what I do. I really want this work to feel emancipatory to people, so much so that I have these ridiculous notions that I should try to embody that work. I can say this now, shamelessly, that I have a kind of insurrectionary feeling of wanting a reader to have an experience in a book of mine that is life changing, not in the sense that you're going to quit your job and become a monk, but that your life changes for that period of time, and that you will experience a different kind of life as you read the work.

That has nothing to do with postmodernism and everything to do with modernism. And in that modernism is the apogee of classicism, and, going back to the Nadeau book, I think you could say that about surrealism, too: that it represents the apogee of classicism, in a way. All of these things could easily be demolished by anyone who's reading these works.

BJD: We'll go with it for now.

ML: We're talking, we're talking, so what the hell? Anyway, every page of the Nadeau book is about how serious this endeavor is. How exhilarating a leap into an unknown world the artists' work is for a human being to have access to now and then. So it's a very genuine, authentic, ridiculously grand project that I feel a part of. ✶

MAUREEN HOWARD

TALKS WITH

JOANNA SCOTT

"ARE YOU TALKING ABOUT THE DANGER OF LOSING THE READER IF WE SHAKE UP THE FORM, OR THE DANGER OF LOSING OUR MINDS?"

Unsung sources of suspense:

The delays of a meandering narrative
The invention of competing voices
Table tennis

Joanna Scott *is the author of two collections of stories and eight novels, most recently* Follow Me *(Little, Brown, 2009). She has lived with her family in Italy, pursuing her fiction, but is settled in upstate New York, where she teaches at the University of Rochester. Joanna is a recipient of a MacArthur Fellowship, a Lannan Award, a Guggenheim Fellowship, and the Rosenthal Prize from the American Academy of Arts and Letters.*

Maureen Howard is the author of nine novels and a memoir, Facts of Life, *which won the National Book Critics Circle Award. The* Rags of Time *(Viking, 2009) is the last in a series of novels celebrating the four seasons. She is the recipient of the Academy Award in Literature from the*

Academy of Arts and Letters. She was born in Bridgeport, Connecticut, and made her way to New York where she has lived for many years with the comfort of family. She teaches at Columbia University's School of the Arts.

Scott and Howard met when they were seated next to each other at dinner at a Houston writing festival one night in 1991, and continued talking at a PEN/Faulkner gathering in Washington, D.C., later that year. Joanna was expecting her first child. Maureen and Joanna have been talking children and writing ever since. Their girls are now well grown. The exchange that follows took place over email in the winter of 2009–2010. (May 2010)

JOANNA SCOTT: Maureen, I've been thinking about your memoir *Facts of Life* and its relationship to the fictional remembering that goes on in your new *Rags of Time.* I wonder if I'm right to sense that the two books share an energizing tension? On the one hand, a home is a writer's necessary refuge—the work gets done behind a closed door. On the other hand, a home can be a "stifling refuge" (a phrase you use in *Facts of Life*), and the world outside the door, with its layered history, is always beckoning. The first thing your fictional writer does in *The Rags of Time* is to head out, away from home, into Central Park.

MAUREEN HOWARD: The exploration of place: I say that as though to introduce a classroom spin. Today we will concern ourselves with Flannery O'Connor's confinement to Milledgeville, Georgia, where she discovered the saved and the damned; to Naipaul's childhood in Trinidad, which became sacred to him in England. Well, if I seem unable to swing free of Bridgeport, even now recalling the *chug-chug* of factories in World War II, it may be to reconsider the best of times. In *Natural History,* both a novel and a history of my city, I romanticized the myths of Barnum's Winter Quarters, and the secrets of City Hall. These many years in New York I'm quite at home, I know the bus routes and where to scout out the Extra Virgin! olive oil, but often turn to the memory bank in a mix of melancholy, mockery, and affection, hoping I have not overinvested in the double feature at the Rialto, the parish church.

I envy your possession of the island of Elba in *Liberation*. In *Follow Me,* you place a map of the Tuskee River to guide both the writer and the reader of the novel. It becomes your Yoknapatawpha County. Mind if I call in the gentleman writer? I must believe that when we leave home, we are ready to leap over the gender gap.

JS : Yes, it's a wonderful freedom we have on the page. We can start by presuming that anything's possible, and then we step across those borders that in the real world might be impassable. But wherever we go, we take the baggage of our memories with us. Your fictional New York is really a version of Bridgeport, stretched to fill a bigger map. That makes perfect sense. New places mirror our first formative experiences, when we were figuring out how to get from one address to another. "Pay attention to here and now," your fictional writer reminds herself as she heads out once again into Central Park: "Delighted to be released from Bridgeport, just for the day." But still "that old stuff" presses in. Bridgeport won't let you forget it.

MH: Actually, she pastes that line on a photo of her parents walking arm in arm on Fifth Avenue, pleased with their adventure just for the day. That old stuff, but then again, Make it New, the old adage of modernism, is with me still. A vintage bottle hasn't lost its fine nose. To discover a form for each story—where to put the journalistic scrap, how to emboss the surface of setting, be it my Park of the new millennium or Frederick Law Olmsted's plan for the Greensward, or the retreat of the Germans in your *Liberation*. We ask the reader to follow the turns of narrative, but if you put a coin in the slot, there are multiple views which may contain the personal story. Collage: the early pasteups, the background of brushstrokes, history fractured with today's news. I think of Sebald walking the byways of East Anglia, milling history for the daily bread of his writing. His discovery of place is more than setting, more than local history; his discovery of past and adjacent lives is self-discovery. In an early collection of stories, you wrote of historical figures—Dorothea

Dix, Charlotte Corday—and appropriated their lives to suit your purpose.

JS: Really, I think they appropriated me to suit their purposes! That's usually the case with my fiction. There I am, just walking along, wrapped up in my own petty troubles, and I hear ghosts whispering from the shadows. I like the feeling of that kind of discovery, when we're caught by surprise, when the world reveals a portion of itself unexpectedly. But it's not enough for fiction writers to collect stories and retell them, is it? Your notion of collage (something you enact visually in your books, with images and blocks of text) is beautifully apt—the past fractured with the present. Writing fiction begins with a process of fracturing. We chip away at known reality, take pieces of it, and then set off to elaborate and assemble in order to try to press toward the part of experience that resists knowing yet tempts us with the possibility of understanding. And because a thing that is individually and lovingly made reveals aspects of the person who made it, the end product of this process of assembling, the collage that is fiction, involves self-portraiture. I'm taking the long route back to your idea about the writer's personal involvement. The author may be absent from the work, but she's left her dirty fingerprints all over the pages. I see you, Maureen, in your *Rags,* not just in your fictional writer but in the very structure and style of the book. You've made something that can contain different points of view, contrasting impressions, and your characteristic blend of past and present. And I sense that behind this multiplicity is an author who remains acutely concerned about the future.

MH: Which future? An agreeable future of nuclear deterrence plotted in Geneva? The future of the great melt? A revival of the gold standard? Of my grandchildren, who, I like to believe, live in a state of innocence? Or the future of our stories, the weight of their fancy? Ranting again, powerless, well aware my soapbox is cheap wood that splinters. I stole that line from Sinclair Lewis, gave it to the writer in *Rags.* Thinking about the responsibility of fiction recently, I came across a prescription for searching out the word: "a word that could stand at the back of all the words covering the page, a word which, if not truth itself, may perchance hold truth enough to help the moral discovery which should be the object of every tale." —Joseph Conrad. If that sounds heavy-duty, so be it. Post it over my desk with a photo of Ethel Merman belting out "Let Me Entertain You." Concerned about the future? Or did you mean the future of the book?

JS: I like to imagine Joseph Conrad and Ethel Merman sharing your wall. About the future, it's an elusive prey for those of us who work with narrative. Isn't it related to the notion of "moral discovery"? I'm reminded of a beautifully intimate production of Chekhov's *Three Sisters* I recently saw up at the Stratford Festival in Ontario. As I walked away from the theater I found myself worrying about the disappointments ahead for those characters, as though the play hadn't really finished. And this made me think about the consequences of all choices that we dare to make. I felt that I was more alert to the impact of my present actions, thanks to Chekhov. If nothing else, we come out of our immersion in an artfully told story with a new sense of urgency. Time is short, and there's so much to do. Time is short and you've managed to complete the whole of your four seasons. It was a daring thing to take on, Maureen. Did you know what you were getting into when you started writing *A Lover's Almanac?*

MH: I knew the stories would continue; the time allotted in the earliest season might not be enough. We were heading to the millennium, a date of reckoning, so the media thought, the computer folk, too. I had no crystal ball, just faith that our stories must go on as they always have—in the cave, the schoolroom, on-screen, and in a generosity of time offered by the novel. I had come across Benjamin Franklin's *Poor Richard's Almanac,* portioning out the year with entertainments, fanciful stories, yet always wise in Franklin's advice.

I have an astronomer friend who calculates the heavens for *The Old Farmer's Almanac,* so the phases of the moon, sighting of the North Star are exact. My almanac is a winter story of late love and young love in need of a thaw. Continuing themes? I presumed I could take Audubon's ambition in *Big as Life: Three Tales for Spring,* place his magnificent folio of American birds next to my birdwatcher's sketches: his big drama, her accuracy of singular observation. Perhaps I thought four seasons would see me out. Out of the workroom into Central Park is all I mean.

JS: Did you begin with themes, then? How did the characters emerge? Looking back at the beginning of *A Lover's Almanac,* I wonder which came first, the name "Louise Moffett" or her predicament?

MH: Little Miss Muffet sat on a tuffet. Not frightened, my Louise Moffett. She packed up, left the farm with her portfolio of drawings, flagged down the bus to New York. I have long been interested in that promise, the bold investment in the future. Way back in *Bridgeport Bus,* I mapped the route to the big city. The predicament? Will she make it? Of more importance, will she make a life? We can call upon characters we once called heroines—Wharton's Lily Bart, Esther in *Bleak House,* Doris Lessing's Martha Quest, your Sally Werner in *Follow Me* all get on the bus for the chapters that lie ahead. Reading Sally's story, I feel you are writing in ballad form, each part of her journey gathering new lyrics, new refrains in her story. Sorting playful from upward and onward, taking the trip each time is the serious game of fiction.

JS: Yes, the journey continues from writer to writer. *The Ballad of Sally Werner* was in fact one of my early working titles. I never meant it to be a final title, but I did have the model of the ballad in mind as I was writing. And a bus really is the perfect narrative vehicle for fiction. Did I ever tell you about the bus trip I took across country when I was eighteen? I went from Portland, Oregon, to New York City with seven dollars in my pocket, a jar of peanut butter, and a loaf of bread. I still have vivid memories of the people I met along the way. That would have been a novel, if I'd known how to write one back then. I had to read Beckett first, and you, and plant myself in the basement of a library for a few years. Also, I had to sharpen my skills on my typewriter, a big pink IBM electric I bought used on Twenty-seventh Street in New York. And then I had to catch up and learn the functions of various word-processing programs. So how does technology come into play? This is a subject that you recently brought up in an email.

MH: Cleaning up my back room after years of work in progress, I came across an article from the *New York Times,* August 19, 2002, testimony to my curiosity in new adventures for readers: a photo of words swirling on a wall with sound effects; an inset photo of traffic on a highway, presumably New York City. Interesting bricolage, but what rocked me was the commentary of a professor at UCLA on electronic writing: "For centuries literature has been delivered in a vehicle with a narrow sensory interface: the print book." She welcomed "richer sensory input." Joanna, do you feel impoverished, undernourished by the page? Do you ever stifle a sob at the end of a moving passage? Not the passing of Little Nell; perhaps Lily Bart embracing death; or laugh at the endless physical impairments of Beckett's fortunate family Lynch in *Watt*? Want to throw a feeble story across the room? Anyway: the same article pictures Robert Coover in a virtual-reality chamber at Brown, computer-generated lines of *Moby-Dick* swirling on the walls. "I'm not convinced that it's going to work to deliver literary art," Coover says, "but I don't want to be excluded from it." Nor do I, and I'm particularly taken by that shot of traffic overprinted with Melville's words—"There now is your insular city of the Manhattoes, belted round by wharves..." "Its extreme downtown is the battery..." and so forth, as the writer jumps ship for the many stops along the way of his great adventure. Recently I sense you have been out of sorts with the well told, so does the cure await in the interactive?

JS: I think what you're referring to is my occasional impolite expression of impatience with tales that threaten to oversimplify experience. It's not that I object to the "well told," as you put it. I love those tales that flaunt their elegance (the stories of Isak Dinesen and Angela Carter come to mind). But I also love wild explorations of madness. I feel a little less alone when I encounter characters who are working through befuddlement. We'll never run out of things to say about the struggle to make sense of confusion. It could be that the notion of the interactive is making narrative more flexible in its rendering of groping thought. But I don't think we've come close to realizing all the possibilities of the printed page.

MH: Poor old printed page, sporting its careful, or do I mean *conservative,* fiction, at times chancing an energetic style, lacking the risk of imagination. Pat, pat, turn the page, for there the reader will find the assurance of ongoing narrative without seeming misdirection, no sidebars. Except, of course, there's Powers and Wallace (RIP), Jeanette Winterson, Zadie Smith, Bolaño just now—his doorstop as postmortem; three voices on the triangulated page of Coetzee's *Diary of a Bad Year.*

JS: Are you saying here that a story that charges toward its end is necessarily conservative? You're arguing in favor of a narrative made up of digressions? But I wonder if those sidebars can be deceptive. I think of the footnotes in Nabokov's *Pale Fire*—these end up moving the plot forward in sneaky ways. Each of Nabokov's apparent digressions manages to add to the suspense. But maybe that's your point. Suspense can come in many flavors. It isn't just generated by a sequence of actions. There might be suspense in the delays of a meandering narrative, or in the invention of competing voices. As a reader, I love to get caught up in paragraphs that are full of vivacious details. Confusion can be very suspenseful, if we're able to move through the murk. I'm convinced that the most essential suspense in fiction is generated within each sentence. There might even be a suspenseful element to this conversation!

MH: As in table tennis? But you are far more agile of mind. You do actually ride horses, set the post high. Where might we end? Not in discord, not likely. Your probing is inspired yet reasonable. Your consideration of what's genuine in a story is right on; while I mouth off on the ingenuous: the weight of discourse in George Eliot; and, after her first novel, the serious play of Virginia Woolf, particularly the endgame of *Between the Acts*. Having parodied all of England's history from prehistoric man, half-human, half-ape, to a day in June 1939. She brings the sweep of history down to a domestic scene between a disaffected husband and wife. "Then the curtain rose. They spoke." The simplicity of the small sentences, their weight. The reader does not have to know that by 1941 the Woolfs had been bombed out of London; that they are leading "a rather vegetable existence" in the country, that Mrs. Woolf was about to write a last note to her husband—"I want to tell you that you have given me complete happiness…"; or that she put stones in her pockets to weight the end of her own story. Revealing diaries, letters, "A Sketch of the Past," the brave adventure of her writing life were over, though she never appeared unmasked in her fiction, a postmodern gesture.

The search for form is dangerous as a cut into stone that makes or defaces the sculptor's work; or like the tailor's stitches ripped to let out the binding collar of linear time. As for your postpartum sorrow for Chekhov's abandoned provincials, their future may be imagined by the writer. Perhaps a Scott appropriation on the fate of Uncle Vanya's medical career?

JS: There's an idea—Uncle Vanya moves to upstate New York. Your last question reminds me to consider dimension as well as direction in narrative. Maybe it's in the depths of their characters, in the hidden sources of singular voices, where writers like Eliot and Woolf and Chekhov establish the assurance of continuity. And at the same time they let us experience the potential for arbitrary turns. But I wonder about your comment that the "search for form" is dangerous. Are you talking about the danger of losing the reader if we shake up the form, or the danger of losing our minds?

MH: Oh, we're performing for the reader: at times a high-wire act; at times the comfort of telling a fireside tale, the love story again. As for losing my mind? It was lost long ago. I gave over so thoroughly to the pursuit of fiction. You write reviews and criticism, though I think your devotion is to stories, to the construction of novels in particular. Is it addictive? I have seldom taken a break that wasn't claimed by the pleasures or problems of family life. Or teaching: I recall being envious of you the semester when you'd read just Dickens with your class. I've never had the opportunity to do that: delve.

JS: I'm surprised that you would say you don't delve. What about Woolf, or Cather? Or P.T. Barnum, for that matter? Or Olmsted or Audubon? I'd call you a supreme delver! And I know you're thinking about the possibility of delving into something new. We talked about this the other day on the phone. You've just finished years of an ongoing project. What's next? the world asks. And you're asking: what do we do when we're not writing? Well, there's always life to keep us busy. And we can read about other people's lives. If we're lucky, we might be able to stand close to paintings and examine the brushwork. Some of us go to parties or travel or play music or drink. I admit I find it hard to know what to do with myself, or at least with my imagination, when I'm between projects. But yes, it's time to get recharged, to gather up influences and discover what we missed while we were absorbed in our dreams.

MH: What are you working on? I call that a provocative question.

As though the dough must be rising, if the bread is not already in the oven. I'm about to teach a course in self-portraits—written portraits, of course, but also a look-see at the many self-portraits of Rembrandt—costumed, flamboyant when young, signs of illness in old age. And that moving study by Alice Neel, revealing herself naked in old age. I was ticked off by a review of my *Rags* that reported me as eighty. I am seventy-nine, says so in the virtual page of my story. I might try my hand at biography, not the biopics I've loved writing, but fear I might lose the years left to another life. Thomas Hardy went back to poetry, but I'll not try friends with attachments of my versification. Questions: Add to a book of stories never collected over the years? That's the easy way out. I do have a model, a book like Fitzgerald's *The Crack-up,* the confession, arrogance intact, pathos of letters to his daughter. Delete Bridgeport? I'm losing my mind, as you suggest.

JS: Those are all wonderful possibilities. And I'm so heartened by your determination. I read just the other morning that the last bookstore in Laredo, Texas, has closed. Now if you live in Laredo and want to browse in a bookstore, you need to drive 150 miles to San Antonio. And the cover story of this week's *New York Times Magazine:* a best-selling writer farms out his ideas to coauthors while devoting most of his own time to marketing the franchise of his fiction. We'll see how it plays out. But you're right, the point is to press on with new explorations. Until we give up on words altogether, we'll need literature to keep teaching us how meaning can be made.

MH: Or sought in the next lap of our stories. *Yes, a voice comes to me in the dark. Scripto ergo sum.*

JS: Well, I'm impressed, Maureen. You're looking forward toward a new book, though your seventy-nine-year-old self hasn't even completed the year. I'll be turning fifty this summer; you'll be turning eighty. So what if we can't keep track of our errant minds? We must celebrate! I was supposed to hang upside down from a trapeze on my forty-fifth birthday. Just my luck, a storm moved in while I was waiting to climb the ladder, a bolt of lightning lit up the sky, and my trapeze swing was canceled. Maybe we should try that high-wire act you mentioned earlier? Wouldn't it be something to be as fearless as Philippe Petit, who walked on a tightrope from the top of one Twin Tower to the other? I hear he does occasional reprises on a low rope in Washington Square. He also can push a baby in a stroller while riding a unicycle. Maybe we could learn how to do that.

MH: I sign off now. Only words in my teetering balance. *In the middle of the journey of our life... Stately, plump Buck Mulligan... Lolita, light of my life, fire of my loins... I will arise and go now, and go to Innisfree... In my younger and more vulnerable years... And God called the light day and the darkness he called night... I was born... Mrs. Dalloway said she would buy the flowers herself.* ✶

GEOFF NICHOLSON

TALKS WITH

WILL SELF

"SHOULD WE PERHAPS NOT SIMPLY ACCEPT
THAT ALL WE ARE DOING IS GOING FOR A WALK?"

Similarities between sex and walking:

Basic, simple, and repetitive
Capable of great sophistication and elaboration
Sources of pleasure that can feel like hard work

I had always thought of myself as a "good walker." I walked *farther, more tirelessly, more willingly than most people I knew. If I went out walking with friends, they'd be ready to go back long before I was. I didn't have Will Self among my friends, but I knew he was part of the Iain Sinclair psychogeography brigade, breezily undertaking thirty-mile walks, leaving unwary companions limping and bloody. So perhaps I wasn't as good a walker as I thought.*

While living in London and New York, two of the great walking cities, I'd walked every day as a way of getting around, and as a means of urban exploration. Later, when I settled in L.A., a city where nobody walks, I continued to walk as best I could, but it was an effort, a deliberate decision to go against the prevailing culture. It seemed unnatural, an act of protest or eccentricity, but I wasn't protesting anything and didn't want to be willfully eccentric. I just wanted to walk. And so I found myself wondering why I wanted that, what walking meant to me, what it meant in history and in the contemporary world. These questions ultimately led me to write a book titled The Lost Art of Walking.

Of course I knew I didn't have this territory all to myself. There was, for instance, Rebecca Solnit's Wanderlust, *and Joseph Amato's* On Foot, *but these seemed to be academic in a way I knew my own writing wouldn't be. However, when I learned that Will Self was walking and writing, and publishing the results in the* Independent *and in a book called* Psychogeography, *I felt worried that we might be treading on each other's toes.*

I didn't know Will Self before we had this epistolatory exchange, but book reviewers had compared our novels. Received wisdom had me as a warm, humane satirist whereas he was the glacial, snarling, druggy mad dog of English letters. The two of us communicated, knowing that we were talking in public. We both consider ourselves, in part, entertainers, and we tried to amuse each other and our putative audience.

I led the way in these exchanges, and god knows Will Self has more deadlines to meet than I do, but he matched me for diligence and enthusiasm. I would send off emails that I hoped would provoke a response, and I'd get one back within half a day. There was nothing glacial or mad or druggy about my correspondent, but Will has a reputation for baroque vocabulary, and he lived up to that. I learned a new word from this exchange— verglas. *Look it up: I had to.* —Geoff Nicholson (June 2009)

I. SEDATED WALKING, PROGRAMMATIC WALKING

Hi Will,

In the same week that my publisher agreed to commission *The Lost Art of Walking*, I set off for a long walk around the Hollywood Hills, not too far from where I currently live. I'd been walking for about half an hour when, for no reason I could see, I stumbled, fell over, and broke my arm in three places.

Once I'd been operated on, had metal pins put in my forearm, and while I was still in a cast and sling, I thought I'd better start walking again. And I did—being suitably medicated with (prescription) opiates. Naturally I thought of [Thomas] De Quincey, and about you, and I also thought of an old girlfriend of mine who liked to walk around London having taken LSD. She said she observed things—architectural details, street furniture, things in people's windows—that she'd never notice without the benefit of psychedelics.

My own, limited experience of walking in the city while tripping (in the LSD sense) was that it was horrible. I imagined I could read the minds of all the people walking toward me in the street, and they all had profoundly ugly minds. When I talked to Iain Sinclair about this, he said he thought I was very wise to avoid mind-expanding substances while walking, since there was something monstrous lurking just below the surface of the city, and getting in touch with it was to be avoided. I take his point re: psychedelics, and yet wandering around London and even more so New York, a couple of drinks to the good, seems to me one of life's great pleasures. Guy Debord [walker, situationist, definer of psychogeography], as far as I can see, was pissed almost continuously.

So, since I think you know infinitely more about addiction than I do, I was wondering if you had any thoughts on being addicted to walking as opposed to being addicted to anything else, possibly even to writing. I know that I feel bad if I haven't walked for a while, and also if I don't write for a while.

What say you?

Geoff

Well, Geoff,
My drinking and drugging days certainly saw plenty of walking: on acid, on dope (which I smoked, more or less continually, for over twenty years), on coke (a notable coked-up midnight troll

included passing the Natural History Museum in South Kensington, with its facade featuring bas-reliefs of the Linnaean chain of being, and becoming convinced that it was a small-scale model of all organic evolution), and even on opiates. Although, mostly, one walked through the city to score (absurd now, but in the late 1970s and early '80s, in London, it was actually difficult to get your hands on junk) and then sat still.

Initially, I've been scathing about the idea of walking-as-addiction: walking is expansive—addiction contracts; walking is about oneself-in-the-world, addiction about retreat from the world; walking—or at any rate, the kind you and I do—is about being open to vicissitude, losing control—addiction is a highly controlling undertaking: an attempt to modulate the psyche (and the body) and hence all experience—and so on. However, I have to concede that the 4/4 rhythm, the sense I have on long walks—both urban and rural—of being rather disembodied: a head floating above the ground; the meditational aspect, whereby I allow my mind to "slip its gears"—all of these do seem akin to the kind of altered experience I sought in drugs. The bizarre thing is that while walking can produce these effects more reliably, I don't feel driven to it too compulsively... yet.

Best,
Will

Hi Will,

I agree with you about the disembodied, meditative aspect of walking. I often find, especially if I'm walking a long way, that I start out very thoughtful and attentive, observing things, having lofty thoughts, making sentences in my head, but then after a few hours I've stopped all that. I'm just putting one foot in front of the other, just walking. I think this a good thing.

Sebastian Snow, who's one of my favorite walking writers—mildly demented old Etonian who walked the length of South America, 8,700 miles from Tierra del Fuego to the Panama

Canal—says in his book *The Rucksack Man,* "By some transcendental process, I seemed to take on the characteristics of a Shire, my head lowered, resolute, I just plunked one foot in front of t'other, mentally munching nothingness." I like that.

And this is one of the problems I've always had with walking in overprogrammatic ways—you know, walking the entire length of Broadway, or back and forth over every bridge that crosses the Thames, or every street in Hampstead Garden Suburb. Sure, you can do it, but at some point you find yourself wondering whether it actually needs to be done.

I remember an interview of yours where somebody asks you what's the difference between a psychogeographic act and a stunt. And you reply, "I'm too old for stunts." Surely not, Mr. Self.

Geoff

Geoff,

I very like the "munching on mental nothingness" line, and it does apply to me perfectly well, too. I liken it—again—to meditation: I set off thinking programmatically—or perhaps only troubled by what they call, in German, "the ear worm," perhaps some ghastly mid-'70s pop ditty the lyric of which I can't chak, or maybe a more rarefied composition of lines, tropes, and imagery, drawn with great intent from what I see and hear and smell and feel. However, in the fullness of time the steady beat of the feet usually manages to subdue all this. I pursue very high mileages for this reason: twenty-five, thirty—even thirty-five miles in a day. Up at these high mileages (like, I would imagine, high altitudes, although such a notion is inimical to me: I adore mountaineering literature, but only read it when I'm lying in a hammock in the delta), I find that I become—like your Old Etonian—absorbed into the landmass, feeling its contours as you might those of a body one is seeking carnal—or, at any rate, sensuous—knowledge of.

As to the gestural—yes, I am too old for walking lobsters on a leash through the Tuileries, or negotiating Florence by dice, or finding my way around Berlin using a map of Hartford, Connecticut. I distrust the idea that the society of the spectacle can be torn down in this fashion—although I do believe long-distance walking can undermine it. I cleave to airport walks for this reason: walking to the airport, taking a flight, then walking at the other end. Not only does this negate the way prescribed folkways banalize the sublimity of international jet travel, but because the physical perception of distance is so much more vivid than the mental, it actually feels as if Manhattan has been rammed into the Thames Estuary: in place of the special relationship, a hideous miscegenation of cities.

I also agree with you as to the sense of purposelessness engendered by these gestural walks—or stunts. But, I ask you, might the need to feel our peregrinations have a purpose be part of our problem? In other words: should we perhaps not simply accept that all we are doing is going for a walk?

Best,
Will

II. TRESPASSING, FUNCTIONAL WALKING

Dear Will,

I was some way into writing my book before I became aware of your Psychogeography columns in the *Independent,* and of course I didn't dare read any of them. Even so, somebody sent me a copy of your piece "Down and Out in Beverly Hills" which bears (let's call 'em) parallels to a piece I published in a very obscure literary magazine that I'm absolutely sure that neither you, nor anybody else, ever read. My piece was called, wouldn't you know it, "A Long Walk in Hollywood." God knows the writing life is hard enough without worrying about this stuff.

What I suspect this may be about is that Englishmen of a certain literary bent—you, me, Aldous Huxley, Reyner Banham, to name very few—we all respond to many of the same things about

Los Angeles—its essential strangeness, how it doesn't match with any of our English expectations of what a city is and does.

And yet we try out our English sensibilities and habits on the city, including walking, and we find that they fit rather well: suburbs, well-tended gardens, lots of small, quirky shops, a surprising number of decent bookstores. Sure, you have to do some driving—but, you know, try living in a small English town without a car these days.

And if L.A. isn't the most walkable of cities, it's all part of the perverse English nature to do what isn't expected, walk where we're not "supposed" to walk. Try walking past the Scientology Celebrity Centre if you really want to experience the evil eye from a security guard. Of course I walk past it all the time since it seems to annoy them so much.

I come originally from Sheffield, adjacent to the English Peak District, and walkers there still like to think of themselves as part of a great radical tradition that found its apotheosis in the Kinder Scout mass trespass, hundreds of walkers asserting their right to roam over land that was used just once a year by the wicked landowner for his grouse shoot.

I know you used to walk with your father when you were a kid, and so did I. My dad was one of those guys who thought that KEEP OUT and NO TRESPASSING signs applied to everybody except him. One of the more intense and excruciating moments of my childhood was walking with my dad and wandering past KEEP OUT signs onto somebody's private land and being chased off by a man on a horse who said, "How'd you like it if I came and rode my horse in your garden?" Since we lived in public housing at the time—a row house with a minute front garden—I found this rather delicious.

Have you done any interesting trespassing?

Best,

Geoff

Geoff,
Well, I take your point about Englishmen d'un certain age, although

I am an Anglo-American myself—American enough, and raised enough in the States not to feel any visceral strangeness about the urban topos there, whether it's L.A. or Chicago (where I recently walked from the Loop to the nearest Walmart, an economic traverse, if you like—it was nine miles).

I so identify with you and your experiences of your father. Surely this is the primary ambulatory relationship? My dad was relatively timorous, although a lion when it came to trespassing, standing on the edge of cliffs—the higher and more vertiginous the better—and licensing laws.

But recently I've been walking with a still more insouciant trespasser, the artist Antony Gormley. When Antony sees a KEEP OUT sign, he charges toward it. We went for a walk across Foulness Island in the Thames Estuary, which has been an army artillery range since 1916 and can only be reached by boat, then traversed by a couple of rights-of-way. Our objective was "the broomway," an ancient medieval causeway that is only accessible at low tide, since it heads out from the island onto the estuarine mud, then runs for six miles upstream until coming ashore at Southend.

Needless to say the start of it was festooned with STOP! GO BACK! notices, warning of instant discorporation from unexploded ordnance if you dared to go farther. Antony was not to be warned off: "Oh, they're just saying that," he bellowed, and ramped on across the mud. It was one of the eeriest and strangest walks I've ever taken— out there in brown verglas, the great stacks of the power station at Canvey Island rising up out of the haze as, like ambulatory ships, we slopped our way upriver.

Whenever I tell people I'm going to walk somewhere utilitarian—like an airport, or even a long-distance walk that seems quite prosaic to me, they always ask: "Is it for charity?" Do you get the same response? And how do you respond to such inanity?

Cheers,

W

Fellow ambulator, Will,

"Are you doing it for charity?"—I think it brings us back to what you were saying an email ago about walking just for the simple hell of it rather than to chart zones on atmospheric unity. (Have I got the right Debordian usage there?)

Of course for an author there's another wrinkle to this. So many terrible situations become much more tolerable if you know you can write about them afterward, and a walk that's too easy and pleasant, and done for no "good" reason, just may not provide enough gutsy raw material. So what was the point of doing it?

I guess Werner Herzog's walk from Munich to Paris—depths of winter, 1974 (written about in *Of Walking in Ice*), was the supremely "useful" walk. He did it to save the life of Lotte Eisner, "walking in full faith believing that she would stay alive if I came on foot." And she did. She didn't die until 1983. She edited *Paris, Texas,* a movie with two of cinema's greatest walking scenes.

I have a personal functionalist Herzogian humiliation. I wanted to get Herzog to say something flattering about my book that could be emblazoned across the jacket ("Walking is virtue—Nicholson is a god among walkers" type of thing), and I knew that sending a copy to his production office wasn't going to work, so I found his home address, and I took it over there in person, on foot, and dropped it in his mailbox with a humble and (I thought) winning letter, in full faith that having walked all the way from my house to his (thirteen miles round trip, including a jaunt up and down Laurel Canyon Boulevard—a nightmare for a walker, steep gradient, blind curves, no sidewalk, and fast-moving drivers who never in their wildest dreams expect to see some idiot pedestrian in the road)—I'd get what I wanted. My full faith was misplaced. No word as yet from Mr. H.

I once asked Iain S. what he thought was the worst place to walk in London—he reckoned the Rotherhithe Tunnel.

Any improvement on that?

Geoff

Ha! Small world, Geoff,
On my 120-mile circumambulation of Los Angeles, the only really dicey moment—I simply don't count being dicked by gun crews in South Central, this is standard—came on Laurel Canyon Drive. Foolishly, I had ventured up through the park to Mulholland Drive on the (non-pedophile) assurance that there would be a sidewalk on Laurel Canyon. When I got there, there was nothing but the Divine Right of Drivers in full spate, and darkness was falling fast. I set off down the canyon, but about halfway to Sunset Boulevard seriously feared for my life (I was having to cross from side to side to avoid being invisible to drivers on the bends), and ended up cowering in a carport.

I was saved by a Virgil, in the form of a guy in silk shorts and a trim goatee who emerged from nowhere, walking insouciantly down the gutter of the roadway. He told me he walked up and down all the time to his house, and that sometimes in the dead of night he went down on his extra-length skateboard. As Burroughs observed: "You wade through shit—and then there's a Johnson."

I agree: some purpose is required for a long walk, and what better purpose than having to do something functional. On my L.A. walk I went to meet with Michael Lynton at Sony Pictures in Culver City. It took me a day to walk there from Hollywood, and then a day to get back. So what if the meeting was only half an hour long.

Your Herzogian experience sounds... well, rather romantic, frankly. Difficult to imagine Aguirre turning from the wrath of God to blurb a book.

Vale!

W.

III. SEX-WALKING

Will,
I've been thinking about what you said somewhere back there

about feeling the landscape's contours as you might those of a body. There was a time when I was trying to "sex up" my book by writing about the connections between walking and sex.

In the days when I had a real job and worked in an office, I lived for the lunch hour, when I could get out and walk the streets and look at all the women who were also walking the streets in their lunch hour. Once in a while some looked back, but I don't flatter myself that anyone ever thought I had a sexy walk. In his book *The Flaneur,* Edmund White says that in Paris, heterosexuals cruise each other just as much as homosexuals: I've yet to be convinced. (Incidentally, my spell-check suggests *Flamer* as a correction for *Flaneur.*)

Gay cruising sounds really difficult and time-consuming to me: walking up and down at a park or dockside or somewhere, eyeing each other, making some kind of complex negotiation based on body language or eye contact or whatever. The walking is definitely a part of the seduction process, but I suppose it's not part of actually having sex. So I began making a list of the ways that walking was like sex and ways it wasn't.

Essential similarities: They're both basic, simple, repetitive activities that just about everybody does, and yet they're both capable of great sophistication and elaboration. They can both be sources of fantastic pleasure, but there are times when they can both feel like hard work. They're both things that some people like to do alone, that some like to do with just one other person, and that others like to do in groups of various sizes. And some people like to wear special clothing while they're doing it. And then, essential differences: One: although I'm sure you can catch various diseases while you're walking, they're different from the sort you can catch while having sex. Two: whereas walking is the kind of activity that can be happily and legally undertaken in public with a dog... At that point I abandoned my ruminations; this seemed too flippant even by my standards. I score pretty high on flippancy.

So, if you have some final thoughts about the sexuality of pedestrianism, something suitably steeped in sensual gravitas, that might be a perfect way to bring this correspondence to a close.

Yours,

Geoff

Ah, yes, Geoff—
Walking and sex. In my youth the madman lolloped ahead, his drool spattering the thighs of oncoming walkers, and I daydreamed of random acts of alfresco lovemaking. But I am old, Father Geoff, and nowadays I have to tug the fucker along by his chain, and he only ever drools on me.

Well, I am being a little disingenuous when I suggest that I'm entirely beyond such things—but not altogether. Recent comments, in conjunction with promoting my psychogeography book, and that were also made at an "in conversation" Iain Sinclair and I undertook at the V&A in London, led to something of a backlash: these were to the effect that while plenty of women are dedicated walkers, the conjunction between less innate interest in the minutiae of spatial orientation and the quite understandable anxiety that can afflict women walking alone in strange places has meant—I think—that the kind of stuff we do is more of a male preserve. The obvious examples of women walker-writers were slung back at me—but I can't help but believe that these are the exceptions rather than the rule.

And perhaps that's where the desexing of walking exists for me: since I am, de facto, heterosexual, an extempore—or even planned—ambulatory sexual encounter is not likely. And to cruising, I don't agree—I think it sounds like enormous fun, and quite understand that even with greater liberalization, gay people—men in particular!—still feel the urge to go out, have a walk, and score. Bliss!

Very best,

Will ✶

JOAN DIDION

TALKS WITH

VENDELA VIDA

"I DON'T KNOW HOW MANY TIMES YOU HAVE TO
LEARN THINGS LIKE YOU'RE GETTING OLDER,
BUT IT TURNS OUT TO BE QUITE A FEW MANY MORE
TIMES THAN YOU WOULD THINK.

The writing platforms of Joan Didion, reverse-chronologically:

"Real Apple" computer
"Fake Apple" computer (DOS)
Standard Royal or Olivetti typewriter
Big Five tablet

Joan Didion *is the author of five novels, including* Play It
As It Lays *and* A Book of Common Prayer. *She is also
the author of ten works of nonfiction, including* Slouching
Towards Bethlehem, *her essay collection about the 1960s
counterculture in California that forever changed the way
we think about the '60s and journalism. Her other acclaimed books of nonfiction include* The White Album, After Henry, Where I Was From,
and, most recently, Blue Nights. *With her husband, John Gregory Dunne,
she wrote the screenplays for the films* The Panic in Needle Park, Play
It As It Lays, A Star is Born, True Confessions, *and* Up Close &
Personal. *In 2005, Didion was awarded a gold medal from the American*

Academy of Arts and Letters, and she won the National Book Award for nonfiction for The Year of Magical Thinking.

But saying all this does not really communicate the effect Joan Didion has had on millions of readers' lives, and on countless writers' lives as well. I know, because I am one of those writers she has influenced to a degree that makes me sheepish to admit. When I was growing up in San Francisco, I knew from a young age I wanted to be a writer, but there was a problem: I didn't know any writers. And there was nothing around me telling me this was a reasonable dream. The posters that hung in my grade-school classrooms showed pictures of astronauts—not helpful. Or Einstein—again, really not helpful.

It wasn't until high school that I came across Joan Didion's Slouching Towards Bethlehem. *From her author bio, I learned she had grown up in Sacramento, and because Sacramento was not so far from San Francisco I thought maybe I could try to be a writer too. Flash forward to the first book I tried to write, which was a collection of essays about California. And because Joan Didion got her title for* Slouching Towards Bethlehem *from a Yeats poem, guess who started reading a ton of Yeats? But I know I'm not alone in admiring her precision, her wit, her ear for dialogue, and her incredible ability to reveal just the right detail at just the right moment. Who is better at revealing the ways we strive as a culture to make our news stories conform to a particular national narrative? And who is better at communicating the disappointment our society experiences when they do not?*

I interviewed Ms. Didion for the City Arts & Lectures series in San Francisco on November 15, 2011. The audience greeted her with a rapturous applause, and laughed a great deal. She was witty and honest, and seemed unafraid of any question, or any answer.   *—Vendela Vida*

VENDELA VIDA: Welcome to San Francisco.

JOAN DIDION: Well, thank you.

VV: What is the first thing you do when you come to San Francisco?

JD: Turn up the heat.

VV: Turn up the heat?

JD: Yeah. I mean, I grew up in the Sacramento Valley, so…

VV: When you were growing up in Sacramento and you would come to San Francisco, what would you do here?

JD: Oh, I would always get sick on the ferry. There was still a ferry, you know, to go home. You crossed the bay on a ferry, and I would always get sick on the ferry. It was a very glamorous trip, until that moment.

VV: I have this image of you frequenting places that no longer exist, but places that I grew up knowing about, and which I read about in your works of fiction and nonfiction, places like the restaurant Ernie's and the department store I. Magnin.

JD: Ernie's and I. Magnin were big issues, yeah.

VV: They were big, big things for you?

JD: Yeah. My cousin Brenda and I used to play a game which involved an I. Magnin elevator. It was one of those games that little girls play to scare each other. The elevator crashes…

VV: That's an exciting game.

JD: [laughing] Yeah.

VV: I was just thinking that in *Blue Nights,* I. Magnin makes an appearance because you talk about how you used to buy cases of I. Magnin soap.

JD: Right.

VV: And then your daughter, Quintana, when she was young and you were living in Southern California, she would actually make a business—a soap factory—out of these soaps. Can you talk about that a little bit?

JD: She had this idea—she and a friend, the only friend that she had on the beach. We lived on quite an isolated beach, and it was cut off by the tide twice a day. Twice a day we were totally alone on this beach. So Quintana and her best friend on the beach decided that what they were going to do was have a soap factory and sell the soap to passersby on the beach. So they melted down all my I. Magnin soap.

VV: All your nice soap.

JD: Yeah, which was kind of an ivory color and, by the time they finished with it, it was kind of a dishwater color.

VV: Lovely.

JD: And then I, because nobody else was on the beach to buy the soap, I bought it back from them.

VV: Do you remember how much they charged you, to buy the soap back?

JD: No, probably more than I. Magnin did.

VV: I want to talk a little about your childhood in Sacramento, because I get the impression that you started writing at a very early age.

JD: I did.

VV: And do you remember what it was? I read in "On Keeping a Notebook" that your mother gave you a notebook when you were very young—a Big Five tablet—and your mother gave it to you with, quote, "the sensible suggestion that [you] stop whining and learn to amuse [yourself] by writing down [your] thoughts." What do you remember about this notebook and what thoughts did you write down?

JD: I wrote a story, or a novel, as I thought of it, which had to do with the young woman who was its protagonist, and found herself in an extreme weather situation. She discovered that she was—I can't remember whether the first thing that happened was the snowstorm, or whether that was the second thing that happened and the first thing that happened was that she stumbles onto the Sahara desert. But in any case there were quite extreme weather situations.

VV: I also read that when you were first learning to write and teaching yourself to write, you would retype passages from Hemingway novels, and I'm wondering what appealed to you about Hemingway's work, and which novels in particular you would retype?

JD: I would retype the beginning of *A Farewell to Arms,* all through the retreat from Caporetto.

VV: Oh, wow.

JD: And then, I would retype a short story called "Hills Like White Elephants." And years later, we were asked—John and I were asked by HBO—they were doing kind of an anthology of short stories and the producer asked us if we would pick a short story and do it, and, like magic, "Hills Like White Elephants" came to mind, and it was already written exactly like a screenplay.

VV: Right, it's all dialogue.

JD: It's all dialogue [*laughs*]. And so we did that, and they got Tony Richardson to direct it, and they shot it in Spain with James Woods and... someone else. And it was a very gratifying payoff after having so often retyped it.

VV: What kind of typewriter were you typing on then?

JD: I was always typing on a standard Royal (because my father had bought a lot of standard Royals at a government auction) or an Olivetti that I bought with the first money I ever made, which was I was stringing for the *Sacramento Union*. And the *Sacramento Union* doesn't exist anymore, but it was the morning Republican paper in Sacramento, and with the first money I made there I bought an Olivetti, the classic little Lettera 22 or whatever it was called, and I can remember my father saying, "Well, you'll never be able to get parts for that thing." He's saying this because it was Italian, right.

VV: And *were* you able to get parts for it?

JD: I was able to get my parts for it. I was able to get parts for it rather easier than I got parts for the Royals that he bought. [*Laughs*]

VV: And do you still type on a typewriter, or...

JD: No, I had to change because I couldn't get parts for any typewriter anymore, or get them fixed or anything. So I started using a computer and it was infinitely... [*pauses*] When I started using a computer, it was when everybody was using DOS systems. And they were so infinitely much more logical than I was, that it was... You know how they always tell you in school that algebra will make you logical? Well, I never got algebra and I never got logical. But DOS—I mean, it was like gold, it just made everything logical and made me infinitely more logical than I had ever been in my life. And then DOS became Windows—I mean, everybody was suddenly using Windows systems, which was like the fake Apple.

VV: Right.

JD: So I was not happy. But because no one uses DOS anymore, I finally switched to real Apple.

VV: And that's what you use now?

JD: That's what I use now. Real Apple. [*Laughs*]

VV: It seems like your mother was very instrumental in your writing career. She gave you your first notebook. And I believe it was also your mother who first encouraged you to apply for the essay contest that you ended up winning during your senior year at Berkeley. You applied for an essay contest sponsored by *Vogue*. Is that right, that it was your mother's idea?

JD: Yes, that was my mother's idea. Although when I *did* win it, I drove home to Sacramento and showed her the telegram and said, "And it was you who told me I could do this," and she looked doubtful and said, "It was?" [*Laughter*]

VV: What was your essay about?

JD: It was about an architect named William Wilson Wurster, who was sort of the father of the Berkeley style which was later, well, it later was all over California, but at that time—

VV: He was new?

JD: Yeah.

VV: And what was the prize, for winning the contest?

JD: The prize for winning the contest was a job, or consideration for a job, and one thousand dollars.

VV: A job at *Vogue*?

JD: Yes. So they brought me into New York and interviewed me and gave me the job, which I think was quite a pro forma thing. I think they just brought you in as part of the prize. Anyway, I worked there for eight years. It was a perfectly wonderful place to work because they had a personnel director, and it was like a family—they had a personnel director who would stop you in the hall and ask when you called your mother last. And then, if you said, "a week ago," she would march you into her office and point to her phone and you would call her. Call your mother in front of Miss Campbell. [*Laughs*] And also they had a nurse, and the nurse, every morning she would put a table in front of her office door and on the table she would line up little cups full of phenobarbital for [*audience laughter*], you know, girls who had had nervous nights. I mean, really, it was kind of *in loco parentis*. It was a great place to have as your only real job. I mean, after I quit *Vogue* I never had another real job. I don't mean I had no job; I was sitting at home freelancing.

VV: You were also freelancing when you were working at *Vogue*, right?

JD: I was writing a few pieces, yeah.

VV: And weren't you working on your first novel, as well?

JD: I wrote my first novel while I was working for *Vogue*, yeah. It was published while I was working for *Vogue*.

VV: That seems very ambitious, to finish your first novel while you're actually working a full-time job and calling home and—

JD: I took six weeks off as a leave of absence from *Vogue* and finished it. I wrote the last half of that novel in six weeks at home.

VV: Would you advise writers to actually have magazine jobs or newspaper jobs in which they have to meet deadlines, because then they get better at actually finishing things?

JD: Yeah. I think it forces you into addressing the situation, whereas it's kind of all-too-easy not to address a book, if there's any excuse for it.

VV: In your essay "Goodbye to All That," you talk about when you were living in New York in the Nineties in one of your first apartments. You hung a map of Sacramento County up on your bedroom wall "to remind me who I was," you wrote. I'm wondering if you can talk about what you meant by that. What did you need to be reminded of and how would that map remind you?

JD: I needed to be reminded of where I came from, that I had a place in the world, because I felt very loose in the world during those first years in New York because I didn't belong there, and everybody I knew in New York was from New York. Or they were from places with a tradition of coming to New York, like they were Southerners and they all kind of knew each other. And I knew no one. No one from Sacramento went to New York at that time. I was maybe the first person I ever knew who went to New York. So it was important for me to keep the geography, keep where I came from in mind.

VV: And in 1964, you married John Gregory Dunne, who was at the time a writer for *Time* magazine, and shortly after that you moved to Los Angeles with the intention of staying for six months, and then you ended up staying for two decades, right?

JD: More.

VV: More than two decades. What was it about Los Angeles and Southern California that appealed to you?

JD: Well, it took me about two years to get it, but once I had made that investment it seemed like some place to stay. I got it, finally, one day when I was stuck on the freeway. I was on my way to an appointment, I was doing a piece, and I was late for the appointment, and it was raining, and I'm on the freeway, and I kept thinking, Is this all there is? [*audience laughter*] and suddenly it occurred to me, This *is* all there is. There isn't any more. And then I got Los Angeles. And from then on, New York seemed sentimental to me after that.

VV: In *The Year of Magical Thinking,* you write about how you and John often went to Hawaii when you were working on a script because, you said, "No one in New York could ever get the time difference straight, so we could work all day without the phone ringing." I'm wondering, what were those days in Hawaii like? Because you also write about them in *Blue Nights,* and I'm wondering what your days looked like.

JD: Usually in the seasons we chose to do this, it was almost always raining all the time, because it was often Christmas time; it was the winter season, usually. And so we'd be in this room with the rain coming in and we would work until about nine o'clock at night, and then we would go to a Chinese restaurant, and that was how the day went. They were perfect days. You know, I can't think of a better kind of day for a writer than just working on that one thing, that total focus. Because when we were in Hawaii working on a movie, it was always a rewrite for somebody, you know, it was a crash situation. They were very intense days, and it was a very good place to work on something intensely.

V V: I've read that before you start a novel, you always reread Joseph Conrad's *Victory*, and I'm wondering if there's a movie or a script that you turn to? When you were working on a movie, was there a movie, a perfect movie that you returned to, or a perfect script you kind of held up as an ideal?

JD: The one with Joseph Cotten and Orson Welles, Harry Lime, *The Third Man. The Third Man* is just a perfect script.

V V: And Graham Greene...

JD: Well, I don't think Graham Greene wrote the final draft, but he wrote it. Actually we timed a sequence in the movie where there is a penicillin scam. It's a post–World War II penicillin scam. The whole thing is explained in about four lines, literally in about eight seconds of screen time. It's quite stunning. Take a look at it the next time—well, I was going to say the next time you rent it, but that shows how... I think there are faster ways to get movies now. [*Laughs*]

V V: There's an amazing passage in *The Year of Magical Thinking* when you're describing your last birthday spent with John, and there was a snowstorm on your birthday, and so your plans to have dinner with Quintana and her husband were cancelled. And before dinner, you said that John was sitting by the fire and re-reading one of your own novels, *A Book of Common Prayer*, and he was trying to figure out how you had accomplished something technically. And at one point, he said—and I'll quote here from *The Year of Magical Thinking*—"'Goddamn,' John said to me when he closed the book, 'Don't ever tell me again you can't write. That's my birthday present to you.' I remember tears coming to my eyes, I feel them now." That passage strikes me on so many levels, every time I read the book, partly because, as you write a couple sentences later, there's no one else who could have given you that gift.

JD: No.

VV: No one else, because you worked so closely.

JD: That's right.

VV: Also, whenever I read that passage, I think, Wow, that's saying that you have doubts about your writing. And I sometimes think, If she has doubts, what hope is there for the rest of us?

JD: Like, every day.

VV: Every day. And what do you do, then, when you sit down to write, how do you overcome those doubts?

JD: Well, sometimes if you sort of keep at it, you hit one paragraph or image, or not even one paragraph—one image. Actually, this new book, Blue Nights, I was going crazy with it. I wasn't getting anywhere with it at all. And suddenly it occurred to me that I could call it Blue Nights, and then it seemed worth pursuing, worth trying another day or two, and once I had tried another day or two, something else caught my attention and it kind of pushed me through that, over the edge, into doing it.

VV: You started writing Blue Nights on what would have been Quintana's seventh wedding anniversary. You've said in the past that you don't know what you're thinking until you write it down, so I'm wondering: were you surprised, when writing this book, to discover the directions that it took you in?

JD: I was totally surprised. As I said, it wasn't called *Blue Nights* at first, so clearly I had no idea that it was about the dying of the brightness and about aging. That kind of came to me as we went along. When I say "we," I mean "I," because this was a true non-"we" project. So yes, this book came as a total surprise to me.

VV: When you read it now is it a surprise? Or does it make sense?

JD: Well, it makes sense to me in light of the blue nights aspect of it.

VV: That was the unifying theme for you?

JD: Yes.

VV: There are several lines you repeat throughout the book, usually quotes from Quintana. For example, when she is very young, she is haunted by a figure who she calls the Broken Man. Can you describe what the Broken Man was?

JD: Well, the Broken Man was so specific that I gradually became as afraid of him, as Quintana was. The Broken Man she described as wearing a certain kind of shirt, which is the kind of shirt you've seen about a million times on the guy who works at the gas station, and she was very specific that this shirt had his name on it, and his name was "one of those ordinary kinds of names." Then she named her idea of ordinary kinds of names. As I say, it was so specific I developed an idea that he was lurking around the house, and kept looking for him, you know?

VV: You would go out to the deck and look behind the curtains...

JD: I would go out to the deck, yeah. And I would sort of look suspiciously at anybody who came to work on the house, you know.

VV: You quote a line where she says: "After I became five I never dreamed about him." That line and a few others are repeated almost like lines of a poem throughout the book, and it's very affecting, this repetition. I'm wondering, when you're writing those lines and repeating them, were you trying to achieve a mirroring of your own thought process?

JD: It's a mirroring of—yeah. I find myself repeating lines a lot, and it seems to be the most efficient way I know of expressing what's on your mind without saying it straight out.

VV: At the end of the amazing introduction of *Slouching Towards Bethlehem,* you write, "Writers are always selling somebody out," and I'm wondering what you meant by that, because it's often quoted as meaning one thing, but I'm wondering what you meant.

JD: Yeah, I didn't mean the way people sometimes interpret it. When they quote me, it's kind of as if I was making an accusation or saying something revealing about writers, but no. It was perfectly simple: all I meant was that writers see you in a way you don't always see yourself. If you are written about, particularly if you aren't used to being written about, you are going to think you were a little bit betrayed by the writer because you're not going to see yourself exactly as you see yourself. And that's just an inevitable fact of being written about or writing, and that's what I meant by "selling out."

VV: So when you write about yourself, when you turned the focus on yourself as you did in your last two books, in *The Year of Magical Thinking* and *Blue Nights,* how does that pertain to you? Do you see yourself in a different light afterward than you—

JD: Yes, you do.

VV: And do you see yourself that way when you're writing the book, or is it only when the book is completed that—

JD: I think it's only when the book is completed, because you don't know where the book is going while you're writing it. That seems impossible, but it turns out to be, at least in my case, unfortunately true. You've got no picture of where you're going. Things would move much faster if you did.

VV: What do you think you learned most about yourself after writing *Blue Nights,* as a parent or a writer?

JD: I don't know what I learned about myself as a parent because I think I probably fretted more than I needed to about my own role as a parent. It wasn't, in the end, all that important, I mean, in Quintana's development. It wasn't as important as some other things in her life. I mean, one of the most important things I learned during the course of writing it—I totally acknowledged that I was getting older, and that may strike you as late and it *was* late. But I am, you know, a slow study on this stuff, on life stuff. [*Laughs*] So I would have thought that I had gotten used to being older. Right after John died it occurred to me that I no longer saw myself as twenty-four because he was the last person who saw me as twenty-four. But that was nothing compared to later. I mean, I don't know how many times you have to learn things like you're getting older [*laughs*], but it turns out to be quite a few many more times than you would think.

VV: It seems, from the outside at least, that the editors you have worked with have been very integral to your writing experience. You named a collection—one of my favorite collections, *After Henry*—after your beloved editor Henry Robbins—

JD: Right.

VV: —who was your editor and, I believe, John's editor.

JD: He was John's editor and my editor, yeah.

VV: You've also had a very close relationship with Robert Silvers of the *New York Review of Books*.

JD: Right.

VV: I'm wondering, when you're working with these editors and having these close relationships, how many of the ideas that you bring to him are turned into stories and how many times is it the other way around, that he comes to you and says, "Do you want to write about this?"

JD: Usually it's something that I go to the editor with. Not that I haven't done a lot of pieces that were an editor's idea, but usually that's those few editors with whom I have a very close relationship and they're kind of plugged into the way I think, so ideas that come from them are generally almost like ideas that come out of my own head.

VV: You were working on *Blue Nights* with—who is your editor now?

JD: My editor now is Shelley Wanger at Knopf.

VV: And did you show her things as you were going along or did you give her the whole book?

JD: No, I gave her the whole book. I think. I can't remember. I think I gave her the whole book, yeah. It's such a short book, I mean. [Laughs]

VV: I read somewhere that you feel that all books should be able to be read in a single sitting.

JD: In a single sitting is the ideal thing, yeah.

VV: Because you just don't lose the reader that way, is that why? So they can actually—

JD: You don't lose your own attention.

VV: That's important, too.

JD: That's key, yeah.

VV: Do you know what you're going to write next?

JD: No. I hope it's going to be something really surprising.

VV: To you?

JD: To me, yeah.

VV: Do you think you'll write fiction any time soon?

JD: I don't know. I had made some notes for a new novel before John died. I had thrown a lot of notes and clips into a box, and I haven't opened that box since he died. It had nothing to do with his dying, except after he died, Quintana was in the hospital and there was no moment when I would think about starting a book because who knew what was going to happen? And so I just left them in that box and they're still in that box. So I had this idea that maybe after Christmas, when things quiet down, I will open the box and see what's in it, and maybe—if there's anything in it that clicks something, maybe I will write fiction again.

VV: Do you think you'll be surprised by what's in the box, or do you hope to be surprised?

JD: I hope to be surprised, but I'm a little scared [*laughs*] that I won't be. So I don't want to check too soon. ✷

CONTRIBUTORS

Philippe Aronson has published French translations of over two dozen books by American and English writers, including Zadie Smith, Patrick deWitt, Pauline Kael, Frederick Exley, and Sam Shepard. His own work in English has appeared in *Fence*.

Tom Barbash is the author of the novel *The Last Good Chance* and the *New York Times* bestselling *On Top of the World*. His short-story collection *Stay Up With Me* will be published by Ecco/HarperCollins in September. His stories have appeared in *McSweeney's, One Story, Tin House, VQR, Narrative, Best American Nonrequired Reading,* NPR's *Selected Shorts,* and other publications, and his book reviews have appeared with regularity in the *New York Times* and *San Francisco Chronicle.* He is on the faculty at California College of the Arts.

Brian Joseph Davis is a screenwriter and the author of *Portable Altamont,* a book that garnered praise from *Spin* for its "elegant, wise-ass rush of truth, hiding riotous social commentary in slanderous jokes." He is a cofounder of the literary website *Joyland,* and his work was recently included in *Against Expression: An Anthology of Conceptual Writing.*

Sarah Fay is an editorial associate at the *Paris Review.* Her work has appeared in the *Atlantic,* the *New York Times Sunday Book Review,* and the *New Republic,* among other publications.

Kaitlyn Greenidge is originally from Boston. A 2010 graduate of Hunter College's fiction MFA program, she lives in Brooklyn.

Sheila Heti has been publishing interviews in the *Believer* since 2006 and began working as interviews editor in 2010. She is the author of several books, most recently the novel *How Should a Person Be?* and, for children, *We Need a Horse*. She lives in Toronto.

Noy Holland is the author of three collections of short fiction, *Swim for the Little One First, What Begins with Bird,* and *The Spectacle of the Body*. Her stories have appeared in the *Quarterly, Conjunctions, Black Warrior Review, Ploughshares, Open City, NOON,* and other publications.

Joshua Jelly-Schapiro is a writer and geographer at the University of California, Berkeley.

Drew Nellins lives in Austin, Texas.

Geoff Nicholson is the author of the novels *Footsucker, Bleeding London,* and *The Hollywood Dodo,* among others, and nonfiction such as *Sex Collectors* and *The Lost Art of Walking*.

Nick Poppy is a writer and filmmaker living in Brooklyn.

Ross Simonini has served as interviews editor at the *Believer* since 2007. His interviews and writings appear in the *New York Times, Frieze, Interview,* and regularly in the *Believer.* He is a founding member of the band NewVillager.

Suzanne Snider's work has been published in the *Believer,* the *Guardian,* the *Washington Post, Guernica,* and *Triple Canopy.* She is the founder/director of Oral History Summer School and is currently completing a book about rival communes on adjacent land.

Amy Sohn is the author of the novels *Run Catch Kiss, My Old*

Man, Prospect Park West, and *Motherland.* She has written for *New York* magazine, the *New York Times, Harper's Bazaar, Playboy,* and the *Nation,* among many other publications.

Wells Tower is the author of the short story collection *Everything Ravaged, Everything Burned.* He lives in North Carolina.

Deb Olin Unferth is the author of the story collection *Minor Robberies,* the novel *Vacation,* and the memoir *Revolution: The Year I Fell in Love and Went to Join the War.* Her work has been featured in *Harper's, McSweeney's,* the *Believer,* and the *Boston Review.*

Vendela Vida is the author of four books, including the novels *Let the Northern Lights Erase Your Name* and *The Lovers.* She is a founding coeditor of the *Believer* magazine and the editor of *The Believer Book of Writers Talking to Writers.*

Zoe Whittall is the author of the novels *Holding Still for as Long as Possible* and *Bottle Rocket Hearts.* Her third and latest poetry collection is *Precordial Thump.* Her writing has appeared in the *Walrus,* the *Globe & Mail,* and more.

Leni Zumas is the author of the novel *The Listeners* and the story collection *Farewell Navigator.* She teaches in the MFA program at Portland State University.

ACKNOWLEDGMENTS

Thanks to Melissa MacEwen, Evan Greenwald, Belle Bueti, Sydney Goldstein, Kate Goldstein-Breyer, Holly Mulder-Wollan, and all the tireless *Believer* interns past, present, and future. And a very special thank you to the *Believer*'s managing editor, Andi Mudd.

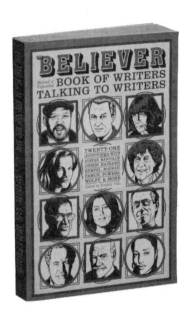

NOT INCLUDED IN THIS VOLUME: INTERVIEWS WITH WALLACE SHAWN NORA EPHRON SHERMAN ALEXIE LAURIE ANDERSON AND SCORES OF ILLUSTRIOUS OTHERS

Published nine times a year, every issue of the *Believer* contains conversations, like the ones in this book, between excellent writers—alongside interviews with people like Maira Kalman, Steve Carell, and Neko Case. Each issue also features columns by Nick Hornby, Daniel Handler, and Greil Marcus, plus terrific essays by writers like Tom Bissell, Sloane Crosley, Jonathan Lethem, Susan Straight, and Geoff Dyer. Subscribe with the form below and, in addition to a special discount, you'll get Nick Hornby's latest collected writings from the *Believer*—*More Baths Less Talking*—free of charge!

visit us online at
www.believermag.com
or fill out the form below for a special discount.

- - —— - —— - —— - —— - —

Please send me one year (9 issues) of the Believer *for just $40—
a $5 discount from the website!*

Name: _____ Street Address: _____

City: _____ State: _____ Zip: _____

Email: _____ Phone: _____

Credit Card #: _____

Expiration Date: _____ CVV: _____

Please make check or money orders out to the *Believer.*

CLIP AND MAIL TO: The *Believer,* 849 Valencia St., San Francisco, CA 94110